D0899891

Urban Renewal Politics

NUMBER ONE: METROPOLITAN POLITICS SERIES

Urban Renewal Politics

SLUM CLEARANCE IN NEWARK

By Harold Kaplan

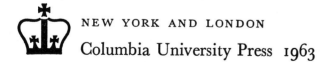
NEW YORK AND LONDON
Columbia University Press 1963

Harold Kaplan, who received his Ph.D. from Columbia University in 1961, is Assistant Professor
of Political Science at York University, Toronto.

Copyright © 1963 Columbia University Press
Library of Congress Catalog Card Number: 63-19076
Manufactured in the United States of America

To My Wife

Foreword

It is now widely appreciated that the United States is not merely an urban nation but a country of large metropolitan concentrations as well, and that it is becoming steadily more metropolitan. The stresses and strains imposed upon our economic, governmental, and social institutions by these trends are also now familiar themes of public discourse. Among the many aspects of a complex metropolitan society, the governance of cities and of metropolitan regions has proven to be one of the most intractable problems. "Solutions" abound, but "progress" is elusive. A major difficulty resides in the fact that knowledge about the existing political systems in urban and metropolitan communities is usually insufficient to provide a sure footing for the governmental and administrative proposals often advanced as remedies for metropolitan ills.

This volume is the first of a series of studies which will examine some of the salient governmental and political dimensions of the New York Metropolitan Region. These studies are a product of a metropolitan study program at Columbia University which began in 1957 and has been supported by a grant from the Ford Foundation. The main purpose of the program has been to provide, as part of the education of candidates for the Ph.D. in political science, an emphasis upon contemporary urban and metropolitan political systems, especially the twenty-two-county, tri-state New York Metropolitan Region. Each holder of a fellowship in the program has written, or is now writing, his dissertation on a New York Metropolitan Region problem. Several of these dissertations will appear in this series.

Harold Kaplan's *Urban Renewal Politics* demonstrates effectively the main themes of the metropolitan study program: a concern with the political process through which the citizens of the metropolitan region attempt to find solutions to their perceived problems, the institutions and the leadership involved in this effort, and the relations of the local and regional systems to each other and to larger systems. In relating how the City of Newark embarked upon and advanced an urban renewal program over a decade of difficulties and accomplishments, he not only portrays the successful performance of dedicated and courageous public officials but also raises significant questions about the distribution of power and the role of leadership in an urban community: for example, what of the frequently assumed indispensability of high-prestige, "leading" citizens in securing rapid, planned change?

Other studies in the series will be concerned with related and complementary aspects of metropolitan government and politics, including transportation, land-use planning, interest groups, and political parties.

The faculty committee supervising the metropolitan study program, and serving also as editors of this series, consists of Professors Richard E. Neustadt, Wallace S. Sayre, and David B. Truman, of the Department of Public Law and Government of Columbia University, and Dr. William N. Cassella, Jr., of the National Municipal League.

WALLACE S. SAYRE
Eaton Professor of Public Administration
Columbia University

New York City
June, 1963

Preface

This study originally appeared in 1961 as a Columbia University Ph.D. dissertation. Most of the research for the dissertation was carried out during 1959 and 1960. As part of that research I interviewed close to fifty people in Newark and reinterviewed about fifteen of them. In the summer of 1959 I was employed as a Redevelopment Analyst by the Newark Housing Authority.

In revising the dissertation for publication, I concluded that to reinterview participants and to make an exhaustive study of the urban renewal system since 1960 would not be feasible. Therefore, the present study remains an account of the 1949–60 period; a concluding chapter briefly summarizes the major events of 1960–63.

A number of people have contributed to this study, but several deserve special mention.

Professors Wallace S. Sayre and David B. Truman have taught me most of what I know about politics and government. I have been particularly fortunate in having both of them as advisers on the dissertation and on this manuscript. They have suffered through the many versions and drafts of this study and have never failed to provide insightful criticism and encouragement.

This study would not have been possible without the cooperation of many people in Newark, most of whom prefer to remain anonymous. The members of NHA's staff proved particularly generous with their time and made all relevant documents available to me. Of all those in Newark who provided help and encouragement, special mention must be made of Joseph Nevin, Director of Redevelopment of NHA and my boss for one summer. If there is any item of consensus in Newark's urban renewal system, it is the great esteem in which he is held.

Professors H. Douglas Price and David Rogers read Chapter VIII and made very useful suggestions. I also benefited from criticisms of my dissertation made by Professors Conrad Arensburg, Lawrence Chamberlain, and Ernest Fischer.

Needless to say, the conclusions arrived at in this study are my own and are not the responsibility of anyone in Newark or at Columbia University.

My wife served as editor, typist, stern critic, sympathetic listener, and discourager of hesitancy. If this book is at all intelligible to those readers who are neither political scientists nor housing officials, the responsibility is hers.

Mr. Robert Tilley, Mrs. Trudy Ruth Hayden, and Mrs. Kathryn Sewny of the Columbia University Press helped bring this study to the publication stage. Mrs. Helen Allen of York University provided additional editorial assistance.

Finally, it is my pleasant duty to thank the New York Metropolitan Region Program of Columbia University and the Ford Foundation for financing my graduate training and for making possible this publication.

HAROLD KAPLAN

Toronto, Ontario
May, 1963

Contents

Foreword, by Wallace S. Sayre   vii

Preface   ix

Abbreviations of Agencies and Organizations   xiii

I   Introduction   1

II   NHA: The Strategy of Slum Clearance   10

III   The Politicos   39

IV   The Civic Leaders: Neighborhood Rehabilitation   61

V   The Civic Leaders: Economic Development   93

VI   The Planners   114

VII   The Grass Roots   135

VIII   The Urban Renewal System in Newark   165

IX   Postscript: 1963   184

Notes   193

Index   207

Tables

1. Federal Funds Spent in the Fifteen Leading Urban Renewal Cities, 1949–1960   3
2. Ralph Villani's Vote in the First Ward as a Candidate for City Commissioner, 1949 and 1953   144
3. The Negro Population Explosion in Newark, 1920–1960   149
4. Dispersion of the Negro Population in Newark, 1950–1958   149
5. Federal Funds Spent in the Fifteen Leading Urban Renewal Cities, 1949–1962   186

Figures

1. Newark's Slums: Percentage of Residential Structures Lacking Central Heating, 1959   13
2. Urban Renewal Projects in Newark, January, 1960   14
3. Newark's North Ward: Election Districts Where Ralph Villani Polled His Largest Number of Votes as a Candidate for Mayor, May, 1954   145
4. Newark's North Ward: Election Districts Where Joseph Melillo Polled His Largest Number of Votes as a Candidate for the City Council, May, 1954   147
5. Newark's North Ward: Election Districts Where Joseph Melillo Polled His Largest Number of Votes as a Candidate for the City Council, May, 1958   148
6. Population Changes in Newark's Neighborhoods, 1950–1958   150
7. Election Districts Where Leo Carlin Polled His Weakest Votes as a Candidate for Mayor, 1954 and 1958   160

Abbreviations of Agencies and Organizations

BMR	Bureau of Municipal Research, Inc.
CHC	Citizens' Housing Council
CHNC	Clinton Hill Neighborhood Council
CPB	Central Planning Board
FHA	Federal Housing Administration
NAACP	National Association for the Advancement of Colored People
NAHRO	National Association of Housing and Redevelopment Officials
NAREB	National Association of Real Estate Boards
NCNCR	Newark Committee on Neighborhood Conservation and Rehabilitation (after 1958 the Newark Commission on Neighborhood Conservation and Rehabilitation)
NEDC	Newark Economic Development Committee
NHA	Newark Housing Authority
NJAHRO	New Jersey Association of Housing and Redevelopment Officials
NJAREB	New Jersey Association of Real Estate Boards
PHA	Public Housing Administration
REBON	Real Estate Board of Newark
SOHC	Save Our Homes Council
URA	Urban Renewal Administration

Urban Renewal Politics

CHAPTER I

Introduction

In the summer of 1949 the United States Congress took action to meet the spread of slums and the dearth of standard housing in urban areas throughout the country. For close to a decade urban spokesmen had urged Congress to supplement its public housing activities with a new housing program addressed to the needs of middle-income families. After years of intensive effort these demands were eventually embodied in Title I of the 1949 Federal Housing Act.

Title I provided federal aid to urban communities for the clearance of blighted areas. The cleared sites were to be sold at write-down values to private redevelopers who would agree to build middle-income housing or other projects appropriate to those sites. The federal government agreed to pay two-thirds of the net project costs (two-thirds of the difference between the costs of clearance and the sale price of the site) if the local government agreed to pay the remaining third.

Supporters of the 1949 Act had viewed federal aid as the *sine qua non* of a substantial attack on urban slums. Yet, the response of local communities to this Act, during the first decade after its passage, proved disappointing to most of the Act's supporters. There were, of course, some notable examples of renewal success in New York, Chicago, Cincinnati, and Philadelphia. But most cities responded slowly, and some responded not at all. There could be no denying the need for middle-income housing or the severity of the slum problem in most urban areas. There could be no minimizing the incentives provided by federal aid. Yet, serious obstacles to the achievement of successful slum clearance were still evident after ten years.

Most professional housing officials trace this lag in achievement to factors that are national in their impact: the red tape of the Urban Renewal Administration (URA), congressional stinginess, the caution of private redevelopers, and the policies of the Federal Housing Administration (FHA) on the insurance of mortgages. These national factors, important as they may be, are only part of the story. Factors peculiar to specific communities, though less often cited by housing officials, are probably just as important in explaining the over-all lag. Local factors, moreover, are indispensable in explaining the different levels of achievement of various cities.

This study concerns itself with the question of the differential renewal achievements of various cities. The general problem is to determine how some cities have overcome the obstacles to clearance and to identify the local concomitants of successful renewal.[1] For this reason, local variables rather than nation-wide variables are stressed.

This is a case study of one highly successful city—Newark, New Jersey.* More specifically, it is a study of the Newark Housing Authority (NHA) and describes how this agency launched nine clearance projects during its first ten years in Title I. An attempt is made to identify the concomitants of successful slum clearance in this particular urban area. The analysis of an atypical case should suggest some reasons that urban renewal has been less successful elsewhere. It should also provide some clues to the causes of success in other atypical cities.

Throughout this study the term "success" is used synonymously with high levels of clearance activity. Defined in this way, success may be measured by the number of blocks cleared, the number of new dwelling units constructed, or the total amount of funds spent. It is a quantitative, not a qualitative, index; it deliberately avoids questions involving the appropriateness of particular versions of renewal policy. Of course, the quantitative index may not be free of its own implicit value judgments, but it is more operational and easier to work with than most qualitative indices. It is

* For an outline of Newark's slums and a summary of the renewal program see Figure 1 (p. 13), Figure 2 (p. 14), and project summary on pp. 8–9.

also the index of success generally used by URA and the professional housing officials.

Measured in these terms, Newark has one of the most successful renewal programs in the country (see Table 1). Only two other

TABLE 1

FEDERAL FUNDS SPENT IN THE FIFTEEN LEADING
URBAN RENEWAL CITIES, 1949–1960

(1) City	(2) Total Federal Funds Spent (in millions of dollars)	(3) Federal Funds Reserved but Unspent (in millions of dollars)	(4) Funds Spent per Capita * (in dollars)
New York	65.8	94.6	8.3
Chicago	30.8	77.2	8.4
Philadelphia	17.3	87.6	8.6
Washington, D.C.	16.1	40.4	20.9
New Haven	13.5	24.1	88.8
Norfolk	11.7	14.4	38.2
Baltimore	9.2	43.0	9.8
St. Louis	8.6	37.0	11.5
Pittsburgh	8.2	24.8	13.6
Boston	8.1	18.3	11.6
Detroit	7.5	22.2	9.5
Minneapolis	7.2	10.2	14.9
San Francisco	6.0	9.1	8.1
Buffalo	5.6	18.9	10.5
Newark	5.4	34.3	13.3

* Column 2 divided by the city's 1960 population.
SOURCE: U.S. Housing and Home Finance Agency, Urban Renewal Administration, *Urban Renewal Project Directory* (Washington, D.C., 1960).

cities of comparable size—Norfolk, Virginia, and New Haven, Connecticut—have bettered Newark's achievement. The large amount of federal funds reserved for Newark, but not yet spent (Table 1, Column 3), indicates that the city's renewal program will become increasingly impressive in the 1960s.

One major assumption has conditioned the author's approach to Newark renewal and has largely determined the format of this study. It is assumed that success in urban renewal is, at its root, a political question. It is a question of negotiating with an array of independent actors who have different perspectives on the renewal program. Renewal stands or falls on the ability of some entrepreneur (in this case the Newark Housing Authority) to elicit the necessary support and to neutralize the existent opposition. Those individuals and groups at the federal and local level whose participation is essential to the launching of a project must be persuaded to cooperate. Those whose interests are affected adversely by a project must be bypassed, accommodated, or persuaded to weaken their opposition.[2]

The problem that confronts a local redevelopment agency is the problem that confronts almost all administrative agencies: that of surviving in a controversial or political environment in which there is no consensus on goals. Much of the lag in renewal achievement can be explained by the highly diffuse and unstructured environment in which most local redevelopment agencies find themselves.

Before a clearance project can be launched, the local redevelopment agency must first muster a professional staff capable of making the necessary surveys and plans. The URA Regional Office must then be persuaded to grant loans for further surveying and planning and to reserve a capital grant for eventual clearance. To retain its eligibility for aid, the local agency must satisfy a host of URA's requirements on land acquisition, relocation, land disposition, and other aspects of clearance. If the local agency deems public housing necessary to its renewal plans, the Public Housing Administration (PHA) must be persuaded to cooperate. The local agency must also recruit prospective private redevelopers from the community and from cities across the nation. Leading financial institutions must be encouraged either to serve as redevelopers or to provide mortgage funds for other redevelopers. An agreement by the FHA Regional Office to insure the mortgages of private redevelopers is usually indispensable to a project.

Behind these direct negotiations lie the possibilities that the President or the Washington offices of URA or FHA will decide to alter federal housing policies or the amount of federal funds available. Another key actor is Congress, which can alter the provisions of the federal housing law and which holds ultimate power over the amount of money appropriated to urban renewal.

Every stage of the local agency's dealings with federal agencies must be ratified by the local governing body—in Newark's case, by the mayor and City Council. The local governing body must also be asked to approve the redevelopment agency's relocation plan and urban renewal plan for each project. In many states, as in New Jersey, the local planning board must declare all Title I sites blighted before clearance can begin. In addition, the planning board must approve public housing sites, realignment of streets, changes in the zoning ordinance, and other detailed aspects of renewal projects. The City Hall agencies involved in public construction must be persuaded to coordinate their efforts with the clearance program and to provide the necessary supportive action for projects. Local redevelopment agencies must also be attuned to the attitudes of bond buyers, site residents, neighborhood organizations, public housing tenants, and a variety of other local groups that are affected, in some way, by urban renewal policy.

These environmental factors help explain why more is not accomplished in the field of urban renewal. Renewal achievement is apt to be the by-product of a local redevelopment agency's successful accommodation to an unstructured, hazardous environment. The over-all lag in renewal achievement is not surprising. What does seem surprising is that certain agencies, like NHA, have managed to deal successfully with such an environment.

This, then, is a study in the politics of urban renewal. It attempts to describe NHA's political environment and the Authority's efforts to function within this environment. It examines the structure of relations among those who participate in slum clearance politics. The major problem treated in this inquiry may now be rephrased more broadly. What kind of local political structure lies at the base of Newark's achievements in urban renewal? What kind of local political structure is conducive to rapid, planned change?

The following account describes Newark's urban renewal power structure by examining, in turn, each of the major components of that structure. The focus of this study is on the role that each major actor plays in the renewal system, on how these roles emerged, and on why they persist. Chapter II examines the Housing Authority, its basic strategies, and its dealings with nonlocal participants; Chapters III through VII look at the "politicos," the realtors, the corporation executives, the city planners, and the grass roots organizations. An attempt is made in each chapter to characterize the typical patterns of interaction over a ten-year period between a particular bloc of interests and NHA. Chapter VIII outlines the structure of the renewal system in Newark and relates this structure to the question of renewal success.

MAJOR PARTICIPANTS IN NEWARK URBAN RENEWAL *

Hugh Addonizio	Congressman, 1948–62; Mayor, 1962–
Murray Bisgaier	Executive Secretary, NJAHRO, 1947–
Michael Bontempo	City Councilman At Large, 1954–
Salvatore Bontempo	City Commissioner, 1953–54
Paul Busse	Executive Secretary, NEDC, 1956–62
James Callaghan	City Councilman At Large, 1954–62
Kenneth Carberry	Executive Director, Chamber of Commerce, 1953–59
Dennis Carey	Essex County Democratic Chairman, 1954–
Leo Carlin	City Commissioner, 1949–53; Mayor, 1953–62
Joseph Cocuzza	Member, CPB, 1954–
Agnes Coleman	Chairman, NCNCR, 1953–
Henry Conner	Executive Director, BMR, 1948–
Louis Danzig	Executive Director, NHA, 1948–
Meyer Ellenstein	City Commissioner, 1949–54
Herbert Greenwald	Former President, Metropolitan Corporation of America, redeveloper of North Ward project
Robert Hoover	City Planning Officer, 1956–58
James Keenan	City Commissioner, 1949–53
Edward Kennelly	Superintendent of Schools, 1953–
Jack Lehman	President, United States Realty and Investment Company, redeveloper of Hill Street project
Alexander Matturi	NHA Commissioner, 1949–54
Joseph Melillo	City Councilman, North Ward, 1958–
Stephen Moran	City Commissioner, 1949–53
Joseph Nevin	Director of Redevelopment, NHA, 1949–60
George Oberlander	City Planning Officer, 1959–
H. Bruce Palmer	Chairman, NEDC, 1955–60

* Only those participants referred to more than once in the text are listed. Only positions or offices relevant to Newark renewal are mentioned.

Jack Parker	President, Jack Parker and Associates, New York City, redeveloper of South Broad Street project
Theodore Pettigrew	NHA Commissioner, 1955–
Albert Rachlin	Chairman, Subcommittee on Industrial Sites, NEDC, 1955–62
Harry Reichenstein	City Clerk, 1933–
Mariano Rinaldi	Business Administrator, 1956–62
Peter Rodino	Congressman, 1948–
Gerald Spatola	NHA Commissioner, 1957–62
Raymond Stabile	Member, CPB, 1954–62
Oscar Stonorov	Head of Central Business District Survey, 1959
Irvine Turner	City Councilman, Central Ward, 1954–
Milford Vieser	Financial Vice-President, Mutual Benefit Life Insurance Company; Chairman, Subcommittee on the Financing of Enterprises, NEDC, 1955–62
Ralph Villani	Mayor, 1949–53
Samuel Warrence	Director, Division of Tenant Selection and Relocation, NHA, 1949–
Edmund Wollmuth	Executive Director, Chamber of Commerce, 1948–53
William Zeckendorf	President, Webb and Knapp, New York City
Joseph Zeller	Member, CPB, 1955–60

URBAN REDEVELOPMENT AND RENEWAL PROJECTS IN NEWARK, 1949–1960 *

Project Name	Description	Estimated Net Costs (in millions of dollars)	Date of Announcement	Status as of January, 1960
North Ward Redevelopment (First Ward)	Clearance of about 10 blocks for public housing with redevelopment on either side.	7.9	January, 1952	
Columbus Homes	A 2,000-unit public housing project on the North Ward redevelopment site.		January, 1952	Open for occupancy in September, 1955.
Broad Street	Two 22-story apartment buildings privately redeveloped for middle-income housing.		January, 1952	Ready for occupancy early in 1960.
Branch Brook Park	One 22-story apartment building redeveloped for middle-income housing.		January, 1952	Ready for occupancy shortly after the Broad Street project.
Central Ward Renewal (Old Third Ward)	The renewal of a 60-block area to contain public housing, redevelopment, rehabilitation.	17.4	March, 1955	Urban Renewal Plan in final stages of discussion with URA; execution to begin sometime in 1961.
Wright Homes	A 1,206-unit public housing project in renewal area.		March, 1955	Open for occupancy in December, 1959.
Mercer St. Project	A 1,680-unit public housing project in the 60-block area.		January, 1958	Relocation almost completed. Demolition by sections began in the summer of 1959.
Jeliffe Avenue Renewal (Light Industrial)	Clearance and rehabilitation of a 25-block area for light industry and housing.	11.0	November, 1957	Urban Renewal Plan to be completed and sent to URA late in 1960.

Project	Description		Date	Status
Colleges Expansion (North Broad St. Renewal)	Clearance and rehabilitation of about 15 blocks for expansion of Rutgers and Newark College of Engineering.	12.0	September, 1958	Urban Renewal Plan for the first section of the area to be completed and sent to URA sometime in 1960
Hill Street Redevelopment (Lehman)	Clearance of 2 blocks for middle-income apartments.	5.7	May, 1959	Federal planning funds received. A capital grant reserved permitting entire area to be cleared.
South Broad Street Renewal (Parker)	Eventual clearance and rehabilitation of 125 blocks for apartments and commercial uses.	24.0	June, 1959	Federal planning funds received. A grant permitting clearance of first section reserved by URA.
Seton Hall Redevelopment (Educational Center)	Clearance of 3 blocks near present campus for expansion of educational and religious facilities.	4.5	June, 1959	Planning funds received. Grant permitting clearance of entire area reserved by URA.
Penn Plaza Redevelopment (Newark Plaza)	Clearance of about 15 blocks for 17 new apartment buildings and some commercial uses.	20.1	October, 1959	Planning funds received. Grant permitting clearance of first section of the area reserved by URA.
Essex Heights Renewal (Turner-Galbreath)	Clearance and rehabilitation of about 25 blocks for housing and commercial uses.	31.1	November, 1959	Planning funds received. Grant permitting clearance of section of that area reserved by URA.
Clinton Hill Renewal	Rehabilitation of 12 blocks administered by NCNCR.	2.5	December, 1956	Urban Renewal Plan to be completed late in 1960; execution to begin in 1960 or 1961.
Demonstration Grant Project	A study of planning techniques in urban renewal, administered by CPB.	.3	January, 1958	Second interim report published in 1959. Final report due in 1960.

* All projects executed by the Newark Housing Authority unless otherwise stated.
SOURCE: Newark Housing Authority.

CHAPTER II

NHA: The Strategy of Slum Clearance

The ability of any redevelopment agency to realize its goals is circumscribed by the attitudes and responses of local organized interests.[1] Many factors contributing to its success are attributes of the local political environment and are beyond the control of agency officials. As later chapters will document, NHA's success can be explained in large part by the permissive character of its local environment.

Environmental factors, however, are a necessary but not sufficient cause of NHA's success in redevelopment. Less adroit agencies might fail to perceive the permissive character of their local environment, and more timorous agencies might fail to exploit it for the benefit of the program. That NHA officials are painstaking strategists, attuned to the problems of successful redevelopment, is highly pertinent to that agency's long-run achievements. This chapter examines the process by which the Authority's staff made its clearance decisions from 1949 to 1959, the substance of its policies, and the strategies it developed for exploiting this permissive environment.

"GETTING THE JUMP"

Newark was the first city in New Jersey and among the earliest in the nation to begin an urban renewal program.[2] Less than eighteen months intervened between the passage of the 1949 Housing Act and the announcement of Newark's first slum clearance project. Many in the Housing Authority now cite this "jump" as an important contribution to their subsequent success. By submitting a concrete clearance proposal earlier than most other cities in the

United States, Newark was able to secure a prior claim to federal funds and to acquire a reputation for competence among federal officials.

Newark could move swiftly in the field of redevelopment because a large municipal organization, the Newark Housing Authority, led by an aggressive Executive Director, Louis Danzig, was poised to act immediately after passage of the 1949 Act. The Housing Authority of the City of Newark had been created in 1938 under the terms of the U.S. Housing Act of 1937 and the New Jersey Local Housing Authorities Act of 1938. Like housing authorities throughout the country, it was an independent public corporation responsible for the construction and management of low-rent housing projects. It was managed by a locally appointed board of six housing authority commissioners and was sustained by federal subsidy, the rent from its projects, and federally guaranteed housing authority bonds. By 1949 NHA was, with the exception of the Board of Education, the largest spender of funds and the largest dispenser of contracts in the city government.

Danzig and his staff had recognized the shortcomings of public housing for some time and had lobbied for legislation on urban redevelopment. Even before Congress and the New Jersey Legislature took final action in 1949, Danzig had his legal staff prepare an ordinance making NHA the city's official redevelopment agency. Immediately after passage of the federal and state legislation, Danzig submitted this ordinance to the city commissioners. The good relations that he had established with the commissioners during the public housing years facilitated rapid approval of the ordinance.

This quick start not only gave NHA the jump on most other cities; it also provided the Authority with a strategic edge over most local interests. These local groups failed to recognize the significance of the new program until several clearance projects were under way. By the time these groups were mobilized and prepared to make demands on the Authority, NHA had already established good working relations with the key federal and local officials.

Danzig did not wait for the federal Division of Slum Clearance and Urban Redevelopment to get organized before launching his own survey of potential sites. When federal officials indicated that funds for preliminary surveys would not be available until spring, 1950, Danzig went ahead with staff and funds borrowed from NHA's public housing accounts. Here, once again, Danzig could utilize the resources and organization that NHA had amassed in the 1940s to get a quick start on the new program.

It was during one of his frequent trips to Washington, and one of his frequent attempts to prod federal officials into faster action, that Danzig met Joseph Nevin. Nevin had been an initiator of public housing in New Jersey and had over twenty years of public housing experience behind him. He was recognized as one of the leading housing officials in the nation. Danzig did not succeed in getting federal officials to move faster on the new program, but he did persuade Nevin to leave the Public Housing Administration in order to serve as NHA's Director of Redevelopment. By the close of 1949 NHA had the jump in another sense. It had acquired and retained a staff of housing officials, lawyers, and administrators —a staff which combined experience in housing, sound political instincts, and a strong loyalty to the clearance program.

THE DECISION-MAKING PROCESS

Newark's urban redevelopment policies are products of the interaction of two elements: the goals of NHA's professional staff and the demands of certain nonlocal participants, like the Urban Renewal Administration, the Federal Housing Administration, and the private redevelopers.

NHA officials often say that their clearance decisions are made on the basis of "technical" rather than "political" criteria and that projects are planned in a "nonpolitical" environment. In one sense, those statements are true. NHA's clearance policies have not been the result of open conflict among local interest groups. Such conflict over slum clearance has been rare and has not affected the substance of NHA's decisions. NHA has provided the initiative for all clearance projects. The work of its expert staff has been shielded from random interference by local interests. Though the demands of such interests are often anticipated and taken into account by

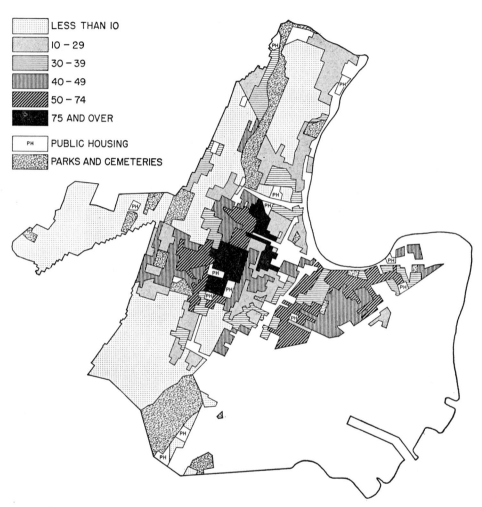

LESS THAN 10
10 – 29
30 – 39
40 – 49
50 – 74
75 AND OVER

PH   PUBLIC HOUSING
PARKS AND CEMETERIES

Figure 1. NEWARK'S SLUMS: PERCENTAGE OF RESIDENTIAL STRUCTURES
LACKING CENTRAL HEATING, 1959
SOURCE: Newark Central Planning Board

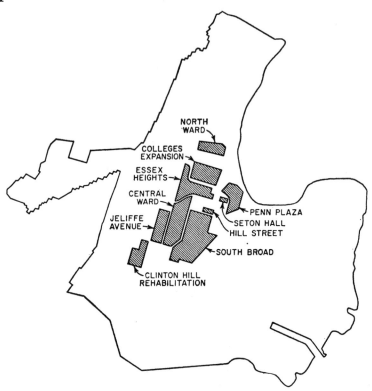

Figure 2. URBAN RENEWAL PROJECTS IN NEWARK, JANUARY, 1960
SOURCE OF MAP OUTLINE: Newark Central Planning Board

NHA's staff, decisions on projects are made in a low-temperature atmosphere and are often delegated to middle-rank staff men.

By a nonpolitical environment, Authority officials also mean that the cues of redevelopers and federal officials, rather than those of local interests, necessarily govern NHA's clearance decisions. Negotiations with nonlocal actors are conducted by Nevin and his immediate subordinates; dealing with local interests is deemed political, and this is handled by Danzig. Both are bargaining relations. Since the nonlocal participants largely determine the success or failure of local redevelopment, NHA's negotiations with them have a greater impact on the substance of clearance policy.

The initial goals of NHA's redevelopment officials were derived from their own experiences in public housing, from the values of the housing profession, and from the wording of the 1949 Act. These officials defined Newark's redevelopment problem as a lack of standard housing for middle-income families and an excess of substandard or slum housing. The purpose of the new program was to find the most dilapidated areas in the city, to clear them, and then to sell the areas to private redevelopers who would build moderately priced housing. NHA summed up its goals in one phrase: "Middle-income housing on cleared slum sites."

During Newark's first decade in urban redevelopment NHA discovered that these goals were only partially attainable within the Title I program as it was then defined. From 1949 to 1959 NHA had to learn which portions of its initial program were acceptable to private redevelopers, FHA, and URA, and which parts were not. This, briefly, was the course of redevelopment policy making during the first ten years.

NHA officials also learned that a rigid commitment to the initial goals and a refusal to accept half-victories would foreclose all clearance action. They eventually came to place greater emphasis on winning some kind of clearance than on obtaining clearance strictly in accordance with their initial purpose. As far as NHA officials were concerned, it had to be either pragmatism and flexibility in the planning of projects or no projects at all.

THE NORTH WARD: ADJUSTMENTS IN PURPOSE

In beginning the search for an initial redevelopment site, NHA was guided by its original definition of the program's purpose.[3] In the early part of 1950 Nevin and his staff identified the sixteen most blighted areas in the city, ranked these sixteen according to degree of blight, and assigned top priority to four of the worst areas. Discussions were then held among NHA's top men to determine which of the four sites should be selected for immediate action. During these discussions, however, Danzig and Nevin soon realized that an extrapolation of their experiences in public housing would not guarantee success in urban redevelopment. They realized that there were two new actors to contend with. The participation of FHA and the private redevelopers was not required in the earlier program; it was essential in urban redevelopment.

The key question about any redevelopment site was whether a private firm could make a profit on middle-income housing in that area. If the answer was negative, no redeveloper would buy the site, and no FHA official would agree to insure mortgages for construction there. In public housing NHA could afford to select sites according to the degree of blight present. In urban redevelopment the acceptability of a site to the two new participants had to take precedence in site selection, or NHA would later be stuck with unmarketable vacant land.

There seemed, in fact, to be an inverse correlation between the degree of blight in an area and its acceptability to FHA and the redevelopers. Middle-income housing probably wasn't feasible in the midst of a hard-core slum or a Negro ghetto. At least, FHA and most developers believed it was so, and that was the important thing. They argued that no market for middle-income housing existed in these areas and that few people could be induced to move there. Moreover, projects in the midst of slum areas, as public housing experience showed, tended to be rapidly inundated by the surrounding blight.

The ideal solution, from NHA's point of view, was to tear down the entire ghetto and build a "city within a city." But the federal Division of Slum Clearance would not finance such massive operations, and NHA didn't know where it could get the redevelopers to buy all that land. The more NHA officials pondered this problem, the more convinced they became that the Title I program contained an internal contradiction. Newark probably could not have the construction of middle-income housing in addition to the clearance of its worst slums until some changes were made in federal legislation or policies.

The result of this soul searching was a fresh start in site selection. In its second effort NHA sought areas that were in need of clearance but that also were acceptable to FHA and redevelopers. This subordination of slum clearance to site feasibility forced NHA to bypass the hard-core slums of the Central Ward and to select instead a site in the North Ward. This site was within the area marked for clearance by the Central Planning Board's Master Plan and, thus, was a defensible choice for NHA's initial effort in redevelopment. It was also on the outer edges of the slum belt and in better condition than most parts of the Central Ward. The North Ward site, in short, was not sufficiently blighted or inter-racial to repel redevelopers or FHA.

In setting the boundaries and format of this project, NHA sought to protect redevelopment from the encroachment of the surround-ing slum areas. NHA's decision to draft an ambitious proposal covering about fifteen blocks and to think in terms of area re-development rather than a redevelopment project was motivated by its earlier experience with the "disappearance" of public hous-ing projects. The locus and contours of this site were dictated by a search for natural boundaries (a railroad, a park, and a major thoroughfare) to contain the project as a community within itself and protect it from its immediate environment. NHA officials were so strongly committed to the clearance of a large area surrounded by natural boundaries that, when federal officials cut back the area slated for redevelopment, they refused either to reduce the size of the clearance area or to sacrifice one of the natural boundaries. Instead, they proposed to retain redevelopment along the outer boundaries of the site and to fill in the middle spaces with public housing. This, then, was the final format of NHA's first effort in urban redevelopment: a 1,550-unit public housing project bor-dered on both sides by privately redeveloped housing.

NHA officials knew they were acting cautiously, but they were very eager to make their first effort a success. They were prepared to gamble on redevelopment in a hard-core slum, but not on the first project. Indeed, no one at that time knew whether redevelop-ment was feasible on any site in Newark. Perhaps Newark's high wage rates, high taxes, and high costs of construction would pre-vent the building of true middle-income housing anywhere in the city. Perhaps there was no market for middle-income housing in Newark or its environs. NHA officials realized that, if the first proj-ect did not answer these questions in Newark's favor, there would be no second project. For this reason, they saw the North Ward as a pilot project which would demonstrate the viability of redevelopment in Newark to FHA and the redevelopers. For the same reason, they were taking no risks in site selection at this initial stage.

But NHA officials had not weakened their commitment to slum clearance. Despite the problems of site feasibility in the Central Ward, they knew that they could not continue to ignore that area. In 1952, after the announcement of the North Ward project, they began reconsidering sites in the Central Ward.

THE CENTRAL WARD: REDEVELOPMENT IN THE GHETTO

The expansion of the urban redevelopment concept by Congress in 1954 encouraged NHA to try redevelopment in the Negro ghetto.[4] Since early 1950 NHA officials had been convinced that no mere project, not even one as large as the North Ward project, would be safe from slum encroachment in the Central Ward. Only a full-scale demolition of the ghetto, or total neighborhood redevelopment, would succeed in that area. The 1954 Federal Housing Act renewed the slum clearance provisions of the 1949 Act and added a program of federal aid for local renewal activities other than clearance. This legislation permitted local agencies to designate an entire neighborhood as an Urban Renewal Area. Within this area the local agency would be empowered to conserve all sound structures, rehabilitate the sound but deteriorating structures, and clear the structures that were beyond saving. Under the terms of this Act NHA could launch a varied and comprehensive attack on the Central Ward.

NHA officials began with the hard core of Newark's slum belt, a section known at that time as the Third Ward. They then expanded their proposed renewal area, first to establish natural boundaries for the site in the form of major commercial thoroughfares, and then to include some fringe areas suitable for private redevelopment. The Housing Authority's plan was to concentrate public housing construction in the Negro area, with private redevelopment in the less dilapidated areas to the west. Tearing down the entire ghetto was not feasible; area-wide renewal seemed to be the best alternative.

These plans were dashed when URA concluded that the 100-block area was too large and eliminated forty blocks on the west.

NHA decided to proceed with the renewal of this sixty-block area and made its formal announcement in April, 1955. Renewal would begin with a public housing project, NHA said, to help relocate those who would subsequently be displaced by clearance for re-development.

But URA had eliminated all those blocks suitable for private redevelopment and had left NHA with nothing but public housing sites. In addition, by cutting down the area and restricting the amount of funds available for clearance in the reduced area, URA made it impossible for the Authority to leave any major imprint on the ghetto. Central Ward renewal, then, would amount to the clearance of a few sites in a hard-core slum, without any attempt to alter the basic character of the slum.

NHA officials realized that home builders would not participate in Central Ward redevelopment under these terms. The fear of being left with vacant sites led NHA to reduce the area slated for clearance even below the federal limit. The Authority's staff knew that most buildings in the Central Ward should be torn down, not dressed up. "The real question," as one official put it, "was what we were going to do with all that cleared land."

Yet, NHA was dubious about the chances of private redevelopment even in this diminished clearance area. Eventually, Housing Authority officials decided to build their own public housing projects on two of these cleared sites and to sell the rest to the City, the Board of Education, and the Boys' Club of Newark. Redevelopment by public or quasi-public institutions helped NHA avoid some of the problems involved in attracting private builders to a Negro ghetto, but it did not eliminate the problem of site feasibility. Such institutions had their own special needs and usually did not want to build on the sites NHA most desired to clear. For its own public housing projects, however, NHA could select two of the most blighted areas in the Central Ward.

NHA's inability to achieve either private redevelopment or "a city within a city" was demonstrated in the Central Ward Urban Renewal Plan, completed early in 1960. It revealed that thirty-two blocks in the renewal area would be either rehabilitated or left untouched. Fifteen blocks would be cleared for two public housing projects; ten for redevelopment by public institutions. Three blocks would be cleared for private redevelopment, including the construction of a new supermarket. Thus, of the sixty blocks in the renewal area, only two would be redeveloped for middle-income housing. This, moreover, was to come in the last stage of the project.

NHA officials view this plan as a major achievement, no less significant because it falls short of the Authority's initial goal. To them, it is something of a miracle that any Title I activity proved feasible in the Central Ward.

INDUSTRIAL REDEVELOPMENT: ALL RULES HAVE EXCEPTIONS

The initiation of light industrial redevelopment on Jeliffe Avenue was a departure from the way in which most clearance projects in Newark were begun.[5] Only here can one say without question that a local group significantly affected NHA's initial planning or that a project hinged on NHA's negotiations with a local interest.

In 1955 NHA drafted a proposal asking URA either to restore the forty blocks it had lopped off the Central Ward renewal area or to designate these forty blocks as another renewal area. At the same time NHA learned that a subcommittee of realtors from the Newark Economic Development Committee (NEDC) had selected four tentative sites for a privately financed industrial redevelopment project. One of the sites was a fifteen-block zone within the forty-block area NHA had resubmitted to URA. For reasons more fully explored in Chapter V, Danzig was eager to involve local corporations in the redevelopment program. He was willing to accommodate them with concessions even on matters of substantive policy. He tried to convince NEDC members that they would be unable to clear the area without federal aid. He then offered to incorporate their plans for industrial redevelopment into his forty-block proposal.

The businessmen were difficult to sell on Title I, but they finally agreed. Shortly afterwards URA officials cut back the area to twenty-five blocks, though retaining the entire industrial zone. Jeliffe Avenue, then, turned out to be more of an industrial redevelopment project than NHA had originally planned.

The extent of NHA's concessions, however, should not be over-estimated. To begin with, the Authority had applied for this forty-block area before it began its campaign to sell Title I to NEDC. Secondly, since light industry was the only usage suitable to the Jeliffe Avenue area, NHA probably would have proceeded in that direction in any event. What NEDC apparently viewed as a con-cession was simply NHA's next logical step. Thirdly, local business-men did not actively seek a role in planning this project; they were persuaded by NHA officials to become a part of the planning process. Finally, after the formal announcement in November, 1957, NHA's control of project planning on this site was absolute.

RUTGERS AND SETON HALL: REDEVELOPMENT
FOR INSTITUTIONAL USE

Housing Authority officials see themselves operating in a tightly confined box created by the terms of the 1949 Act, by the needs of private redevelopers, and by the policies of federal housing agencies.[6] One way out, as they learned in the North Ward, is to find a site where middle-income housing might prove possible. An-other is to modify the Authority's emphasis on housing and to have institutions redevelop the land for their own use. Colleges building new facilities or corporations building new home offices need not worry about finding middle-income housing markets or making a profit. They presumably find enough benefit in central city loca-tion, moreover, to absorb the high costs of construction. NHA learned another lesson from the Central Ward project: that it is often more efficient to secure redevelopers first and then to negoti-ate the appropriate site with them.

In 1955 and 1956 NHA's program moved toward such redevelop-ment for institutional use. A major effort was made to have local corporations, colleges, labor unions, and hospitals consider build-ing under Title I. A plan for the expansion of Rutgers University in Newark, under the 1949 Act, had been drafted by NHA's staff as early as 1950 but had been laid aside. For the reasons stated earlier, Danzig had preferred that NHA's first project demonstrate the viability of middle-income housing in Newark. Furthermore, the various branches of Rutgers had been unable to agree on a concerted effort, and Governor Alfred Driscoll had been opposed to any expansion of Rutgers at state expense.

In 1955 Danzig renewed the idea of a college expansion project and began an intensive selling campaign that went on for two years. Seldom have NHA officials worked harder to arrange a project.

First, Danzig brought the various branches of Rutgers University together and led them to agreement on a common expansion plan. He also worked through the New Jersey Association of Housing and Redevelopment Officials (NJAHRO) to sell the idea of a school construction bond issue to Governor Robert Meyner and the New Jersey Legislature. As NHA also persuaded the Newark Museum, the Newark Public Library, and the Newark College of Engineering to join in constructing new facilities on the site, the project gradually grew into a "cultural center." In September, 1958, the Authority announced the designation of a fifteen-block renewal area, just south of the North Ward project, for the expansion of local educational and cultural facilities.

Danzig also sought the participation of the local Catholic university, Seton Hall. A proposal for the construction of new educational and religious facilities under Title I had been broached much earlier to Seton Hall officials, but now NHA stepped up its efforts. Since all other local colleges were involved in Title I, it was both fair practice and good policy to include Newark's Catholic college. While Seton Hall was eventually drawn into the program for entirely different reasons, its inclusion probably served to neutralize the Catholic Church as a source of potential opposition to the college expansion project and to the state bond issue.

Seton Hall officials also had to be sold on the idea of Title I. After long negotiations they agreed to participate, but only if their project would be kept separate from the other college project. Thus, in April, 1959, NHA announced the clearance and rehabilitation of two blocks surrounding Seton Hall's downtown campus. It was to be a second college expansion project, one mile away from the proposed cultural center.

Redevelopment by public institutions may have helped NHA

avoid some of the problems involved in redevelopment for middle-income housing, but it did not give NHA any greater flexibility in site selection. The colleges generally insisted on redeveloping areas adjacent to their present campuses. In order to protect its separate identity, Seton Hall insisted on a site removed from that of the other college project. None of the institutions was any more willing to redevelop sites in the hard-core slums than private home builders would have been. Once again, NHA found itself unable to select sites solely on the basis of the degree of blight, the presence of natural boundaries, or the absence of mixed land uses and other persistent blighting factors.

REAPPRAISAL AND DEPARTURE

Many of NHA's practical rules of thumb became definite policies in 1958.[7] During that year a crisis in the North Ward project led NHA officials to reappraise their entire program. In the course of this reappraisal NHA officials made explicit the lessons of their first eight years in redevelopment and systematized the day-by-day tactics they had been pursuing. They now see this new awareness and strategy as the key to their remarkable success in 1959.

By spring, 1956, NHA had not received any expressions of interest in the North Ward site from either local or nonlocal redevelopers. Authority officials realized that, unless they immediately started an intensive search for redevelopers, any attempt to dispose of the land by competitive bidding would be a fiasco. After an anxious and busy year Danzig and Nevin stimulated several respectable bids. In May, 1957, bids were received, and the land was sold.

The site lay vacant for six months, however, while NHA, the redeveloper, and FHA argued on the terms of mortgage insurance. In November the redeveloper announced that he could not come to terms with FHA and that he was withdrawing from the project. The site lay vacant for another few months before NHA convinced the Metropolitan Corporation of America to assume responsibility for the project. In order to salvage the project and to meet FHA's requirements, NHA permitted this company to raise the rentals and to revise the redevelopment plan. The Metropolitan

Corporation also wanted a guarantee that their redevelopment proposal would be accepted by NHA and that the competitive bidding procedure would be a formality.

NHA officials regard their difficulty in disposing of the North Ward site as the worst crisis of their redevelopment program. The lessons contained in the loss of one redeveloper and the securing of a second were not lost on them. They were determined not to begin another project without first having secured a redeveloper and tailoring the project to his needs. "We took an awful chance in the North Ward," one official said, "by guessing at what redevelopers wanted. Then we had to go around peddling vacant land. Now we let the redevelopers *tell* us where they want to build." What was the point of having the staff prepare a redevelopment plan, if the redevelopers later found it unworkable? The new rule was: "Find a redeveloper first, and then see what interests him."

NHA became convinced that the redevelopers want to negotiate agreements at the outset of a project and that they will shy away from cities trying to dispose of already cleared sites by competitive bidding. NHA also came to realize that the competitive bidding requirements need not be unduly constricting. Without prior arrangement, bids for a site are not forthcoming. The Authority found it necessary to make arrangements with a redeveloper, then advertise for bids, and, finally, sell the site to the only bidder.

The North Ward crisis and several other events also convinced the Authority's staff that local business corporations would never participate in redevelopment to the extent that NHA had originally expected. Despite years of campaigning, Danzig could not persuade even one local corporation to redevelop a site in Newark or to finance redevelopment by others. When local interests, like Rutgers and Seton Hall, agreed to participate, NHA discovered problems that were not present in its dealings with outside redevelopers. In dealing with Seton Hall, NHA was bargaining not merely with a redeveloper but with a religious institution. In dealing with Rutgers, NHA found itself bargaining with the city's leading corporation executives who sat on the colleges' boards of trustees. In short, redevelopment by local interests increased both

NHA's negotiating problems and its involvement in local politics. Apparently for these reasons, Danzig and Nevin decided to focus their attention on attracting nonlocal, nationally known home builders like Zeckendorf, Turner, and Parker.

If the important men in home building were to be drawn to Newark, NHA realized that it would have to make the lure attractive. In talking to redevelopers, Authority officials discovered that they had to make choice sites available and let the builders suggest the appropriate rentals. It is not surprising, then, that NHA's efforts led to projects involving high-priced apartments on sites immediately surrounding the central business district. Insistence on slum sites or moderate rents would have destroyed the venture before it began. NHA once again discovered that if the city's worst slums were to be cleared, it would have to be for public housing.

THE DOWNTOWN PROGRAM

NHA's new efforts were prefaced by a small, locally sponsored project.[8] After years of intensive effort by NHA, Jack Lehman, president of the United States Realty and Investment Company, agreed to sponsor a middle-income housing project. In so doing, however, he rejected all of NHA's site suggestions in order to build on South Broad Street, perhaps because United States Realty owned a good deal of property there. He cautiously insisted on a two-block project, moreover, even though NHA argued that projects of this size were not feasible. As one informant phrased it: "The Lehman proposal wasn't a project, it was part of a project." Other redevelopers would have to be drawn into that area to support United States Realty's plans. This project only heightened NHA's interest in attracting outside redevelopers.

The crisis in New York City's Title I program, which broke in spring, 1959, was a windfall for NHA's new venture. A number of prominent home builders, including Jack Parker of Long Island, were told by Robert Moses, head of New York's clearance program, that there would be little clearance activity in New York for a while. Allegedly, Moses referred them to Newark for the interim. They quickly found that Danzig—like Moses—was both flexible and autonomous as a negotiator.

Parker, the first builder to be rerouted to Newark, insisted on the clearance of a massive area which would give him room enough to build luxury apartments over the next ten years. Parker and NHA officials negotiated for several months before agreeing on a vast 125-block site in the South Broad area. Parker was interested in some choice downtown sites and in some sound residential areas. NHA drew the boundary lines to include these, as well as certain hard-core slum areas. The final site was suitable to NHA because it bordered on the Central Ward project and might entice Parker into some further redevelopment in the ghetto. The site also bordered on, and served to buttress, the two-block Lehman project.

After reaching a detailed agreement with Parker, but prior to a formal announcement of their plans, NHA officials sounded out URA on this procedure. The Washington office could not publicly condone the selection of redevelopers before the selection of a site. The Philadelphia office, however, embarrassed by the large number of vacant sites in the region, gave NHA its informal blessing.

With the announcement of Parker's proposal NHA discovered that the nation's largest redevelopers tended to follow each other. As soon as NHA had captured one "big name," Newark became known among that small clique of home builders as a good place to build in. Now that the program had caught on and Newark was "hot," NHA's long months of pressure on these redevelopers began to pay dividends. Within a few months of the Parker project NHA was ready to announce two more ambitious proposals.

The Penn Plaza proposal involved the clearance of fifteen blocks in a run-down commercial area near Pennsylvania Station for the construction of luxury apartments, stores, and office buildings. Since plans to clear "Skid Row" had been circulating for at least fifteen years, the site and boundaries of this project were set largely by tradition. Oscar Stonorov, an architect hired by the City to supervise a study of the central business district, helped NHA persuade the Gilbane Construction Company of Providence, Rhode Island, to undertake redevelopment in this area.

The Essex Heights proposal, announced in December, 1959, was the result of a long campaign by NHA to bring the Turner Construction Company to Newark. Prolonged negotiations had yielded agreement on a twenty-five-block site straddling a good part of the downtown area but also extending west into the hard-core slum. By adding some slum areas to a downtown redevelopment project, NHA had once again encouraged home builders to risk limited activity in the ghetto.

By January, 1960, the total number of renewal projects in Newark for which federal commitments had been received involved clearance or rehabilitation of well over 300 blocks. Over $700 million in local and federal funds was required for the completion of these projects. Although URA committed funds for the completion of all NHA projects then current, it insisted that such funds be spread out over a ten-year period. In January, 1960, URA gave NHA $26 million in a lump sum as the first annual installment of this plan.

Although Housing Authority officials realize that the downtown projects will be the focus of their attention for the next decade, they have not shut the door on negotiations for additional projects. NHA has conceded that the local demand for new housing will be met by these downtown proposals, but it has continued to consider new proposals for nonresidential redevelopment or for redevelopment by public institutions. Early in 1960 it seemed likely that NHA's next proposal would be an expansion in medical facilities by the United Hospital Foundation of Newark. Preliminary discussions were also being held on a light industrial project to be sponsored by William Zeckendorf and on a central office building for local organized labor. All three projects would be in the downtown area.

THE MEANING OF SUCCESS

High quantitative achievements in project building have been attained through a highly flexible application of NHA's initial values. Thus, the Authority has not always been able to obtain the construction of moderately priced apartments or to clear as much of the hard-core slums as they would like. Some local observers who say that NHA has been overly accommodating to the redevelopers would quarrel with a characterization of the program as successful. It also is said that no one really knows whether the current middle-income housing projects will ultimately prove successful for the redevelopers.

The term "success" is used to indicate effective action or project building within the limits of the present Title I program. Most of the modifications in purpose that NHA has made are prerequisites to achievement, given the current status of federal legislation, redeveloper demands, and URA and FHA policies. Success is also defined in relation to the limitations set by the locale. Many of NHA's actions have been dictated by the problems of attaining middle-income housing in a city like Newark. Within these limitations NHA has managed to tear down a great deal of substandard housing and to initiate a great deal of new construction. Few agencies in a similar situation could have done more.

One may quarrel with this interpretation of the program and still concede that NHA as an agency has been successful. NHA has been less interested in executing particular redevelopment policies than in taking significant steps to reverse Newark's decline. In 1949 NHA officials set out to improve the local housing situation and to achieve whatever redevelopment action was possible under the circumstances. Those goals have, for the most part, been attained.

STAGING A PROJECT

The nonpolitical context of NHA's decision making does not insure that agency officials can afford to be oblivious to the problem of securing local acceptance.[9] The Authority's staff, in fact, has developed a conscious strategy for facilitating such acceptance, at the same time protecting its flexibility in dealing with outside parties. This strategy centers around the staging of projects or the sequential order of negotiations. To an extent, the procedures described below have been forced upon NHA by the exigencies of dealing with redevelopers and federal officials. But NHA officials are fully aware of the strategic uses of this procedure.

The keys to NHA's staging process are the elaborate, preliminary negotiations involving NHA, redevelopers, and federal officials, and the low visibility of this preparatory stage. The result of these informal, unpublicized negotiations is a detailed project package.

The necessary political support for this package is negotiated in advance in order to avoid public defeats or open skirmishes. Local officials generally must accept the package as is or risk jeopardizing the entire proposal.

NHA's first step in its recent projects has been to find a redeveloper interested in Newark. It is self-evident to NHA officials that decisions on sites and their uses must be adapted to the demands of the investor if projects are to be successful. Such demands, moreover, can best be met if NHA remains the City's sole spokesman in these dealings. No one outside NHA has direct dealings with the redevelopers. Most local participants first learn of a new clearance project when they read the formal announcement by NHA in the newspapers.

It also is self-evident to Authority officials that the formative stages of a project must be protected from excessive public interference. The redevelopers themselves demand secrecy so that they can either back out gracefully or make a dramatic announcement of their plans. In addition, NHA officials feel that the announcement of tentative or alternative plans serves to excite opposition in several neighborhoods, whereas only one area will eventually be cleared. Such a preliminary announcement also gives various local interests the idea that the situation is still fluid and, hence, still amenable to their influence. NHA seldom makes a public announcement until it knows exactly what the project is to be.

NHA's next step, after finding a redeveloper, is to begin discussions with URA in order to secure federal planning funds and a capital grant reservation. Some indication of FHA's willingness to insure a mortgage on the site is also sought. For as long as a year the Director of Redevelopment will shuttle back and forth between the Philadelphia office of URA, the New York office of FHA, and the redeveloper's staff, in search of a plan agreeable to all. From NHA's point of view this is the most crucial stage of a project; it also is the most difficult hurdle to overcome. Once a plan suitable to all interests has been found, the acquiescence of local officials is assured. As one Authority official put it: "There's no point in even talking about a project with the people down at City Hall until Philadelphia [URA] gives the go-ahead." To NHA officials the amazing thing is not that the City backs them fully, but that they ever get URA, FHA, and the redeveloper to agree.

This procedure also has its strategic value. Federal approval of a project makes subsequent local approval extremely likely. If City officials were to try to amend the project, they would disrupt the balanced network of negotiations and probably stop the flow of capital into Newark. When NHA proposals are submitted on the eve of a federal deadline, as they often must be, the pressure on City officials to approve without amendment or delay is even greater.

NHA officials have had good working relations with URA's Philadelphia office from the beginning. The Regional Office has occasionally intervened in local disputes to support NHA's position. When other renewal groups or agencies have tried to deal with URA, they have found that only Danzig and Nevin have good access to the Regional Office. This access has also permitted NHA officials to become the interpreters of federal housing legislation and policies for all others in Newark.

SECURING CITY HALL SUPPORT

NHA's next and final step before a formal announcement is to clear the project with the mayor or, before 1954, with the majority bloc of city commissioners. Even at this early stage the mayor is under pressure to ratify NHA's arrangements with Philadelphia and the redevelopers. If there were any serious political objections to the project, NHA presumably would take them into account. Exactly how far NHA would go in accommodating the mayor is a moot point, for neither Ralph Villani, Mayor from 1949 to 1953, nor Leo Carlin, Mayor after 1953, ever raised any major objections.

The support of municipal agencies involved in public construction related to slum clearance is often as important as the support of the mayor. Any clearance project, but particularly area-wide renewal, requires the widening and repaving of streets, the construction of schools, the relocation of sewers and underground utilities, and other supportive actions by local agencies. To avoid embarrassment after the formal announcement of a project, NHA attempts to extract beforehand a tentative promise of cooperation from the appropriate agencies. Since renewal projects are more palatable to local officials if a large part of the City's one-third share can be defrayed by local construction, NHA has had added incentive for involving public works agencies in its projects.

These agencies have their own good reasons for negotiating with NHA. Most of them find that they can increase their share of the municipal budget and facilitate approval of their projects by linking their activities to an expanding, federally aided program. The Superintendent of Schools, for example, backed NHA's first two projects with public school construction. With URA paying part of the cost of these new schools, approval by the Board of Education was virtually assured, even if it meant slightly increasing the capital budget for those years. This coordination of programs has served, though unintentionally, to weaken whatever control City Hall has over NHA through the City's one-third contribution. The major part of that contribution has been imbedded in the Board of Education's capital budget, where it is less available to manipulation by the mayor or the City Council.

The problem that confronts NHA is how to gain the support of relevant agencies without exposing the project to wholesale intervention by City Hall. How can certain agencies be lined up in advance without accumulating additions or amendments that eventually would make the project unworkable? If the project is ever to get started, the line of participation must be drawn somewhere.

NHA has responded to this problem by distinguishing between those agencies which must be consulted in advance and those agencies whose concurrence usually can be counted upon once the formal announcement has been made. Construction agencies generally fall into the first category; service and regulatory agencies into the second. In the pre-announcement consultations, moreover, NHA tries to extract a pledge of cooperation by outlining the probable effect of the project on the agency concerned and indicating the supportive action required from the agency. Although all questions of the agency will be answered by NHA, the project plans are not made available for general inspection. To minimize potential political interference, NHA's staff members also try, wherever possible, to deal with the corresponding staff official in the agency, not with the top man. Thus, Nevin deals exclusively with the Superintendent of Schools, Edward Kennelly, and lets Kennelly make all presentations to the Board of Education.

The successful nature of these operations was demonstrated in March, 1953, when relevant agency heads were brought together to testify on the proposed redevelopemnt plan for the North Ward. Commissioner Leo Carlin, who probably expected this meeting to point up NHA's lack of communication with City Hall, found that most of his subordinates in the Department of Public Works already had discussed the project with Nevin and had pledged their support. The agencies indicated that they had been briefed on their role, but they revealed no extensive familiarity with the details of the plan. The agency heads who had not been briefed proved unwilling to stand in the way of the project.

Later, Carlin, as mayor, altered his former position and encouraged negotiations between Nevin and the administrative agencies. Only in those rare cases when NHA and an agency are deadlocked do the negotiations rise to the mayor's office and become visible to the newspaper-reading public. The 1954 City Charter's attempt to centralize authority at City Hall apparently did nothing to disrupt NHA's relations with the administrative agencies. In April, 1955, a meeting of agency heads to discuss the Central Ward project showed the same pattern of support for NHA that had emerged in the 1953 meeting.

THE FORMAL ANNOUNCEMENT

About two years generally intervene between the initial selection of a site and the formal announcement of a project. The proposal is not publicized during this time, in part to protect NHA's negotiations with URA, redevelopers, and City Hall, and in part to secure a maximum impact for the formal announcement. By agreement with the local reporters covering urban renewal, a few discreet hints about a project may be periodically released, but the major announcement is saved for a big spread in the Sunday editions.

Outside of its attempt to stage the announcement of a project, however, NHA does not devote any substantial resources to pub-licity or public relations. Authority officials have said that too much publicity often stimulates organized interests that otherwise would have remained inert. The public relations staff of the busi-ness bloc developed an over-all rationale of the renewal program, which NHA officials have been inclined to let stand. Outside of this, NHA's sole public relations efforts have centered on maintain-ing good relations with the press.

The Newark *News* has been a major spokesman for the conserva-tive, reform-minded civic leaders and a leading supporter of charter revision, the Carlin administration, and slum clearance. Because of this concern with good government, critics of NHA generally receive short shrift in the editorials of the *News*. In addition, neither the *News* nor Newark's other important daily, the *Star Ledger,* gives significant attention to NHA's negotiations with local parties. These dailies, like many other newspapers, define "news" as dramatic action or conflict. Since overt conflict among the renewal participants is infrequent, press treatment of local renewal is limited largely to formal announcements by NHA.

Reporters covering local renewal often are baffled by the tech-nical questions involved. By seeking clarification of these questions from Authority officials, the reporters help reinforce NHA's posi-tion as interpreter of federal policies. Through this symbiotic rela-tionship, moroever, NHA has inadvertently gained considerable influence over the treatment of its activities by the local press. It has had no reason to fear newspaper attacks or attempted exposés.

THE ACCUMULATION OF COMMITMENTS

After the Authority announces a project and the mayor approves an application to URA for survey and planning funds, the pressure on the City Council to add its assent is overwhelming. By this time, to quote one informant, the project is "frozen." The councilmen must consider the proposal on a "take it or leave it" basis; rarely have they seriously considered "leaving" a proposal approved by NHA and the mayor.

As the project progresses and the amount of funds and energy expended by NHA, URA, the redevelopers, and City Hall agencies accumulates, the commitment of these participants to the project increases proportionately. NHA may begin a project despite some major problem or disagreement among the participants, confident that the accumulation of commitments will eventually lead to an agreement or solution.

Such an accumulation of commitments also makes effective intervention by local interests increasingly difficult. The City Council must eventually approve an urban renewal plan and a relocation plan, and the Central Planning Board (CPB) must declare the entire area blighted, but such action normally has been routine. As members of the Council and CPB have said, effective local review of clearance proposals can occur only at the very outset of a proposal.

At the later stages NHA follows the same procedure used in launching a proposal. The urban renewal plan, for example, is discussed with the redevelopers, then with URA and FHA, and finally with the administrative agencies at City Hall. After further discussion with the mayor it is presented to the City Council and CPB. At this point the time, energy, and money already expended preclude serious local review.

MAINTAINING THE PACE

In the post-announcement stage NHA, the redeveloper, and URA continue to negotiate in order to determine what specific uses are appropriate to the site.[10] In this way it is not basically different from the pre-announcement stage, although the bargaining becomes more and more specific. The initial plan of a project or the public image presented in the formal announcement may have to be altered substantially as new problems emerge and the demands of participants change. A rigid commitment by NHA officials to the initial plan would strain, if not break, the commitment of other parties to the project. From NHA's point of view the major problem of the post-announcement stage is not to execute the initial plan without alteration but to keep the commitments of outside parties "warm."

One way to maintain such commitments is to maintain a rapid pace throughout the project. Redevelopers and federal officials quickly lose interest in projects that drag on interminably. For this reason, prolonged consideration by the City Council or CPB can prove highly damaging. For the same reason, NHA will hasten to break deadlocks in negotiations, even if it means a further departure from the initial plan.

In October, 1959, when URA told Authority officials that funds for the downtown program would have to be spread over a ten-year period, Danzig and Nevin devised a plan to proceed simultaneously with all projects. Rather than handle each project serially and risk losing some redevelopers who were awaiting their turn, NHA divided the larger projects into stages and sought immediate action on the first stage of all projects. In this way all of the commitments to all of the projects were maintained.

This emphasis on rapid and sustained activity applies not only to particular projects but to the entire program. Since the early 1940s NHA officials have emphasized the importance of keeping active and of always having a few proposals under consideration. Activism draws redevelopers to the city, impresses federal officials, stimulates the morale of the agency's staff, and gives the agency an edge in its negotiations with local interests. In the world of urban renewal, project building seems to yield more project building, and clearance activity seems to acquire a momentum of its own. After a certain point successful agencies can do nothing wrong. They are rarely involved in political skirmishes because they are rarely challenged.

There also seems to be a cycle of failure. Inactivity, a loss of status among redevelopers and federal officials, and increasing vulnerability to local political interference seem to reinforce each other. As some NHA officials see it: "a program either catches fire or it doesn't."

One further comment about NHA's strategies should be made. It may be said that the Authority's rules of thumb provide no help in securing local approval of a ten-year redevelopment plan or a long-range scheme of interrelated projects. In fact, NHA's emphasis on gaining approval of the particular project at hand and on avoiding general policy statements is deliberate. NHA believes that ten-year redevelopment plans are impractical, cannot be realized, and only serve to impede the Authority's negotiations with outside parties. It is also convinced that the difficulty experienced in securing local approval of a proposal increases in direct proportion to the all-encompassing character of that proposal. Agencies should not submit a proposal until they know exactly what they want. Proposals should be worded in the most specific terms possible, and more general questions on "where the program is going" should be avoided. Publicizing long-range policy statements or seeking local approval of a ten-year plan is unnecessary to renewal achievement. More than that, it invites disaster.

THE "CLEAN DEAL"

Ask most Housing Authority officials to explain the success of their redevelopment program, and they will reply that private redevelopers and federal officials know they can get a "clean deal" in Newark. When taking part in a slum clearance project in Newark, these outside participants do not have to make separate arrangements with a variety of local officials, yielding concessions at each step in the negotiations and often getting embroiled in local politics. Instead they conduct all their business with a few men in the Housing Authority. These men have the freedom from local interference to bargain flexibly and are sufficiently confident of their control of local renewal processes to make broad commitments. Having once reached a settlement with Danzig, private redevelopers need not concern themselves with having to amend the agreement or with making political payoffs in order to facilitate its local acceptance. The officials of URA, moreover, need not worry that the project will become a local political football once federal funds have been committed. NHA not only has the autonomy to deal freely with these participants, it also has the capacity to deliver on all its promises in record time.

One observer may have exaggerated NHA's importance, but not by very much, when he said: "They [NHA] own the slums. They can sell any piece of real estate in that area to a redeveloper before it's even acquired. And they don't have to check with anyone [in Newark] before they do it. City Hall has got to back them up." This is another way of saying that the Authority has attained its major goals: a free hand to deal with outside participants and a guarantee of unqualified local acceptance of the resulting clearance proposal. To NHA officials a local redevelopment program stands or falls on whether it attracts the necessary outside commitments. A redevelopment agency that has transformed local renewal processes into a routine operation will have little difficulty in attracting these commitments.

This, in summary, is the pattern of policy formation in Newark's urban redevelopment program. The pattern depends upon the existence of a stable and permissive local environment where organized responses to the agency's decisions can be predicted—and often discounted—in advance. NHA's aggressive procedures would probably backfire if used in a less firmly structured political situation. Exactly how this type of benign environment emerged is a crucial question and one that cannot be answered wholly in terms of NHA's strategies. It is a question which the remainder of this study tries to answer.

At the same time, it would be unwise to overemphasize environmental factors and to underestimate the importance of NHA's personnel and their strategies. The formal organization of urban renewal in all cities tends to be more or less dispersive. Before a project can be launched, a large number of independent actors must be persuaded to participate. Some person or agency must bring all the parties together, negotiate support for the project, and quiet or mediate opposition. Someone must build an organization to provide the dispersed renewal structure with an informal peak. An acquiescent local environment may make the job of the renewal entrepreneur easier, but an acquiescent environment alone is insufficient. There must also exist in the same person or agency both the awareness of the need for this entrepreneurial function and the political skill to carry it out.

In Newark NHA's top staff have the necessary entrepreneurial abilities. In this group (Louis Danzig, Joseph Nevin, Samuel Warrence, Augustine Kelly, and Joseph Reilly) are combined the skills of the housing official, the administrator, the lawyer, and the politician. These men share a strong loyalty to the program and to Newark, a willingness to put in long hours, and an instinctive feeling for the politics of administration. It is true that their task as renewal entrepreneurs has been facilitated by the permissiveness of the local political environment, but it is also true that they had the insight to recognize this permissiveness and to adopt procedures to exploit it. They also had a hand in shaping that environment, as future pages will testify. NHA's responses to the political environment and its efforts to shape that environment are basic concomitants of Newark's success in urban renewal. One member of the business bloc grudgingly admitted: "Without Lou Danzig and Joe Nevin, there'd be nothing in the city—no clearance, no Jack Parker, no Turner-Galbreath—nothing—just a lot of talk and plans."

CHAPTER III

The Politicos

The interest of the "politico" in urban renewal centers on the detailed application of urban renewal policies to particular individuals or groups. He is less interested in setting general renewal policy than in doing favors. His major concerns are how NHA's actions affect the lives of Newark residents, how these residents respond, and what can be done to help them. His major activity in urban renewal is to make requests of NHA for jobs, favors, and other considerations.

The term "politico" generally refers to an elected official at City Hall, although the phrase will be used to include all those who share the above-defined perspective. This perspective, and the demands the politicos make of NHA, will be called "political," using the word in quotation marks to denote this special sense.

TAKING NHA OUT OF "POLITICS"

The structure of NHA's relations with City Hall was established in the years immediately preceding the launching of urban redevelopment.[1] In summer, 1948, a near scandal in public housing disrupted the arrangements that had existed between City Hall and NHA since 1939 and led to the negotiation of the arrangements that now prevail.

NHA was apparently a highly "political" agency during most of its first decade in public housing. Informants agree that the city commissioners, during these years, freely intervened in site and tenant selection, the awarding of contracts, and most other aspects of public housing. The politicos favored public projects in their neighborhoods, since projects were low-rise, garden-apartment structures built on vacant sites and occupied by people of the vicinity. Each commissioner viewed a project in his home area as an important source of support; the tenants of a public housing project usually turned out record pluralities for their sponsor. The projects, according to informants, were rotated among the city commissioners and thus among the city's major ethnic groups. In 1948 there were two Irish, one Negro, two Italian, and two Jewish projects.

No systematic attempt has been made to determine the exact scope of "political" interference in NHA's decision making during the 1940s, but most informants believe that the scope was broad. In 1948 the Essex County Prosecutor thought he had enough evidence of intervention in site selection to institute a grand jury investigation. Commissioner Ralph Villani, whose department included NHA, was anxious to avoid such an inquiry, particularly since it would occur six months before an election. To avert an investigation, Villani asked for the resignation of NHA's Executive Director and began searching for a new man who would "clean house" at the Authority. He eventually reached into the ranks of his own electoral organization and offered the job to a long-time political aide, Louis Danzig.

Danzig agreed to assume the executive directorship and to clean house in exchange for a set of informal guarantees from Villani and the other city commissioners. First, he insisted that the commissioners help in making the office of executive director the true center of decision and initiative. To meet this requirement, the city commissioners agreed to grant him a five-year contract rather than the single-year agreements heretofore used. They also agreed to transact all their business with NHA through his office and not through the NHA commissioners. Second, Danzig sought full power to take "politics" out of the housing program, that is, to restrict the extent of the politicos' interference in NHA policy making. He insisted on a free hand in matters of policy, along with a guarantee of support for the policies that NHA developed. Danzig made it clear that he wanted no haggling over future projects and that he would make no accommodations or deals to get them approved. This understanding was in part explicit, in part tacit, and often ambiguous. Yet, all concerned seemed to agree that some kind of basic accord had been reached.

In 1948 and 1949 NHA embarked on a new set of public housing policies without first consulting the politicos or giving them an opportunity to intervene. First, NHA shifted its emphasis from low-rise projects in outlying areas to mammoth projects in the midst of the Central Ward slums. For the first time, NHA became engaged in the clearance of occupied sites and in the construction of significant new housing in Negro areas. NHA also began racial integration of its existing projects. The pattern of NHA-City Hall relations that has prevailed in the urban renewal program was foreshadowed by the city commissioners' quick approval of all these shifts in public housing policy.

THE "POLITICAL" AND THE "NONPOLITICAL"

While insisting upon this freedom from political interference in matters of policy, Danzig made it clear to the commissioners that he would give fair hearing to all "political" requests that did not affect the substance of general policy.[2] If the Authority could help the politicos on small favors that left over-all policy unaffected, NHA would have been foolish not to do so. Some of NHA's critics among the civic groups disillusioned by the Authority's continuing immersion in "political" practices ignore one important aspect of the change that occurred in 1948. Danzig established large, "political-free" areas of NHA activity and insisted that the politicos respect the line separating "political" and "nonpolitical." In short, he continued to deal with the politicos on detailed considerations in return for complete discretion on major policy decisions.

One of Danzig's most important achievements, then, was to eliminate "political" considerations from decisions involving the selection of sites, the awarding of contracts, and the naming of private redevelopers. Another achievement was to remove any taint of wrong-doing or personal profiteering from the program. Even its critics concede that the renewal program is scrupulously run. Through continual negotiations with the politicos, moreover, Danzig has steadily whittled down the size of the remaining "political" area. "Political" considerations, he has argued, must be kept within reasonable limits lest they wreck the program. Excessive "political" interference would destroy the expertise and morale of NHA's staff and could result in another public exposé or grand jury probe.

There probably are limits, however, to how far the Executive Director can curtail this "political" area. He must find an optimal balance between the need to recruit skill, to maintain control over the Authority personnel, and to protect NHA from scandal, on the one hand, and the concomitant necessity of ensuring acceptance of NHA's programs by City Hall, on the other. Thus, both NHA's continuing involvement in "political" considerations and its elimination of such considerations from certain areas are necessary to the Authority's success in slum clearance.

Danzig's practices in hiring NHA personnel illustrate the nature of his arrangements with the politicos. The evidence indicates that appointments to minor positions on NHA's permanent staff and to temporary jobs like real-estate appraisal and day labor have been cleared with the politicos and have often been made on the basis of their recommendations. But Danzig fought to break up the little empires each city commissioner had formed among NHA employees, whose security of tenure fluctuated with the political fortunes of their sponsors on the Board. Under Danzig an employee could not rely on his sponsor for continued employment and would be discouraged from maintaining close ties with that sponsor. Danzig has also sought the freedom to fill the top positions in each division of the Authority by merit and to recruit anywhere in the country. He has occasionally bypassed the politicos on other positions as well. If they insisted upon clearing every NHA appointment, Danzig told them, there would be no program at all.

Next to the hiring and firing of personnel, the activities of the Tenant Selection and Relocation Division are the most important focus of the politicos' demands on NHA. It is here that the Authority comes into direct, persistent contact with the public at large. It is here that the politicos make the most requests and here that NHA can take these requests into account without altering general policy.

A public housing tenant, therefore, may find it easier to secure a public housing unit, prevent eviction from a project, secure a unit in a better project, or have NHA reconsider his rent, if he has the right sponsor at City Hall. In the same way, someone owning property or residing in an area slated for clearance may encourage NHA to give him more information on its plans for his block, to re-examine the appraisal made of his property, to delay an eviction or condemnation proceeding against him, or to give greater attention to his relocation problems. After the Authority has acquired his building, but before it has relocated him elsewhere, he may find it easier to secure more heat and more structural improvements from his new landlord by channeling his requests through certain people at City Hall. Of course, there is no guarantee that he or his sponsor will be successful. A phone call from the politico merely guarantees that the client's folder will be pulled out of the file and re-examined by NHA's staff.

It may be argued, then, that NHA has achieved automony in matters of general policy by permitting some degree of "political" intervention in the detailed application of policy. This arrangement has been possible partly because the politicos have appeared less interested in influencing over-all policy than in appearing to help out particular people. It may also be argued that NHA has built the stable relations that sustain its redevelopment ventures by making accommodations in the details of its public housing administration. In one sense, then, vesting redevelopment powers in the public housing agency has contributed greatly to the redevelopment program's success.

NHA AND CITY HALL POLITICS, 1949–54

The sharp curtailment of NHA's "political" involvement and of the number of "political" favors it made available to the politicos created some difficult problems of apportionment at City Hall.[3] The city commissioners had to decide how to divide the remaining "political" considerations that NHA was still prepared to give.

Between 1949 and 1953 the Board of City Commissioners was divided into a majority bloc, made up of Ralph Villani, Meyer Ellenstein, and Stephen Moran, and a minority bloc, consisting of Leo Carlin and James Keenan. The position taken by the city commissioners on public housing and redevelopment during this four-year period reflected their status on the Board. The two minority commissioners, Carlin and Keenan, saw NHA as an adjunct to the Villani organization. For this reason they opposed a 1949 ordinance vesting redevelopment powers in the Authority. They continued to oppose subsequent NHA proposals, regarding them as just more "gravy" for Villani, Ellenstein, and Moran. From 1949 to 1953, however, the Villani group held firm and easily passed all of NHA's proposals. In January, 1952, when the Board of City Commissioners unquestioningly approved the North Ward proposal, these previously fostered good relations served to launch NHA's venture into urban redevelopment.

Danzig often sought unanimous, or at least four-to-one, votes on the Board of City Commissioners, primarily in order to impress federal officials. To achieve this end, he occasionally attempted to persuade a minority commissioner to go along. Keenan often voted with the majority for the sake of harmony, but Carlin usually cast lone dissenting votes. By and large, Danzig relied on his good relations with the majority bloc and did not try to pressure city commissioners or build coalitions on particular issues.

All of Danzig's arrangements with City Hall collapsed in April, 1953, when the voters bypassed Villani and Moran in favor of Leo Carlin and another critic of NHA, Salvatore Bontempo. The new Board of City Commissioners seemed to view NHA as a Villani stronghold, unfortunately beyond their power to purge. To add to this disruption of established relations, the voters had approved the creation of a committee on charter revision. It seemed likely that one of NHA's leading critics, Leo Carlin, would soon be the occupant of a new, strengthened mayor's office. NHA, then, was faced with a major threat to the continuance of its clearance program. By fall, 1953, however, Danzig had come to an understanding with Carlin on terms similar to those of his previous arrangement with Villani.

Under the provisions of the New Jersey Optional Municipal Charter Act, often referred to as the Faulkner Act, the boards of commissioners of local redevelopment and public housing authorities or agencies are to be appointed by the local governing body. Under the form of government Newark was planning to adopt, this would mean appointment of NHA commissioners by the new, nine-man City Council. The Act also said that the terms of all Housing Authority commissioners then holding office would lapse with the change-over in government. It followed that Newark's first City Council would have the rare opportunity and power to name an entirely new NHA Board.

Danzig viewed this power of the City Council to name a new NHA Board and to maintain its control over NHA Board appointees in the ensuing years as a threat to the Authority's hard-won freedom from "political" interference in policy making. The inevitable result, he thought, would be a "Roman holiday" for patronage grabs in the redevelopment program. Although no friends of Danzig, the "good government" groups agreed that NHA should not be tossed to the wolves. In fall, 1953, they brought Carlin and Danzig together to discuss an amendment to the Faulkner Act which would shift the power of appointing NHA commissioners from the City Council to the mayor with consent of the Council.

During discussion of the amendment Danzig made it clear that he much preferred dealing with a single centralized source of authority at City Hall to contending with nine demanding councilmen or with fluid majorities on the present Board of City Commissioners. NHA's Executive Director indicated that he had no present loyalties to the deposed Mayor and that he was not interested in promoting Villani's comeback. According to reports, Danzig said that he was prepared to deal with Mayor Carlin as he had dealt with Villani. Danzig apparently insisted on the same discretion in policy decisions and the same moderation in handling "political" requests that had prevailed under his earlier arrangements with City Hall. The Council's "political" requests would be channeled through the mayor's office. Danzig refused, moreover, to conduct any purge of personnel regarded as Villani appointees, since he felt this would impair the morale and smooth functioning of his staff.

To prevent interference in NHA's activities by either the mayor or the Council, and to prevent a return to the pre-1948 system, Danzig had his legal staff draft additions to the amendment. One clause said that if the Council were to reject the mayor's nominee for Housing Authority commissioner, the retiring commissioner would continue in office with full voting rights until the mayor and Council agreed on his successor. Another clause permitted the present NHA commissioners to serve out their regular, five-year, overlapping terms. This would minimize the disruptive influence of charter revision and would delay the appearance of a Carlin majority on the NHA Board for at least another three years.

Although few in 1954 saw these additions to the Faulkner Act as anything more than a further accretion to the new Mayor's powers, the negotiations leading up to these amendments and the settlement expressed by the amendments established the basic pattern of NHA-City Hall interaction for the future. With the transition from Villani to Carlin and from city commission to mayor-council government successfully managed, NHA officials now moved ahead on negotiations with URA over the proposed renewal project in the Central Ward. Early in 1955, after Carlin had been elected as Newark's first "strong mayor," the Housing Authority was ready to outline to the Mayor its plans for Central Ward renewal. Carlin readily endorsed the proposal and forwarded it to the City Council for ratification.

NHA COMMISSIONERS AND THEIR STAFF

The Board of Housing Authority Commissioners, established as the governing body of NHA by federal and New Jersey statute, has vested large amounts of discretion in the hands of its staff.[4] The members of the Board see themselves as reviewers and overseers who should refrain from interference in the work of the experts and the administration of NHA's programs. Since 1948, when Danzig became Executive Director, there is no case on record of a staff proposal being rejected or modified by the commissioners, and there are very few cases of split votes.

In addition, the various members of the Board have outdone each other in praise of their Executive Director. In 1953 they renewed Danzig's five-year contract without one dissenting statement or vote, and they later endorsed a resolution granting him tenure.

This pattern of staff-Board relations did not always prevail. Some of the previous executive directors, according to informants, came to Board meetings without carefully prepared proposals, permitted aimless and chaotic debate among the commissioners, and often proved unable to answer questions on the activities of their staff. As one NHA official noted: "He [a former executive director] wasn't on top of the program. . . . The Board meetings were a shambles." Danzig, on the other hand, carefully plans the agenda of all Board meetings, directs the legal staff to prepare resolutions to submit to the commissioners, explains all staff activities and resolutions to the Board members, and answers whatever questions they might have about the staff or the program. Where quick action is necessary, Danzig can proceed on his own, confident that the Board will endorse his action when it is described to them at the next meeting. If Danzig anticipates some opposition to a proposal, he will discuss it informally with various members of the Board. This problem, however, rarely occurs.

The members of the Board have resisted suggestions that they alter their present form of interaction with the NHA staff. In December, 1958, when Commissioner Gerald Spatola urged the Board to caucus without Danzig before each formal meeting, the commissioners unanimously denounced him for trying to interfere with the staff's work. Nevertheless, Danzig agreed to submit an agenda to the commissioners one week before each Board meeting. To Spatola's charge that the Executive Director "rams" through proposals at the Board's meetings, Danzig pointed out that the commissioners had expressed satisfaction with their overseer role and had willingly avoided any significant part in policy initiation.

The NHA commissioners have proved less interested in the over-all lines of policy than in its detailed application; their interest is engaged when NHA's actions directly affect particular people. The Board generally scrutinizes with great care all actions of the staff involving the hiring, classification, and compensation of Authority personnel, the appraisal and acquisition of properties, the awarding of contracts, the maintenance of NHA-owned property, the selection of public housing tenants, the rents charged, and the relocation of displaced families. In a sense, the commissioners are part of the local political environment, making claims on NHA's staff in the "politically" sensitive areas of clearance policy.

Commissioners tend to be chosen from those individuals who are already dedicated to the redevelopment and public housing programs. In addition to helping NHA attain its goal, the commissioners see themselves and are seen by others as spokesmen for particular groups, there to make sure that the Negroes, the Catholic Church, the Jews, organized labor, and others receive fair treatment from the staff. Some have been politicos in the more narrow sense of the term, trying to build a personal organization with NHA favors in the hope of securing elective office. But most commissioners have served on the Board to help improve the local housing situation and to ensure a fair share of NHA's rewards for their constituents. Whatever influence of personal following they may acquire as a result has been incidental.

If Danzig can satisfy the commissioners on questions of fair treatment and fair shares, he has little difficulty in getting his policy proposals approved. Much of what a commissioner knows about urban redevelopment issues has been learned from Danzig. A commissioner's stand on the substantive aspects of redevelopment policy largely reflects that of the Executive Director. If a commissioner should rebel on a matter of general policy or procedure, as Spatola did, the root cause generally is some dissatisfaction with Danzig's response to a particular request.

NHA COMMISSIONERS AND CITY HALL

In the first decade of public housing the NHA commissioner tended to be spokesman for an electoral organization at City Hall and to play a greater part in NHA's decisions.[5] His major role was to protect and expand the enclave of NHA personnel loyal to him and to the city commissioner who named him. NHA commissioners ceased to be the spokesmen of the city commissioners' electoral organizations when first Villani and then Carlin agreed to deal directly with Danzig on "political" requests. There had always been a religious-ethnic balance on the Board. After 1948 the members gradually became independent political entrepreneurs who made requests for their respective interest groups and not for anyone at City Hall.

The new pattern of interaction that emerged when Danzig became Executive Director, then, sharply reduced the total amount of favors and considerations available to NHA commissioners. After 1948 the staff tended to view the mayor and the NHA commissioners as separate, sometimes competing, sources of request. Of course, the mayor generally received preference. At first there was some assorted grumbling about the declining role of the commissioner, but the Board seemed incapable of any concerted resistance to this restructuring. Danzig's five-year contract, moreover, permitted him eventually to educate a new crop of Board members in these new arrangements.

During charter revision in 1954, however, Danzig insisted that the NHA commissioners then in office be permitted to serve out their term and that the new Mayor be denied the power to name an entirely new Board. Danzig seemed to feel that a Board united by loyalty to one politico at City Hall might prove difficult to deal with. Carlin, moreover, might be tempted to expand the role of NHA commissioners in order to bypass the staff or improve his bargaining position with it. Whether Carlin entertained these notions in 1954 is unclear, but he showed no inclination to resist Danzig's demand in 1954 or to expand the role of NHA commissioners in succeeding years. By 1958 the Mayor had had a chance to name four new commissioners, but the appearance of a Carlin majority on the Board had little effect on its relations with the staff.

Many of those outside the Mayor's office and NHA retained their former image of the Housing Authority commissioners. Many city councilmen, for example, continued to see the commissioners as "Carlin men" and as the major instruments of his control over NHA's "political" decisions. While it is true that most of the recent commissioners were drawn from the group that backed charter revision and Carlin's candidacy, most of them were not active politicos or part of Carlin's electoral organization. During their term in office they rarely interacted with the Mayor or with any member of his organization. When differences between Carlin and Danzig appeared, they usually supported Danzig. Thus, in 1958 the Board unanimously denounced Carlin's attack on public housing.

It is true that most NHA commissioners endorsed Carlin's bid for re-election in 1958 and mobilized toward that end whatever influence they might have accumulated as Board members. These actions, however, were taken without any prompting by or communication with the Mayor's electoral organization. When interviewed in 1960, several NHA commissoners spoke frequently of their independence and said that they would resent any pressure from Carlin's office. Any man who knuckled under to the Mayor, one said, was unfit for the job of commissioner. Most city councilmen, then, tended to overestimate the extent of the commissioner's command over NHA's "political" decisions and to exaggerate the extent of his involvement in the Carlin organization.

The persistence of these older attitudes among the public at large places the present commissioners in an awkward position. Most Newark citizens tend to equate NHA with its Board and to assume that the commissioners initiate most policy. Thus, the Board members often bear the brunt of attacks on NHA policy leveled by displaced persons, small businessmen, or neighborhood groups. For those seeking favors from the Authority, the commissioners seem to be the most visible, approachable, and responsive part of that organization. Most commissioners are deluged with requests for consideration far in excess of their capacity to deliver. To some commissioners, like Gerald Spatola, who took the job under the influence of older perspectives, the role can be a particularly frustrating one. Far from dominating NHA's decisions, the new commissioner finds himself on the firing line for anyone with a gripe against the Authority. One commissioner summarized the role well: a "shock absorber" for the staff.

The commissioner also serves his constituents as a channel of access to Danzig, Nevin, and Warrence on "political" considerations or on matters of general policy. When realtors or property owners want further information on NHA's plans for a particular area, their first act is to "reach" one of the commissioners. The commissioner will either introduce his client to the Director of Redevelopment, Joseph Nevin, or obtain the information from Nevin himself. When the West Hudson–Essex CIO Council first considered the construction of a central headquarters under Title I, they began by approaching labor's man on the Board, Commissioner Irving Rosenberg. When Negro leaders get excited about tenanting practices in public housing, their first move is to phone their contact on the Board, Theodore Pettigrew. Danzig always gives the commissioners a sympathetic hearing on the requests or complaints of their clients, although he is not always able or willing to meet such demands.

There is one other function that the present commissioners play, and that is to gather support for NHA's policies among their constituents. Most NHA commissioners try to describe the staff's point of view to various segments of the community, explain why certain steps were necessary, and answer questions or criticisms. The staff, however, has not pushed the commissioners into this role nor consciously used them as "transmission belts." Most staff men see the product of this proselytizing as extra support which can't hurt, but neither can it make or break the program.

THE POLITICS OF ACQUIESCENCE, 1954–58

If the City Council has not been close to the center of redevelopment decision making, it is partly because it was so intended in the 1954 charter and partly because the councilmen acquiesced to it.[6] The civic groups and local newspapers leading the campaign for charter revision preferred a city-manager form of government. They settled for a strong mayor, a strong business administrator, and a weak City Council. Most of the revisionists seemed to view the future councilmen as vestiges of the old political order, as men who would subordinate public policy to "political" purposes if given half an opportunity. The reform groups eventually agreed on Plan C of the Faulkner Act, which denied the City Council powers to initiate action or to create standing committees and which prescribed a half-salary for the councilmen.

The first City Council, sitting from May, 1954, to May, 1958, acceded to almost every major proposal submitted by Mayor

Carlin. On most matters the councilmen followed the lead of their staff, the executive staff of the city clerk's office. The City Clerk himself, Harry Reichenstein, proved particularly influential in guiding Council decisions. On "politically" sensitive proposals, however, the councilmen generally undertook their own investigations and listened less to Reichenstein. Their only serious rebellions against the administration during this first term were on the making of appointments, the awarding of contracts, and the treatment of public employees.

If the city councilmen thought they were to become little city commissioners, each with his own empire of public employees, they were quickly disabused of this idea. Carlin persistently refused to share appointments and other decisions with the councilmen, and the Council eventually decided to concede. Some, like Michael Bontempo, Irvine Turner, and Jack Waldor, rebelled against the Mayor's monopoly of decision making. But most councilmen cooperated with the Mayor, assuming that he would lead a slate of pro-administration councilmen in the 1958 elections and thus would bring his friends on the Council under the umbrella of his electoral organization.

The Council's settlement with Mayor Carlin extended to NHA. Although the councilmen saw NHA as part of Carlin's organization, they grudgingly accepted Carlin's arrangements with Danzig and approved whatever proposals NHA and the Mayor submitted. On the other hand, critics of the administration, like Bontempo, Turner, and Waldor, also tended to be critical of NHA.

If the councilmen have any attitude toward urban redevelopment apart from their complaints about NHA's treatment of their "political" requests and apart from their personal opinion of Carlin and Danzig, it is one of considerable skepticism. Many councilmen see NHA as "the Negro's agency" or as the agency that has hastened the racial invasion of white areas. The city clerk's office generally is credited with expanding the councilmen's understanding of renewal concepts, quieting their distrust of slum clearance, and making them more receptive to NHA's proposals.

A request by NHA for the Council's approval of a survey and planning application to the federal government is the first and crucial step in launching any renewal project. The councilmen immediately refer these proposals to their staff in the city clerk's office. In most cases these applications are reported upon favorably by that staff in less than two weeks and are unanimously passed by the Council at its next meeting. This review is an "independent check." Its purpose is to gather more information, to iron out inconsistencies, and to calculate the impact of the proposal on other areas of local policy, like city finance. At no point in the city clerk's investigation is outright rejection or wholesale amendment of the project ever seriously considered. The clerk's staff has seen little point in examining the project from scratch and thus duplicating NHA's work. Besides, the clerk's office knows that it could not adequately review the work of a large, expert staff of housing officials.

Before the proposal is reported out, Danzig will be invited to attend one of the Council's executive sessions. The purpose of these invitations is to have Danzig answer requests by the city clerk's office for further information. Danzig is rarely challenged at these caucuses or requested to justify aspects of the proposed project. Occasionally, a few councilmen may try to cross-examine Danzig, often because they are tired of being "pushed around" by NHA. But Danzig has little difficulty in besting city councilmen in a debate on urban renewal, and Reichenstein discourages such individual forays. After the Council has "let off some steam," the proposal is passed.

On several occasions the Council has sent proposals for clearance projects to NHA, but the Authority's staff has found none of them feasible and has taken no action on them.

NHA AND THE 1958 ELECTIONS

Carlin's troubles with the City Council began early in 1958, when the Mayor announced that there would be no administration ticket in the forthcoming city elections.[7] Mayor Carlin decided that he would not make any endorsements for city councilman and would not permit his name to be bracketed with any of the councilmanic candidates. Since the Mayor had monopolized the "politically" relevant decisions during the Council's first term,

most of the incumbent councilmen were running without significant electoral organizations of their own. Carlin's decision was a
particularly hard blow to the pro-administration incumbents, who
had gone along with the Mayor in the hope of seeking re-election
as part of his organization. Thus, while Carlin handily won re-
election, two of his major supporters on the Council (Mario
Farco and Michael Gallagher) were defeated, and two other pro-
Carlin incumbents (James Callaghan and Philip Gordon) were
re-elected by narrow margins. Michael Bontempo and Irvine
Turner, two major critics of the administration who had developed
other bases of support, were returned to office by overwhelming
majorities.

As they met for the Council's second session in summer, 1958,
most of the councilmen were determined never again to face the
risks of an election without their own organizations. Their complaints that "something should be done about patronage distribution" might have remained merely unfocused grumbling, however,
had not the Essex County Democratic Chairman decided to intervene.

Except for his endorsement of Carlin for mayor and of several
prominent Democrats who ran for the City Council in 1954 and
1958, the County Chairman, Dennis Carey, had stayed out of Newark's nonpartisan politics. Relations between Carlin and Carey
had been strained, however, by the Mayor's refusal to share some
"political" decisions with Carey and to link his local organization to the county machine in county and state elections. Shortly
after his re-election in 1958, moreover, Carlin had begun a campaign to abolish the Passaic Valley Sewerage Commission, an important source of patronage for the County Chairman.

Carey responded by supporting the City Council's rebellion
and by trying to expand the role of the Democratic organization
in city politics. After the Democrats won control of Essex County
government in November, 1958, he began to tie rebellious councilmen to the regular organization by offering them county positions,
which they could hold while retaining their seats on the Council.
Carey also suggested that the county organization be used to sup-

port certain councilmen in the next election or that an organization slate be constructed.

In view of the widespread belief among city councilmen that NHA was a key element in Carlin's organization, it is not surprising that the Housing Authority became one of the major targets of this rebellion. Most of the councilmen were convinced that NHA had played an active role in the 1958 election and had been a significant factor in determining its outcome.

While the councilmen have overstated their case, there are grains of truth in it. Statements about NHA's influence over the 1958 election are accurate to the extent that many of NHA's "political" decisions had been cleared with the Mayor during the preceding four years and that NHA had given much less attention to the requests of city councilmen. It also is true that some members of NHA's staff and some NHA commissioners, acting as private citizens, had endorsed Carlin and had given him financial or campaign assistance. NHA as an organization did not take a position on the election or urge its members to become involved in Carlin's campaign. The sentiment among NHA's personnel, however, was all pro-Carlin.

NHA was involved in the election, furthermore, because Carlin chose to campaign on the urban renewal achievements of his administration. Throughout the Mayor's first term NHA had been careful to have Carlin make all major announcements on renewal and to avoid undercutting him or leaking items to the press. In this way Carlin benefitted from the drama and publicity value of clearance projects. Early in 1958 Carlin had pressed Danzig for a new project to announce just before the election. After it appeared that NHA would not conclude its negotiations with URA in time for the campaign, Danzig agreed to let the Mayor leak a few cautious statements to the press about a pending project. These leaks apparently confirmed the Council's suspicions about NHA's involvement in Carlin's campaign.

It was assumed by most politicos that NHA would deliver the public housing vote for Mayor Carlin in 1958, just as incumbent city commissioners had been able to command these votes in the

1940s. Early in the campaign Carlin's opponent began accusing Danzig of using threats of eviction and rent increases to pressure tenants into backing Carlin. In fact, there are indications that Mayor Carlin did hold Danzig responsible for a strong pro-administration vote in the public projects. The evidence indicates, however, that Danzig strongly opposed using pressure on public housing tenants and that his views eventually won out. After the results of the election had been examined at City Hall, the Mayor was reported to be dissatisfied with the electoral showing of the city's twelve public housing projects. In the weeks following the elections relations between Carlin and NHA were reported to be at a low point.

THE CITY COUNCIL IN REBELLION, 1959

Notions about NHA's intimate involvement in the Mayor's 1958 campaign for re-election help explain why the Authority was caught in the cross fire of Mayor-Council warfare. The launching of a downtown redevelopment program in fall, 1959, provided the City Council with the opportunity for a direct assault on NHA.

Here Danzig made a miscalculation in strategy. Assuming that the Seton Hall and Parker projects had exhausted Newark's share of federal aid for 1959, Danzig asked the City Council in October of that year to approve an immediate start on the Penn Plaza proposal under the new "three-fourths program." By the terms of this program, if cities began the planning of projects entirely at their own expense and URA later approved the plans, federal aid would defray three-fourths of the costs rather than the usual two-thirds. Proceeding under this rule would permit NHA to begin planning for Penn Plaza without waiting for federal approval, but it would require the City to appropriate $500,000 in planning funds to NHA. Since the site included a great deal of city-owned land, Penn Plaza's future also hinged on the willingness of the Council to sell or donate this land to NHA. Here, then, was the leverage over Danzig that the Council had heretofore lacked. Here was a choice opportunity for rebellion.

When the Penn Plaza proposal was introduced, the City Council took the unprecedented step of forming three ad hoc committees to investigate the project. The councilmen and the city clerk's office appeared reluctant to "give away" choice, city-owned land to "outsiders" for a project whose feasibility had not yet been determined. They also expressed concern about the fiscal impact of withdrawing so many revenue-producing downtown parcels from the tax rolls. In private conversations some councilmen indicated that they objected mainly to the appropriation of $500,000 to a powerful organization allied with the Mayor. As one councilman put it: "I'll be damned if I'll give Lou Danzig a half-million bucks for him to spread around."

On November 4, the day slated for final passage, the City Council voted to postpone consideration of Penn Plaza pending further study. By this time Danzig had decided to proceed under the usual two-thirds arrangement. He also made some minor concessions in the proposal to allay the Council's concern about the temporary decline in tax ratables. But he had waited too long in making these accommodations. On December 7, a few days before the proposal was due to come before the Council once more, Councilman James T. Callaghan issued a sweeping attack on the administration and on NHA, indicating that he was completely dissatisfied with the Authority's execution of urban redevelopment. Callaghan, who had been the Mayor's floor leader in the Council's first term, but who had become very close to Dennis Carey in more recent years, urged that either a new agency be created specifically for the Penn Plaza project or NHA be stripped of all redevelopment powers.

As the debate shifted to the question of whether NHA had acquired too much power, Danzig became increasingly anxious to terminate the Penn Plaza issue quickly. He reportedly advised Carlin to channel some favors to the Council with the hope of splitting the opposition and releasing the Penn Plaza project from caucus. When Carlin rejected this advice, Danzig decided to deal directly with some of the councilmen. There is little evidence on the conversations between Danzig and the councilmen or on the methods he used to break the back of the resistance. But there is good evidence of his success.

At the same time, Mayor Carlin was anxious to get some final action on the project before the forthcoming referendum on the question of returning to commission government. He visited the Council's caucus on December 8, denounced Callaghan, demanded immediate passage of the proposal, and threatened to break the deadlock by submitting the project to a referendum. According to the accounts of several councilmen, Callaghan's motion to postpone consideration of Penn Plaza pending an investigation into the transfer of redevelopment powers had been approved at an earlier caucus. But, under the Mayor's threats and probably through Danzig's intervention, the majority dwindled to a minority of four. Rather than reveal the exact line of division within the Council, the remaining opposition added their votes to make the approval of Penn Plaza unanimous.

Though the Penn Plaza project emerged from the Council unharmed and unaltered, the foregoing events did point up some long-range threats to the prevailing system. Carlin was reported to be angered at Danzig's direct dealings with members of the City Council. The rift was apparently lessened when Danzig brought in the Turner-Galbreath project just before the referendum on a return to commission government. Moreover, the failure of Callaghan's motion and the passage of Penn Plaza did not indicate a collapse of the Council's rebellion. In the ensuing weeks most of the councilmen concluded that the delaying of particular projects was an ineffectual tactic. While pondering their next step, the councilmen agreed to forestall further attacks on the administration until after the referendum. Without delay or debate the Council approved the Turner-Galbreath proposal on December 20. Shortly after the electorate had voted to retain mayor-council government, however, the Council began a campaign to repeal the amendment that Danzig and Carlin had added to the Faulkner Act in 1954. The councilmen instructed an ad hoc committee to draft a resolution giving the Council power to appoint the commissioners of all independent boards and authorities.

The threats to NHA's arrangements with City Hall, then, did not arise from any basic dissatisfaction on the Mayor's part. Mayor Carlin seemed content to play the role of catalyst or broker and to leave policy initiation to NHA. Of course, there is the question of how Carlin's successor will feel about these arrangements, but NHA has survived such change-overs in the past without having to slacken its pace or alter its course. A more significant threat might be the growing fractionalization of the mayor's power at City Hall, implied in the rebellion of the City Council and the intervention of the Democratic County Chairman. There also is a good chance that the office of business administrator will emerge in future years as a rival to the mayor for control of the executive branch. If these trends do develop, NHA may have to abandon its policy of relying solely on its good relations with the mayor to secure City Hall approval of its projects. The Authority may have to expand its network of negotiations at City Hall. Whether NHA could maintain its present autonomy in policy questions and also meet the requests of a wider circle of City Hall participants remains to be seen.

THE POLITICAL SETTLEMENT

At the root of NHA's relations with City Hall lies a political settlement first negotiated in 1948 and later carried over to the new administration. At the root of NHA's relations with other local interests and of its success in slum clearance lie similar settlements, embodied sometimes in written resolution or ordinance, sometimes in a set of tacit and diffuse arrangements. The events just described marked the breakup of an old settlement between NHA and City Hall and the creation of a new one on different terms. In other instances the settlement ended a long-standing feud between the Authority and a local interest group. In NHA's separate dealings with the politicos, with the planners, and with the neighborhood rehabilitation bloc, the two parties consciously sought to negotiate their differences. In NHA's dealings with businessmen, mutually acceptable forms of interaction gradually emerged.

In every instance the local interests have recognized that a basic change has occurred in their relations with NHA. The resulting settlements have served to close certain outstanding questions between the parties and to establish certain expectations about their future behavior. The behavior of local participants in specific renewal events reflects the requirements and prerogatives of previously defined roles. The events involved in the local approval of a clearance project are structured, predictable, and routine.

The various settlements also have a basic similarity in content. The local groups generally have agreed to refrain from interfering in NHA's negotiations with URA or with private redevelopers and to avoid making public attacks on the resulting policy. Demands and criticisms of NHA are still made by local groups, but they are rarely made in public and are rarely pushed to the point where they would strain the groups' good relations with NHA. The local groups generally try to see Danzig informally to talk out their differences.

Private negotiations, then, have replaced public agitation and overt conflict in Newark urban renewal. By removing a major issue from contention and by establishing a framework for persistent interaction between NHA and some local group, the basic political settlement has permitted other small differences or new differences to be resolved through informal bargaining. The settlement does not resolve all the differences between two parties; if such differences can be settled at all, it is through continual, day-to-day negotiation. The settlement simply makes it more likely that such daily negotiations will occur.

In return for these promises of noninterference, various concessions were made by the Housing Authority. The crucial fact, however, is that NHA's concessions did not involve accommodations in the substance of its redevelopment or its public housing policies. The Housing Authority may be viewed as a thriving governmental enterprise with the power to dispense a number of values or rewards unrelated to the substance and procedure of its major decisions. Thus NHA can attain large amounts of discretion in the policy realm through the appropriate manipulation of these other resources.

CHAPTER IV

The Civic Leaders:
Neighborhood Rehabilitation

The single most significant characteristic of Newark politics in the last quarter-century has been the alienation of the city's business and professional groups.[1] Throughout the 1940s the city's corporation executives, lawyers, realtors, and educators fled Newark for suburban residence. While this exodus of upper-income, white Protestants is by no means unique to Newark, it seems to have been accompanied by an extreme case of political withdrawal. The result has been a chasm between the city's former civic leaders, on the one hand, and the politicos, the neighborhood associations, the ethnic societies, the small merchants' groups, and the Catholic Church, on the other.

At one time these upper-middle class groups were the backbone of the civic improvement associations and the reform movement. In more recent years their participation in Newark politics has been sporadic, half-hearted, and ineffectual. The Chamber of Commerce, the Real Estate Board of Newark (REBON), the Downtown Association, and other civic groups traditionally manned by the civic leaders continued to operate after the exodus and continued to press for economy and efficiency in government. But the civic leaders' commitment to such groups was tenuous and the impact of these groups on public policy negligible. Behind the façade of civic leader participation were a few activists and the civic groups' professional staffs, whose major problem was to keep the organizations alive from year to year.

It is doubtful whether the civic leaders or civic elite were ever as important in Newark politics as their names imply. Yet, most local informants agree that whatever political influence these groups had had in the past was severely diminished during the 1940s.

The conditions responsible for this flight from the city and subsequent abdication of power are similar to those present in other urban areas: the deterioration of the city's housing supply, the immigration of nonwhites, the political emergence of newer ethnic groups, and the prevalence of pre–civil service, "machine politics" at City Hall. To most of the civic elite who sought political isolation in the 1940s, Newark was being governed in a highly sordid fashion by "the worst kind." The decline in participation that generally accompanies the shift from family businesses to absentee-owned corporations was also apparent. The large corporations had no stable commitment to Newark, and the corporation executives had no motive for involvement in local politics. While most of these trends are apparent in other central cities, particularly in the older cities of the Northeast, they seem to be more fully developed in Newark. Perhaps this explains why the political alienation of the upper-middle class has been more extreme here.

There is one qualification that must be added to this portrait of a civic leadership that does not lead. If these leaders failed to participate in local politics as reformers or members of civic groups, they did participate as individuals and as "fixers." Those doing business in Newark recognized the necessity of coming to terms with the City Hall "system," much as they may have disliked its ground rules. The indications are that most businesses made individual arrangements with City Hall officials to secure favorable property assessments, token enforcement of certain regulations, insurance against labor trouble, and other benefits. The civic leaders' opposition to public housing, for instance, did not discourage individual businessmen and realtors from seeking certain kinds of benefits or favors from NHA. Such personal accommodations helped weaken the individual's commitment to the public goals of his own civic groups and helped create within the reform ranks a strong resistance to change.

Throughout the first decade of public housing in Newark the business, real-estate, and civic improvement groups staunchly opposed every step of NHA's program.[2] They objected to its allegedly unfavorable impact on local revenues and to its interference in the housing market and in the rights of private property. They deplored City Hall's "overemphasis" of the housing problem and its neglect of other needs like the alleviation of downtown traffic and parking and the attraction of new business. Their attack on the "system" at City Hall, moreover, could be easily extended to NHA, since "political" interference in site selection and other public housing decisions was widely suspected.

In August, 1949, when NHA introduced an ordinance making it the city's official redevelopment agency, civic groups united in a major effort to kill the proposal. The incident aptly illustrates the civic leaders' role in public housing politics during the 1940s and their role during the initial years of urban redevelopment. The civic groups would have remained inert in this incident if the members of their professional staffs had not prodded them into action. Henry Conner, Executive Director of the Bureau of Municipal Research (BMR), and Edmund Wollmuth, Executive Secretary of the Chamber of Commerce, were the first among the civic leaders to recognize that urban redevelopment was not simply another form of public housing. In fact, they saw this new program as an excellent opportunity to achieve the civic groups' traditional goals of neighborhood rehabilitation, attraction of new ratables, and salvation of the central business district. In NHA's hands the program, as they saw it, would be directed primarily toward housing.

The staffs also thought that the redevelopment program might catch the interest of the civic leaders and serve as a vehicle for their re-entrance into local politics. The traditional pressure group activities of the Chamber and BMR, however, would not be dramatic enough to evoke civic leader participation. The civic leaders would have to be given a quasi-official role in urban redevelopment, an institutionalized share of public policy formation. To achieve this end and to shield the program from NHA's "housing biases," the staffs proposed that redevelopment powers be placed in a committee of leading citizens. In August, 1949, Conner and Wollmuth asked the Chamber of Commerce, REBON, and the Broad Street and Merchants Association to endorse this proposal.

While the civic group officials responded to prodding and endorsed the proposal, they did not fully accept or understand their staffs' position. Most civic leaders, at this time, viewed urban redevelopment as an extension of public housing and continued their blanket opposition to all forms of federal aid for housing. They backed the Conner-Wollmuth proposal largely because they opposed any extension of NHA's functions or political influence. Only gradually did the civic leaders see that their own goals could be achieved through the new program. Only slowly did the staffs convince the civic leaders that they should try to guide redevelopment policies rather than condemn the program or NHA *in toto*.

The most important aspect of this controversy over redevelopment powers was the city commissioners' total indifference to the pleas of civic groups. After permitting these groups to make their protest, the commissioners promptly approved NHA's ordinance by a four-to-one vote. This pattern was characteristic of public housing politics throughout the 1940s. Continued opposition by the civic groups had not prevented the commissioners from approving all NHA proposals, nor had it prevented NHA from executing one of the most active public housing programs in the country.

During the early 1940s the civic leaders' isolation from City Hall made it easier for NHA to gain an initial foothold in public housing, to establish good relations with the politicos, and to amass a number of crucial political resources. In 1949 the civic groups could not break through Danzig's arrangements with the city commissioners and could not stop approval of NHA's ordinance. Thus, the isolation of the civic leaders also made it easier for NHA to carry over its arrangements and resources into the redevelopment program. By the time these leaders attained their own foothold in the renewal program between 1953 and 1955, NHA's position at City Hall was almost impregnable. This is one reason that the civic leaders eventually decided to deal directly with Danzig.

From 1949 to 1953 the civic leaders searched for some way to participate in the new program and to influence redevelopment policy. They sought this influence first as leaders of a grass roots Citizens' Housing Council, then as members of a citizen committee within NHA, and, failing in these, as members of citizen committees attached directly to the mayor's office.

THE CIVIC LEADERS AND THE GRASS ROOTS

One major characteristic of the reform movement in Newark is that it has been dominated by business and real estate and, as a result, has had strong conservative overtones.[3] Few mass associations with a liberal reform bent have appeared in Newark, and none has survived. Labor has been indifferent to local politics and willing to accept the lead of the business–real-estate bloc. The Negroes have been poorly organized. Many other potential sources of liberal reform have fled the city and diverted their attention to state and national politics. As a result, those groups that have urged central planning, charter revision, and vigorous code enforcement are the same groups that have demanded economy in government, reductions in taxes, a city-manager government, and an end to public housing. In Newark the terms "reform" and "conservative" must be bracketed.

It follows from this that the reform movement has generally been associated with the civic elite and has been alien to most city residents, neighborhood notables, and politicos. Except for the election of a "reform mayor" in 1945 and a brief honeymoon thereafter, the reform movement did not leave much of an imprint on local politics during the 1940s. The civic leaders proved no more successful at City Hall with their reform proposals than with their conservative demands.

Some civic leaders occasionally expressed concern at their isolation from the public and tried to bridge that gap. In 1949 a series of Newark *News* articles on the slums in Newark aroused widespread indignation and demands for action. Some members of the civic groups' staffs thought that a broadly based reform movement might serve to reunite civic leaders with the grass roots. At the same time the civic leaders would be drawn back into local politics as the spokesmen of a mass organization. Thus, staff members attended a mass rally in December, 1949, at the auditorium of the Newark *News,* helped organize the Citizens' Housing Council (CHC), and helped place some civic leaders in positions of importance in the new organization.

The Council's officers were a mélange of clergymen, neighborhood notables, ethnic spokesmen, civic leaders, and politicos, dedicated to "improving housing conditions in Newark." Conner and the civic leaders rejected suggestions to endorse rent control and public housing. They argued that a vigorous enforcement of the housing codes was the only program on which the entire Council could unite. To forestall a threatened withdrawal of support by the civic leaders, CHC's officers finally drafted a compromise proposal in which a mild endorsement was given to urban redevelopment but major emphasis placed on intensive code enforcement.

The beginning of door-to-door code enforcement by the municipal building inspectors brought CHC into open conflict with the Authority. NHA's Executive Director concluded that CHC had adopted the unrealistic views of the real-estate lobby. He saw CHC's emphasis on enforcement as a new version of the old ruse that slums could be repainted and made serviceable. Danzig also strongly protested the decision to begin intensive inspections in the heart of the slum belt. Enforcement in the hard-core slum, he argued, only served to place impossible demands on landlord and inspector, to push the problem from block to block, and to inflate NHA's acquisition costs when it got around to clearing the area. The leaders of CHC and the head of the new inspection agency, however, felt that the city's worst blocks were health hazards and should be tackled first.

The Citizens' Housing Council and the enforcement program exacerbated relations between Danzig and the civic groups but failed to provide a suitable vehicle for the resurgence of the civic leaders. By summer, 1950, the widespread enthusiasm of the initial meetings had vanished, and CHC, as a mass organization, was dead. The remaining elected officers tried to continue as a small, select, advisory group of community influentials. When the "leftists" insisted on reviving public housing and redevelopment issues, however, the civic groups withdrew their support from the organization and left it to die.

After the civic leaders had departed, several members of NHA's staff kept CHC alive as a "letterhead organization" in the hope of reviving a mass organization to support public housing and redevelopment. This hope was never realized.

The story of the Citizens' Housing Council demonstrates the difficulties involved in bridging the gap between the civic leaders and the grass roots. It also illustrates the short-lived character of mass organizations in Newark renewal.

THE CIVIC ELITE AND URBAN REDEVELOPMENT, 1949–53

In the years following NHA's designation as the official redevelopment agency, Conner, Wollmuth, and Wollmuth's successor, Kenneth Carberry, made some headway in their attempts to encourage civic leader participation in the new program.[4] During 1950 and 1951 Chamber of Commerce publications began to discriminate clearly between public housing and redevelopment and to suggest that the new program be directed toward economic development goals. Though still critical of public housing, the Chamber now qualified its sweeping opposition to all forms of federal aid.

After the collapse of CHC the professional staffs returned to their earlier faith in a citizen advisory committee as the best device for involving businessmen in local politics. Having failed in their efforts to establish a redevelopment commission, the staffs now proposed an advisory committee attached directly to NHA. Rather than respond to NHA proposals only after their formal announcement and then vainly urge the politicos to reconsider them, the civic leaders could in this way intervene at the formative stage of such proposals. Rather than skirmish with NHA on particular decisions, the civic leaders could quietly imprint their values on the program over the long run.

In response to the urgings of Conner and Wollmuth, the President of the Chamber, Charles Watts, sought out Danzig and met with him informally in December, 1949. Watts came away from these meetings reassured that NHA's Executive Director was eager to have private enterprise solve the housing problem "to the fullest extent possible." He found Danzig fully aware of the need to clear sites for new business and genuinely interested in "bringing businessmen in" on the redevelopment program.

Invited to a meeting of the Chamber's Board of Directors to clarify the role local executives would play in redevelopment, Danzig demonstrated his well-known capacity to "speak anyone's language." He reassured the Board that he would stress fully taxable redevelopment projects to relieve the "oppressive" tax rate. He urged business to assume a significant role in these projects as promoters and redevelopers. On the issue of a citizen committee Danzig said: "If you wish to participate in the planning and development of such projects . . . we shall be glad to deal with you individually or through a committee designated by the Chamber of Commerce. Such a committee might deal with the Housing Authority on one hand and with interested business firms on the other." To the businessmen present this suggestion seemed to reject their proposal entirely and to put in its place nothing more than another committee within the Chamber to interest prospective investors in local development.

Thus, the first attempt at some accommodation between NHA and the business community ended in mutual disappointment. Danzig refused to let "outsiders," whether they be City officials or interest group spokesmen, interfere with the work of his expert staff. Business, on the other hand, indicated no enthusiasm either for investing its own capital in local projects or for acting as publicity agents for local redevelopment.

REBON, always more vocal and more conservative than the other business groups, moved much more reluctantly toward acceptance of redevelopment or participation in the program.

REBON was slower to distinguish redevelopment from public housing, slower to drop its blanket opposition to federal aid, and slower to open any kind of dealings with Danzig. Relations between NHA and REBON remained highly strained through this period. As one informant put it: "The real-estate people called Danzig every name in the book."

Three weeks after the announcement of NHA's North Ward project the New Jersey Association of Real Estate Boards (NJAREB) sponsored a bill in the New Jersey Legislature requiring all communities to hold referenda before proceeding with further public housing. NHA saw this as a deliberate attempt by REBON to kill the new project, since the defeat of North Ward public housing in a local referendum would also destroy plans for North Ward redevelopment. REBON subsequently lent credence to NHA's suspicions by supporting the bill with vigor and by joining the North Ward site residents in their attempt to block the project. Throughout this period the leaders of REBON continued to present vigorous code enforcement as an alternative to clearance and as the answer to the housing problem.

Repeated political setbacks and some major changes in REBON's leadership during 1952, however, led the Board to open discussions on "the realtor's role in urban redevelopment." Returning to the proposals developed two years earlier by Henry Conner and Edmund Wollmuth, REBON's Civic Affairs Committee urged that NHA create a citizen committee on redevelopment consisting of realtors, architects, mortgage bankers, and home builders. Danzig publicly praised this letter as a sign of improvement in REBON's attitude toward NHA. The Housing Authority commissioners even endorsed this idea in principle. It soon became apparent, however, that Danzig still had the same reservations about an advisory citizen committee that he had had in 1951 and 1949. By May, 1953, the realtors gave up any hope of "advising" NHA and, instead, turned their attention to City Hall, where a new administration was taking office.

Danzig's attitude toward such new efforts by the civic leaders to participate in local redevelopment was a mixture of indifference and suspicion. He did not consider their backing indispensable to successful redevelopment and made no attempt to woo them. Of the realtors he asked only that they "leave the program alone" and let NHA's arrangements with City Hall run their course. From the local business corporations and the other business groups Danzig wanted not only passive acquiescence in NHA policies but also active participation in the program as financiers, redevelopers, and publicists. But, if the price for that participation was to be the exposure of NHA's policy decisions to the disruptive influence of a committee of businessmen, Danzig would not pay it.

RE-EMERGENCE OF THE ELITE, 1953–55

After Carlin's election as mayor in 1953 the activists and staffs of the civic groups revived the idea of citizen advisory committees.[5] Encouraged by the improved atmosphere at City Hall, they decided to bypass NHA and propose committees responsible directly to the mayor. Two citizen committees were created between 1953 and 1955, one on neighborhood rehabilitation and one on economic development. These committees, however, were more successful in establishing the form of civic leader participation than the substance. The basis for a quasi-official role in public policy formation was finally established; convincing the civic leaders to play that role proved to be another matter entirely. This situation came about largely because both committees were initiated by a handful of people who secured the acquiescence but not the enthusiasm of other civic leaders.

The Newark Committee on Neighborhood Conservation and Rehabilitation (NCNCR) was invented by Agnes Coleman. President of the local real-estate board from 1952 to 1954, she decided to apply the "Build America Better" program of the National Association of Real Estate Boards (NAREB) to Newark. It was Henry Conner and other members of the business groups' staffs that suggested a citizen advisory committee for this purpose. When Coleman outlined plans for a committee on rehabilitation at a series of luncheons for various civic groups, there were expressions of interest and encouragement but few promises of active participation. Most businessmen assumed that the realtors would take the lead because of their immediate stake in neighborhood improvement. Most observers agree that the proposed committee would have died of indifference had not Coleman been willing to shoulder almost the entire burden of participation.

Conner and Carberry initiated the idea of an economic development committee, as much to stimulate business participation as to achieve substantive policies. They met with even greater indifference than Coleman had encountered. Small business and industry refused to have anything to do with such a committee, claiming that it would become the "puppet" of the giant insurance, banking, and retail corporations. Many of these giant firms, however, saw an economic development committee merely as an attempt to encourage them to invest corporate funds in local construction. Others were hostile because it might damage their personal accommodations with particular officials at City Hall.

The proposed committee made no headway until the Mutual Benefit Life Insurance Company took a part. Having decided to construct a new home office in downtown Newark rather than move to the suburbs, Mutual Benefit now recognized its stake in Newark's economic future. To Mutual Benefit officials the proposed committee was one way of encouraging local and out-of-town investment in Newark. With this in mind they determined to press for the committee's creation.

Most of the other corporations restated their earlier objections and dismissed the committee as "Mutual Benefit's show." But they conceded that, if Mutual Benefit insisted on bringing the proposal out into the open, they could not help but support it. There seemed, in fact, to be somewhat less resistance to the idea than there had been two years earlier. Many firms whose personal arrangements with City Hall had been disrupted by the 1954 charter revision saw in this committee a new channel of access to the politicos. When the committee finally came into being, most of the leading downtown corporations agreed to send a representative but refused to commit themselves beyond this.

The internal organization, legal status, and personnel of both committees were worked out during 1953 and 1954 by the civic groups' staffs in consultation with a few civic leaders, like Coleman, and the officers of Mutual Benefit. Later, the staffs brought their plans to Commissioners Carlin and Bontempo, who made a few minor changes in the format.

The committee on rehabilitation, it was decided, would be a broad-based committee representing all elements of the civic leadership. Conner persuaded Coleman that a board made up entirely of realtors would be ineffective. The Newark Economic Development Committee (NEDC), however, was to be made up exclusively of representatives from the city's largest corporations. It was to be a small, behind-the-scenes "general staff" of Newark's business elite.

The most ticklish problem was to define the position these citizen committees would occupy at City Hall. Here the civic leaders and their staffs shared a strong reluctance to be drawn into City Hall politics and also a fear that the politicos would try to make the committees part of their personal political organizations. The civic leaders had participated in citizen advisory committees before, only to see their advice ignored. Such committees had been created to meet the patronage needs of the sponsoring politico; the civic leaders had been drawn in to lend their prestige to the operation. Thus, in 1953–54, Conner and the other staff men insisted that the two committees be kept outside the City Hall "system" and be made a part of no one's political organization. To ensure this, the personnel of the committees would be named initially by the civic groups and later by the committees themselves. It was also agreed that the committees would retain unofficial status and would rely primarily on private contributions, thus minimizing their involvement and vulnerability at City Hall. Unofficial status would also free the committees from a local ordinance requiring all municipal employees to be residents of Newark.

Negotiating with the politicos about these committees proved much less difficult for the civic groups' staff men than getting their own constituents to support the idea. Commissioner Bontempo insisted on making a few of his own appointments to NCNCR but left unaltered the civic leaders' control of that body. Carlin's only price for the creation of NEDC was that it be delayed until after charter revision.

THE CITIZEN ADVISORY COMMITTEE

After 1953 the political activities of the civic leaders diverged, the corporate businessmen focusing their attention on economic development, the realtors and other civic groups pursuing neighborhood rehabilitation.[6] Thus, the role that each citizen committee has played in urban renewal and its dealings with NHA must be described separately. Before doing so, it is useful to consider the institutional context of their activities—the citizen advisory committee. Here there are common experiences which evoked similar responses. Both NEDC and NCNCR have been plagued by an apathetic membership and an inadequate staff. In response to these problems the committees have developed similar types of internal organization and similar patterns of interaction with NHA.

Most members of NCNCR have not given much time to the Committee. Some have been inactive largely because their occupations do not provide extensive leisure time or flexible working hours. Some have tended to play the role of "careerist," interested in rehabilitation as a fillip to their political or occupational ambitions, or the role of "official delegate," appointed as testimony to the importance of their constituent group.

To a great extent, Coleman, Conner, Carberry, and a few others have acted as the controlling inner core of NCNCR. For the professional staff men in this group active participation is part of the job. In addition, there are certain occupations, like real estate or law, that are conducive to extensive involvement in civic affairs. This inner core, which constitutes NCNCR's Executive Committee, has caucused before each meeting to prepare the agenda and has proposed the personnel and jurisdiction of various subcommittees. Its members have often spent money out of their own pockets to keep NCNCR going. Periodically, Coleman and the others propose changes in the Committee's personnel and try to interest additional civic leaders in active membership.

It would be pointless, then, to catalogue the various interests represented on NCNCR, for this would imply some intent on the part of these groups to influence Committee policy. Several days after the Committee's creation on September 19, 1953, organized labor, Negro groups, and other excluded interests denounced the civic leaders' dominance of NCNCR. Yet, when the Committee was later expanded to include these interests, their spokesmen made no attempt to alter NCNCR's internal arrangements. In effect, most of the interests represented on NCNCR are less concerned with wielding power than with representation or membership per se.

This pattern of minority rule is the product not of usurpation by an inner core but of limited participation by the others. The inner core is frequently reminded that most civic leaders on the Committee have full-time, exacting occupations, an aversion to involvement in local politics, and a vacillating commitment to Newark. Far from coveting their power, several members of the inner core are anxious to return to other pursuits and are restrained only by their colleagues' pleas. Many have sought out their own successors so that they could retire to a more passive role in good conscience.

A lethargic majority and an aggressive minority also have been characteristic of NEDC. While some members have failed to participate actively for lack of time or interest, others have been instructed by their firms merely to "go through the motions." Thus, there is little correlation between the size of a firm and the influence it wields over NEDC. Power within the Committee has gone to those who are interested, aggressive, and willing to devote time to NEDC.

The limited commitment of most members on NEDC and NCNCR has led the inner cores of both committees to pursue concrete achievements or "projects" as a way of heightening member interest. If the civic leaders were to be drawn into greater participation, the emphasis would have to be on specific goals and dramatic proposals rather than on cautious studies or central planning. At the initial meetings of NEDC, BMR's staff and other members of the inner core persuaded the Committee to place top priority on an underground parking garage and the commercial redevelopment of Newark's "Skid Row." The same staff impelled NCNCR first toward a revision of the municipal housing codes and then toward the selection of a particular area in Clinton Hill for a federally aided rehabilitation project. Thus, the citizen committees on urban renewal did not become general planning agencies and made no attempt to intervene in the activities of other renewal agencies. Instead, they chose to employ the strategy of activism and, in so doing, to become operating agencies.

This emphasis on specific projects may have been a dramatic way of stimulating interest in the committees, but it raised some serious problems. The planning and execution of projects require an elaborate, well-trained staff. But the committees had no such staff. Moreover, public funds could not be spent by committees which lacked official status.

To meet this problem, both NEDC and NCNCR introduced ordinances making themselves official municipal agencies. In both cases, however, a number of local interests demanded expanded representation on the committees. In addition, the city councilmen sought control over the appointment of committee members. This was seen as an attempt to politicize the committees, and the ordinances were quickly withdrawn. NEDC did not resubmit its ordinance. NCNCR eventually acquired official status in 1958 and was renamed the Newark Commission on Neighborhood Conservation and Rehabilitation, but it received only minimal funds for a staff.

Inadequate staff and insufficient funds, therefore, have been an enduring problem of the citizen committees. It is a problem which has delayed their projects, forced them to borrow staff from other agencies, and formed the basis of their negotiations with the Housing Authority. NCNCR's relations with NHA are described in the remainder of this chapter; relations between NEDC and NHA are discussed in the succeeding chapter.

NHA AND NCNCR: ROUND ONE

During NCNCR's formative stages NHA and the Committee's sponsors maintained attitudes of watchful suspicion toward each other.[7] To NHA officials the Committee looked like another effort by the real-estate lobby to sabotage the clearance program. Here was a new attempt to convince people that the slum problem could be met with a fresh coat of paint. Yet, NHA was too involved at this time in cementing good relations with the new administration at City Hall to risk an open skirmish with the civic leaders. The Committee's sponsors, aware of Danzig's views, deliberately refrained from consulting him and hoped that he could be kept out of the issue.

In the long run, however, NCNCR needed Danzig's cooperation. Shortly after its creation, the Committee discovered that NHA officials were the only individuals in Newark with extensive experience in housing and renewal. Invited to attend NCNCR's early meetings as a consultant, and later as a full member of the Committee, Danzig announced his presence with a vigorous attack on the "clean-up, fix-up" approach to slums.

The Committee's initial behavior confirmed Danzig's suspicions. At one of its first meetings NCNCR named a subcommittee to tour the Fourteenth Ward, an area in the midst of Newark's hard-core slums. Danzig was greatly disturbed by the implications of the act. Reassurances that this was just a publicity device, unrelated to any specific plans for rehabilitating the area, failed to pacify him. Did the Committee's decision mean to imply that NCNCR would concern itself primarily with the slums and pose rehabilitation as an alternative to clearance in meeting the slum problem?

The inspection tour helped answer Danzig's question. After touring the Fourteenth Ward, NCNCR members and Commissioner Bontempo decided on an unscheduled visit to a nearby public housing project. Accompanied by reporters and photographers from the local press, the group inspected Baxter Terrace. It then issued a press statement attacking NHA's maintenance policies, the slovenly living habits of the tenants, and public housing in general.

Danzig found even less cause for reassurance in NCNCR's activities during the ensuing months. Why did REBON and some members of NCNCR constantly refer to NCNCR as Newark's "slum clearance agency?" Why had NCNCR created a Subcommittee for the Elimination of Substandard Housing in Slum Areas? And when NCNCR decided to stage the rehabilitation of a single building, why did it select a building on Strafford Place, a block which

Danzig considered in obvious need of clearance? A few months later Danzig indicated his support for the amalgamation of existing housing codes into one tough Housing Code but warned that such high standards could not and should not be enforced in the heart of the slum areas. He attacked the claims made by some NCNCR members that this code would solve the slum problem.

An open break between NHA and NCNCR, however, did not materialize. A showdown was averted in 1953–54, largely by NCNCR's decision to stress code enforcement in the fringe areas rather than in the slums. This shift in policy drew NCNCR out of NHA's domain and guided the Committee into areas unrelated to the Authority's clearance activities. Like many other NCNCR policies, it was initiated by the professional staff of BMR. Late in 1953 BMR's staff had come to the conclusion that focusing on block-by-block inspections in the hard-core slums had been a mistake. Executed in this way, code enforcement simply moved the slums from one block to another. A "wall" around the slums was needed to prevent their expansion and to protect the surrounding neighborhoods. Intensive code enforcement could help create this wall, but only if enforcement was concentrated in the fringe areas. The shift to a containment policy was given impetus by passage of the 1954 Federal Housing Act, which held out the promise of aid for local activities in nonclearance areas.

Despite these shifts in position, NCNCR still viewed public housing and redevelopment as mild palliatives that merely altered the location of Newark's slums but not their extent. It urged that priority in the renewal program be placed on the containment of slums and the salvation of deteriorating areas. But NCNCR's shift to containment did help settle some differences between the two agencies. NCNCR conceded the inappropriateness of code enforcement in the slums. In effect, it conceded NHA's right to control all renewal action in that area.

In September, 1955, NCNCR issued its first formal endorsement of slum clearance and urban redevelopment. This new position was made more explicit in a general policy statement issued five weeks later. "The initial goal of NCNCR," wrote the Chairman, was to "improve slum housing through better codes and inspection methods. The next phase of our activity lies in neighborhoods outside the slum area."

Throughout 1955 and 1956 NCNCR demonstrated that it would resist all attempts to extend its activities into NHA's jurisdiction, whether to aid or to criticize the Authority's clearance policies. During spring, 1955, NCNCR rejected suggestions by some of its members that it propose redevelopment sites to NHA, help NHA find redevelopers, or lobby for state legislation providing low-interest capital to redevelopers. It was further suggested by some members that strict Housing Code enforcement be linked to a program of expanding the city's over-all housing supply. If NCNCR failed to link the two programs, it would be doing exactly what it accused NHA of doing, namely, shuffling the problem from one area to another. But the Committee's inner core insisted that deteriorating neighborhoods would be saved by lowering their densities and by enforcing codes in these areas. Additional housing was a problem for NHA to handle.

ROUND TWO: STATE ENABLING LEGISLATION

The question of which local agencies would administer the newly created neighborhood rehabilitation program was not seriously considered in New Jersey until almost two years after the passage of the 1954 Federal Housing Act.[8] In 1955 NJAREB introduced into the New Jersey Legislature a bill to establish local conservation and rehabilitation authorities similar to the public housing authorities first created in the 1930s. The New Jersey Association of Housing and Redevelopment Officials (NJAHRO) countered with a bill to include rehabilitation in the powers of present redevelopment agencies. But neither NHA nor NCNCR had yet reached a point in their programs where this matter demanded attention. In the absence of any pressing demand, the 1955 Legislature adjourned without having acted on either measure.

If the members of NCNCR gave this matter any thought in 1955, they probably assumed that Mayor Carlin intended them to be Newark's official rehabilitation agency. Some members of NCNCR's inner core later claimed that explicit promises to this effect had been made by Mayor Carlin when NCNCR was first created. But if NHA had not raised the issue in 1956, NCNCR probably would not have sought this official designation until 1958, when it was ready to apply for federal aid on Clinton Hill.

Early in 1956 URA officials indicated to Danzig that NHA lacked the legal power to rehabilitate parts of the Central Ward renewal area and urged him to acquire such authority before proceeding. Danzig asked Murray Bisgaier, Executive Director of NJAHRO, to confer with federal officials and to draft the necessary legislation. Bisgaier's bill, like the bill he had introduced in 1955, extended the powers of current redevelopment agencies to include neighborhood rehabilitation.

Agnes Coleman learned about the bill from a member of NJAREB. She denounced the move as a "secret power grab" by NHA. Coleman and Mayor Carlin immediately sent telegrams to leading state legislators urging them to postpone considerations until the City had studied the proposal. In addition, the Mayor privately assured her that he would make no statement on the bill before NCNCR had examined it and issued a recommendation. It may well be that NHA hoped to secure passage of this legislation without alerting NCNCR and other local interests. Whatever NHA's initial strategy, the Carlin-Coleman telegrams forced Danzig to negotiate directly with NCNCR. In April, 1956, he submitted Bisgaier's bill to NCNCR and urged a prompt endorsement.

Despite Coleman's fiery reaction to news of this legislation, NCNCR's inner core was not in complete opposition to Danzig's proposal. On the one hand, NCNCR's leaders were opposed to NHA's becoming Newark's official rehabilitation agency; on the other hand, they recognized the need for enabling legislation on neighborhood rehabilitation.

NCNCR itself was years away from any concrete action or project in this field. A few months earlier it had learned that FHA insurance for home improvement loans would be available only within an area formally designated by URA as an Urban Renewal Area. Before this designation could be secured, NCNCR would have to go through an elaborate project planning process. Before it could acquire the staff needed for this process, it would have to discover a stable source of funds. With federal approval of an NCNCR rehabilitation project at least three years off, most members of the Committee were loath to delay NHA's federally approved plans for rehabilitating and clearing the Central Ward.

Of equal importance was NCNCR's estimate of Danzig's strength. Many on the Committee apparently felt that Danzig would win anyway and hoped that some sign of cooperation would encourage Danzig to relax his virulent criticisms of the Committee. NCNCR had needed Danzig to arrange a meeting with URA and FHA officials and to interpret the federal housing laws. It probably would need him again. In addition, most NCNCR members found political controversy unpleasant and thus sought a quick accord with Danzig. The Mayor, moreover, had refused to intervene in quarrels between the two agencies and had insisted that NCNCR deal on its own with Danzig. Carlin's behavior implied that he was willing to join the reformers and to create a citizen committee, but not to strain his arrangements with NHA.

The net result was a willingness on the part of most NCNCR members to endorse the Bisgaier-Danzig proposal. In fact, the Committee's inner core had to exert pressure on the other members in order to stiffen their resistance and to prevent complete capitulation. Only this inner core realized that NCNCR's endorsement might be used as a basis of negotiation and as the means to a settlement with NHA.

At first Danzig attempted to exploit the Committee's vacillation. By emphasizing URA's threats, he created an atmosphere of crisis and helped maneuver NCNCR into the role of "obstructionist." If Bisgaier's amendment did not pass during the current session of the Legislature, Danzig warned, federal aid to the Central Ward would be stopped. Local businessmen were aroused by concern over the future of the adjacent light industrial project. The local press seized upon NHA's warnings and castigated NCNCR for "playing politics" with the city's future.

At this point Danzig abandoned overt pressure and proposed a device to secure federal funds for NCNCR. He offered to hire NCNCR as "rehabilitation consultants" on the nonclearance phases of the Central Ward project. NHA would add an item called "Advice on Neighborhood Rehabilitation" to the gross project costs for the Central Ward, and the funds in this item would go to the Committee. Thus, NCNCR could secure a staff without first acquiring official status. Most members of NCNCR's inner core seemed willing to accept the offer. Before approving the bill, however, there were some sections that they wanted clarified.

One major question that bothered NCNCR was whether the legislation would vest exclusive rehabilitation powers in local re-development agencies and whether NHA would thereby become Newark's sole official rehabilitation agency. Under persistent questioning Danzig conceded that, in his opinion, the bills did not prevent the Mayor and the Council from later naming agencies other than NHA to exercise rehabilitation powers in areas outside the Central Ward. NCNCR leaders insisted that the proposed legislation be rewritten to make this "local option" explicit, and Danzig eventually agreed to the insertion.

Some other amendments to the bill were proposed by NCNCR and incorporated in the revised version, but these were suggested merely to demonstrate that the Committee would not let NHA run wild. In the end, "local option" remained Danzig's major concession. Although NHA could proceed with rehabilitation in the Central Ward, the exact jurisdictional lines between NHA and NCNCR would be left unsettled, pending a local ordinance on rehabilitation powers. The proposed state legislation, moreover, would not be construed as prejudging this later decision in NHA's favor. As for the other part of the agreement, Danzig promised a "formalization of NCNCR's consultative role" in the Central Ward project immediately after passage of the revised amendments.

Danzig's strategy during the summer of 1956 was to publicize widely NCNCR's endorsement. He strongly encouraged NCNCR to lobby for City Council approval of their "local option" proposal and then for enactment of the proposal by the New Jersey Legislature.

In June, 1956, the leaders of NCNCR introduced an ordinance making their committee an official municipal agency. Some leaders began to question whether their arrangement with Danzig to obtain staff had been necessary. At the same time they began to waver in their support for Danzig's "local option" proposals. On June 6, however, an amendment to the Committee's ordinance was introduced by Councilman Cooper, requiring that NCNCR consist of three members from each of the city's five wards. This amendment would have disqualified almost all of the present members and, presumably, would have given the councilmen a major voice in selecting the new personnel. The Committee denounced this attempt to "politicize" its activities and, soon after, demonstrated new interest in Danzig's proposal. NCNCR lobbied steadily for Bisgaier's bill until its passage in fall, 1956.

ROUND THREE: LOCAL ORDINANCE AND SETTLEMENT

The agreement on state enabling legislation had not settled the jurisdictional quarrel between NHA and NCNCR, and no one knew this better than Danzig.[9] Legislative enactment of the Bisgaier bill closed several questions but left others unsettled. The City Council would have to activate NHA's rehabilitation powers in the Central Ward with a formal resolution, and the question of designating an official rehabilitation agency for the entire city also would have to be resolved. Yet, NHA took no immediate action. Danzig apparently planned to wait until another federal threat to cut off Central Ward funds provoked another local crisis.

This time, however, NCNCR seized the initiative. In May, 1957, it designated an area in Clinton Hill as the site of its first rehabilitation project and began to consider drafting an application for federal aid. Before it could submit such an application, NCNCR would have to obtain a local enabling ordinance and a final specification of the jurisdictional lines between NCNCR and NHA. Since NHA was at that time the only municipal agency authorized to receive federal aid, Newark's Corporation Counsel was asked to clarify the current state law on rehabilitation and to indicate whether NCNCR could receive federal aid for this purpose. The Counsel's opinion was that the City could either designate a single agency with jurisdiction over all rehabilitation projects or retain rehabilitation powers itself and name different agencies for different rehabilitation projects. Either the City acting as the local public agency or any agency designated by the City could seek federal aid for rehabilitation directly. Neither would have to act through NHA.

At an NCNCR meeting in July, 1957, when the Committee was ready to file an initial application for aid to Clinton Hill, Henry Conner brought up the question of which agency would take care of rehabilitation. Danzig seemed prepared to fight any attempt to designate NCNCR as the official rehabilitation agency. He apparently had no intention of working through NCNCR in all NHA projects involving rehabilitation activity. But he found no inclination among NCNCR members in July, 1957, to seek designation as Newark's official rehabilitation agency. Instead, the Committee stressed the importance of not "freezing" the situation. It was urged that the City retain rehabilitation powers and name NCNCR as official agency for the Clinton Hill project. Danzig said he would concur if it were made clear that NHA had powers to participate in the spot clearance phases of the Clinton Hill project.

This is where matters stood between NHA and NCNCR in September, 1957, when Danzig received a letter from URA again threatening to cut off funds for the Central Ward. On October 1 Danzig presented to NCNCR an ordinance embodying their earlier verbal agreement. The City would retain official rehabilitation powers, delegating responsibility for Clinton Hill to NCNCR and responsibility for Central Ward rehabilitation to NHA. NHA would participate in the clearance aspects of the first project, while NCNCR would be consulted on the rehabilitation phases of the second. The ordinance might have been quickly endorsed by NCNCR and forwarded to the Council. But NHA and NCNCR attempted first to clarify its terms.

First, NHA officials wanted to know what their future role in the Clinton Hill project would be. One year earlier, in fall, 1956, Danzig had assumed that he and Nevin would be consulted during the selection of a rehabilitation site and the planning of that project. He had been disappointed to find his advice consistently rejected. Matters had come to a head in January, 1957, when NCNCR began planning land uses for a large vacant site in the Clinton Hill area. Danzig had urged the clearance of a sizeable area around the vacant site and the assemblage of a tract large enough for middle-income housing. Any utilization of the vacant site which failed to alter the surrounding structures, he had said, would soon be immersed in an inundation of blight.

NCNCR had rejected this proposal. Danzig's interest in increasing the total supply of standard, moderately priced dwelling units in the city had come in direct conflict with NCNCR's goal of "saving" a particular area. The Danzig proposal, moreover, apparently had threatened NCNCR's attempts to gain acceptance for the project among neighborhood residents. NCNCR had repeatedly reassured site residents that there would be no acquisition of properties, no dislocation of families, and no housing project in Clinton Hill. Finally, NCNCR's commitment to the goals and ideology of neighborhood rehabilitation had been an additional barrier to the acceptance of redevelopment on the site. The major purpose of a rehabilitation project had been to demonstrate what voluntary citizen participation could achieve without use of condemnation, demolition, relocation, or federal subsidy. Danzig's proposal would have beclouded the purpose of both the project and the Committee. The rejection of his proposal apparently convinced Danzig that he would never be able to impress his values on the Clinton Hill project. He thereafter ceased to attend NCNCR meetings.

In October, 1957, when Danzig introduced his ordinance and asked for a clarification of the role NHA would play in the Clinton Hill project, Coleman only stated openly what the earlier vacant site incident had implied. NCNCR and the City Planning Officer would plan all aspects of the project. They might later call in NHA at the execution stage to carry out spot clearance, but NHA would have no established role in planning Clinton Hill renewal beyond that of personal advisor. NCNCR's commitment to the rehabilitation ideology, moreover, made it unlikely that Danzig's personal advice would have much of an impact on NCNCR decisions.

At the same time NCNCR sought a clarification of its future role in the Central Ward. Indeed, throughout 1957 there was a new aggressiveness in NCNCR's behavior that helps explain both the exclusion of NHA from Clinton Hill planning and the Committee's demand for more information on the Central Ward. Behind this new aggressiveness was the appointment of a City Planning Officer and the creation of a modest planning staff in his office. Since NCNCR now had an alternative source of expert personnel, Danzig and NHA's staff ceased to be indispensable to the planning of Clinton Hill rehabilitation. In addition, Robert Hoover, the first City Planning Officer, had considerable personal influence over the Committee's strategy. By urging NCNCR to get tough with NHA, he added a more aggressive tone to the Committee's behavior.

The ordinance submitted to NCNCR by Danzig in October, 1957, stated that NHA would consult NCNCR on the rehabilitation phases of the Central Ward Project. Hoover and several members of NCNCR realized that Danzig was operating under a threat by URA to stop federal funds. They concluded that this was a good opportunity to "demand a spelling out of the responsibilities and prerogatives of NCNCR" in the Central Ward. The members of NCNCR, therefore, set out to press Danzig further before endorsing his proposed ordinance.

In reply to questioning, Danzig made it clear that he had no more intention of bringing NCNCR in on Central Ward planning than NCNCR had of letting NHA help plan Clinton Hill. NCNCR would be called upon at a later stage to help NHA execute the rehabilitation aspects of Central Ward. In addition, Danzig said that he could not describe in detail what the Committee's activities would be, at what stage it would intervene, and how much it would receive in compensation. NCNCR's role, like other aspects of the project, would have to be developed as the project progressed and as the demands of URA and the private redevelopers were clarified. For this reason Danzig opposed any earmarking of funds for rehabilitation at that time. He preferred to keep the amount open until he was ready to contract for NCNCR's services.

NCNCR's inner core, however, proposed an amendment to the local ordinance which would clarify NCNCR's status in the Central Ward. The proposed amendment said that NCNCR would review the urban renewal plan for the Central Ward as NHA developed it. At the execution stage the Committee would assume exclusive responsibility for rehabilitation. In addition, Danzig would agree to include in the pending federal application a brief description of NCNCR's future role and to include in the Central Ward budget an item earmarked for the Committee. NCNCR urged these changes on Danzig at its October 8 meeting, and he eventually agreed to incorporate them in an amendment to the ordinance.

On October 14, one day before NCNCR's next meeting, Danzig sent Coleman the text of NHA's amendment. It read:

> In the exercise of these powers [in the Central Ward], the Housing Authority of the City of Newark shall cooperate with, and shall have the cooperation of all city officials and agencies and shall consult especially with the Newark Committee on Neighborhood Conservation and Rehabilitation, the Central Planning Board, the Division of Inspections in the Department of Health and Welfare, the Board of Education and the Planning Officer of the City.

Danzig went on to say that NHA would place an item for NCNCR's services in the Central Ward budget. This would be done "at the earliest possible time for which [federal] approval can be secured."

Agnes Coleman, Robert Hoover, and several others thought that Danzig's wording was too vague and that his concessions were nonexistent. But other NCNCR leaders felt that Danzig had conceded as much as could be expected and that further delays would jeopardize the Central Ward project. Their sole request was that Danzig's letter to Coleman include a promise to negotiate with NCNCR at the earliest possible time on the exact nature of the Committee's role in the Central Ward. Danzig penciled in this sentence, and his local ordinance was approved. A few weeks later the City Council indicated that it would pass Danzig's ordinance, and URA renewed the flow of Central Ward funds.

These negotiations, beginning in 1954, and culminating in 1958 with a local ordinance on rehabilitation, did much to define the roles of NHA and NCNCR in urban renewal politics. NCNCR became the agency responsible for rehabilitation areas, while NHA maintained control of all renewal activities in the slum belt. Rather than plan the Central Ward and Clinton Hill projects jointly, with each agency handling its respective renewal function, NHA and NCNCR agreed to carry on separate projects and to call upon each other only at the execution stage. Neither would challenge the other's exclusive control of planning decisions in its own project. Thus, the conflict implicit in the differing functions and values of these two agencies was settled by an agreement involving geographical demarcation and reciprocal noninterference.

THE SETTLEMENT IN FORCE

The agreement on the distribution of neighborhood rehabilitation powers may be seen as a political settlement between the two agencies which was basically the same as NHA's arrangements with City Hall.[10] Beginning in an atmosphere of mutual suspicion and recriminations, NHA and NCNCR gradually eliminated the major sources of contention between them and eventually reached a basis of coexistence. Although NCNCR had not entirely abandoned its objections to clearance, it now kept such objections to itself. Each agency could proceed with its own projects, confident that it had reduced the other's behavior to predictable neutrality. NCNCR succeeded in preventing NHA from acquiring exclusive rehabilitation powers and in excluding NHA from the planning of Clinton Hill. While NCNCR failed to shift emphasis in the renewal program from clearance to rehabilitation, it did succeed in drawing a line around the outer edges of NHA's power. NHA, in turn, achieved one of its major goals: an agreement from the realtors and the rehabilitation bloc to keep their hands off the clearance program and to let NHA's arrangements with City Hall and outside parties continue unchallenged.

The reasons that the members of NCNCR abandoned their intransigent conservatism and sought a settlement with Danzig have been suggested in preceding pages: the limited interest of most Committee members in these issues, the disappointments they had experienced in NCNCR's own program, the Mayor's neutrality, and the Committee's fear of blocking federal aid for clearance. In addition, their aversion to controversy encouraged them to concede points quickly. And their unfamiliarity with the tactics of bargaining permitted Danzig to win points by wearing NCNCR members down. Were it not for the promptings of Hoover, Coleman, and a few others, the Committee would have conceded much more, much sooner. The steady erosion of NCNCR's initial conservatism lessened the ideological gap between the two agencies and made it possible for them to bargain freely. This same erosion continued apace after 1957 and helped maintain the settlement in force.

The original goal of the first neighborhood rehabilitation project had been to demonstrate what private capital and voluntary citizen participation could do through strict code enforcement and FHA-insured home improvement loans. In line with this objective NCNCR had decided to apply to the federal government for an unassisted program, involving only FHA insurance of loans for home improvement. But the rapid progress of Negro invasion, overcrowding, and illegal conversions in that area eventually challenged NCNCR's initial assumptions about the efficacy of private renewal action. The Committee's response, not unlike NHA's response to its own policy problems, was to modify its initial policy goals to save the specific project. Throughout the summer of 1957 the amount of public construction and the extent of spot clearance planned for Clinton Hill steadily increased. In August, with estimated capital expenditures in Clinton Hill well over a million dollars, NCNCR voted to apply to URA for a fully assisted program. Proceeding under Title I, however, would involve NCNCR in a more cumbersome process of federal applications and review. It meant that the starting date in Clinton Hill would be postponed for at least a few years. With the area changing so rapidly and with project execution unlikely to begin until 1961, NCNCR members were hardly sanguine about the project's future.

There were other sources of disappointment. In spring, 1958, Hoover resigned to accept another appointment. With him went most of NCNCR's aggressiveness. At about the same time, the Mayor placed a ceiling on the planning office's future budgets, thus halting the expansion of the professional planning staff. The Mayor's move forced NCNCR to abandon its idea of maintaining a large, expert planning office to do most of the Committee's staff work. Although the present planners would continue working on Clinton Hill rehabilitation, the project would proceed much more slowly than originally anticipated.

Such disappointments with the results of private initiative in urban renewal and with the future prospects of the planning office have further weakened NCNCR's criticisms of NHA. They have also reinforced NCNCR's other motives for maintaining the present settlement in force. NCNCR gained a new respect for the problems of project planning, for the importance of an expert staff, and for the rigors of negotiating with federal officials. Uncertain of its own future achievements, NCNCR has been reluctant to block NHA's progress or to make public comment upon clearance policies, even when urged to do so by others.

In spring, 1958, leaders of the Clinton Hill Neighborhood Council (CHNC) discovered a link between some rapid changes in their area and the Housing Authority's practice of relocating a large number of displaced Negroes in Clinton Hill. When a direct appeal to NHA proved fruitless, CHNC asked NCNCR to intervene. At the same time, the City Planning Officer and the head of the major code enforcement agency were criticizing NHA for relocating persons in substandard dwelling units and for creating new overcrowding violations through relocation. But NCNCR refused to "meddle" in matters of "Housing Authority business" like Central Ward relocation. The solution that NCNCR proposed was strict enforcement of codes in Clinton Hill to ensure that relocation from other projects did not create overcrowded or hazardous living conditions. This solution kept NCNCR within its own sphere of operations and preserved the insulation of the two agencies.

NCNCR also has been unresponsive to charges that NHA has planned clearance projects in rehabilitation areas. In contrast to REBON's position in 1952, the Committee has been uninterested in attempts by site residents to block NHA proposals. In 1959 NCNCR rejected an invitation from a group of merchants and realtors owning property on the sites of the Parker and Lehman projects to help their association save the area though rehabilitation. In fact, a prominent realtor and member of NCNCR warned the group that rehabilitation was not a substitute for redevelopment in areas like South Broad. When the second interim report of the planners' Demonstration Grant Project revealed that many of NHA's recent redevelopment proposals lay outside the clearance area, NCNCR members refused to draw the conclusion that some newspapermen urged on them; they would not concede that NHA was clearing land properly within the jurisdiction of NCNCR. At a meeting of NCNCR in summer, 1959, one member denounced NHA for the secretive, high-handed manner in which it planned its downtown redevelopment program and urged NCNCR to do something about it. His remarks were ruled out of order and outside the jurisdiction of the Committee.

At the time of the final settlement Danzig had promised to negotiate with NCNCR at the earliest possible moment on the exact nature of the Committee's role in the Central Ward. While adhering to its part of the arrangement, NCNCR was sluggish in holding NHA officials to their commitments. NCNCR first approached the Housing Authority to discuss the Central Ward project more than a year after their agreement had been reached. At that time Danzig indicated to NCNCR's spokesmen that funds for rehabilitation had been promised by the URA and that these funds would be made available to NCNCR when the project reached the execution stage. Since Central Ward renewal was still being discussed with URA, Danzig could provide no further information. Another request by NCNCR for information in December, 1958, yielded no better results.

NCNCR did not reapproach NHA officials until it had made use of its new official status to acquire an Executive Director, Dorothy Cronheim. At a meeting in December, 1959, Nevin told Cronheim that the Central Ward Urban Renewal Plan had been approved tentatively by URA. For the first time a general outline of this plan was revealed to a spokesman of NCNCR. But Nevin postponed any detailed discussion of NCNCR's role in the project until after final federal approval had been secured. A summary of the meeting between Cronheim and Nevin was placed in NCNCR's files, but it was not discussed in full committee. Most NCNCR members interviewed by the author in the early part of 1960 revealed little familiarity with the Central Ward Urban Renewal Plan.

The sudden relaxation of NCNCR's aggressive posture after the 1957 settlement had several sources: the Committee's preoccupation with Clinton Hill, its distaste for negotiation, its inability to sustain interest in the Central Ward, and its lack of experience with political negotiation. Most members of NCNCR saw the 1957 agreement as a final and welcome resolution of the differences with NHA. Pleased with this "symbolic victory" over NHA, they failed to realize that it might be nothing more than symbolic. They failed to see that the settlement was simply a framework for further negotiations and that negotiations had to continue if the terms of the settlement were to be made operative. For these reasons NCNCR's foothold in the Central Ward project was greatly weakened, if not entirely lost. In 1960 the Committee knew little more than it had known in 1955 about its prospective role in Central Ward renewal.

POLITICAL SETTLEMENT AND ADMINISTRATIVE COORDINATION

The negotiated settlement between NHA and NCNCR attempted to resolve an interagency conflict by insulating the two renewal functions and guaranteeing the autonomy of each agency in its own sphere.[11] The planners and many civic leaders who adhere to the values of central planning and rational administrative organization claim that this diffused responsibility and lack of coordination could lead to a self-defeating renewal program. Because there is no coordination at a level above both NHA and NCNCR and because the two agencies themselves do not coordinate their activities, the City might produce renewal projects working at cross-purposes. Thus, NHA might move Negroes from the Central Ward, only to have NCNCR later move them elsewhere.

One major characteristic of the network of political settlements in Newark renewal, then, is its departure from the values of hierarchy and coordination. Mayor Carlin rarely intervened in renewal politics, and then only to urge the agencies to reach some kind of agreement. He was more interested in some activity on all renewal fronts than in the exact substance of an agreement between the agencies. When pressed by newspapermen, among others, to establish priorities for the program or to choose between NHA and NCNCR, the Mayor would say only: "We need them both." NCNCR and the Authority themselves have had to work out the details.

Having conceded this much to the critics of the system, two further points must be added. First, the lack of coordination in Newark renewal can easily be exaggerated by noting the passivity of the mayor's office or stressing the confused status of the formal organization and local ordinances. One can quickly create an impression of confusion by rhyming off the various renewal agencies and their similar legal functions. Yet, as this and succeeding chapters try to demonstrate, a network of informal arrangements has structured the behavior of these agencies, provided specialized roles for each, and counteracted the fluid nature of the formal arrangements. The various renewal agencies do not really overlap and are not continually jostling each other for position. Nor do these agencies participate equally in the making of renewal decisions, as the formal rules would imply. The system is more coordinated than it seems because so many of the decisions actually are focused in one agency—the Newark Housing Authority.

Second, some amount of "uncoordination" may be necessary to the program's progress. A number of local informants have suggested a causal connection between the lack of formal coordination in Newark's renewal program and the high output of that program. Most informants have opposed the idea of a department of urban renewal or a renewal coordinator. Such coordination, they have argued, would make it "more difficult to keep things out of the newspapers." Moreover, the present agencies would "stop talking to each other" and would focus on "pressuring the top man." Eventually, one of the agencies might capture the top office. All participants in renewal have agreed that their good working relations with other renewal agencies would be destroyed by such a move.

In short, a centralized structure that requires clear-cut, consistent choice can bring to the surface all the latent conflicts contained in a renewal program. A more diffuse structure may make it easier to avoid conflicts or to resolve them through the give-and-take of informal negotiations. A certain lack of coordination, then, may be one price of significant renewal achievement. If so, it is a price that most officials in Newark have been willing to pay.

CHAPTER V

The Civic Leaders: Economic Development

During NEDC's initial stages varying accounts of its function appeared.[1] Perhaps the most widely accepted notion, and the one that NEDC helped propagate through its own press releases, was that the Committee would be a general planning agency in the field of urban renewal. It would make studies of Newark's economy, land uses, and policy needs, would issue long-range policy recommendations in these areas of study, and would coordinate the relevant municipal agencies in accordance with these recommendations. Another frequently mentioned possibility was that NEDC would become a rival redevelopment agency to NHA, attempting to clear Newark's slums with private investment funds rather than with federal aid.

It is questionable whether NEDC had the political support at City Hall to effectuate a central planning role. It soon became apparent, however, that most of its members had no interest in studies, recommendations, or coordination of other agencies. Instead, their interests lay with specific achievements or projects and with immediate government or private action to bring new businesses into the city and to save the downtown area. Even the originators of NEDC, who initially had not thought in these terms, now hoped that some concrete achievement by the Committee would strengthen the rather weak commitment of most member corporations. This decision not to study, plan, or coordinate various aspects of the renewal program helped reduce NEDC to another operating agency and facilitate a subsequent accommodation with NHA.

The notion that NEDC might become an alternative slum clearance agency and a challenge to NHA's supremacy in this field died more slowly than the fact. Prior to 1955 Mayor Carlin had forwarded all inquiries from prospective redevelopers directly to NHA and had refrained from even discussing the program with these parties. In spring, 1955, however, Carlin brought these inquiries to NEDC and asked if the member corporations were interested in financing site clearance or in providing the mortgage funds. Only the sharp refusal of NEDC members to risk their firm's capital forced the Mayor to return to his earlier procedure.

While Danzig praised the creation of an economic development committee and hoped that it would stimulate local investment in redevelopment, his attitude contained elements of caution. Yet, NEDC showed no penchant either for intervening in the slum clearance program or for grappling with NHA. It was not interested in subsuming NHA's activities under a general plan or in providing an alternate, nongovernmental route for the clearance of slums. In fact, NEDC soon settled on a program for revitalizing the city's central business district that bore little direct relation to the Title I program or to NHA.

Since early in the 1940s representatives of the business bloc, like Henry Conner and Anton Hagios, had been arguing for vigorous local action to stem the city's economic decline. In recent years they had come to the conclusion that Newark's future economic health depended upon a revitalization of its central business district. While sites should be cleared for new firms, the immediate emphasis should be on increased access for suburban shoppers to and from the business district. What Newark needed was a network of elevated highways emanating in radial spokes from the business district to carry the suburbanites quickly and safely over the slums. The City should clear sites for downtown parking lots, not for more tax-exempt public housing projects that use up good commercial real estate and seal off the central business district.

At NEDC's initial meetings its subcommittees on highways and parking captured the imagination of most members. Only a few weeks after its creation NEDC announced, as its first major goal, the formation of an independent parking authority and the construction of an underground parking garage in the downtown area.

For most members of NEDC this proposal was a retreat from their earlier position that business could revive the local economy without any major intervention by government. The proposal involved the use of an independent government corporation, a form of administrative organization toward which local businessmen had been critical since NHA's creation in 1938. The scheme was acceptable to NEDC members primarily because the parking projects would be self-sustaining, because the parking authority would be run by local business, and because federal funds would not be required.

When NHA announced plans for a public housing project in the Central Ward (Wright Homes), NEDC's criticisms of the Authority were made explicit. On June 1, 1955, NEDC's Subcommittee on Highways criticized the project for interfering with the proposed radial network of highways. The project, NEDC argued, would block the proposed east-west freeway and would eventually seal off the central business district from the Essex County suburbs. When Danzig had been questioned on this point at a meeting of NEDC four weeks earlier, he had said that no one knew what the freeway's alignment in the Central Ward would be. But the Subcommittee's report demanded that NHA take the east-west freeway and other highway proposals into account in planning the Central Ward project, even if this meant replanning parts of the project already under way. NHA's reply denied that housing was being overemphasized in Newark. Authority officials minimized the ability of a superhighway system to revive the business district. The city's downtown area could be revitalized, they said, only if suburban customers were drawn back to the city as residents of attractive, new, middle-income housing. The Mayor, moreover, soon dissociated himself from NEDC's criticisms of Central Ward policy. The Committee eventually had to settle for a mild resolution urging the Central Planning Board and NHA to "keep highway considerations before them" when drafting their plans.

At the same time that NHA and NEDC were trading public allegations, Danzig began sending out feelers to several of NEDC's subcommittees. Here he displayed a flexibility and willingness to compromise that surprised many of NEDC's members. NHA officials felt that the game of charges and countercharges had gone on long enough. It was time to talk business.

NHA AND NEDC: THE BEGINNING OF NEGOTIATIONS

Danzig's negotiations with NEDC departed significantly from his dealings with NCNCR and other local interests.[2] The history of animosity between Danzig and the realtors of NCNCR did not exist in NEDC's case. NHA's staff viewed local businessmen as more friendly toward NHA than the realtors were and more capable of making a substantial contribution to the clearance program. Local firms, it was hoped, would act as redevelopers, would provide the mortgage funds for other redevelopers, or would use their contacts in the business world to draw capital into Newark. In its dealings with NCNCR the Authority tried to neutralize a source of opposition and keep that opposition away from redevelopment policy making. In its dealings with NEDC it encouraged local businessmen to participate actively in the program as redevelopers, financiers, or publicists. In NEDC's case, more than in any other, NHA officials proved willing to solicit local support and participation with concessions on policy.

In NHA's first clearance project its staff made some policy decisions in response to the anticipated reaction of local businessmen and even shared some decisions with an important member of the business community. Danzig viewed the North Ward as a demonstration project, which could expand the city's tax base, silence business criticisms of NHA for building tax-exempt public housing projects, and encourage local investment in this or succeeding projects. In accordance with his determination to build a fully taxable project, Danzig consistently rejected proposals for a cooperative housing project, a college expansion program, or a "tax deal" for the private redevelopers. He continued to reject all proposals impairing the fully taxable status of the project, even where the alternative was higher rentals for the new, middle-income housing.

According to informants, in fall, 1954, when Mutual Benefit Life Insurance Company announced its decision to build a new home office, Danzig offered the North Ward site for that purpose. The same informants indicate that, when Mutual Benefit's Financial Vice-President, Milford Vieser, rejected this site, Danzig offered to clear any other site in the city that would be acceptable to both Mutual Benefit and URA. This story, if accurate, demonstrates that Danzig was willing to reconsider his initial emphasis on housing if he could thereby secure a local firm as redeveloper.

Mutual Benefit's decision to build new offices without the help of Title I did not end Danzig's discussions with Vieser. In 1956 Vieser arranged a series of meetings between Danzig and Donald A. Harper, President of the Tung-Sol Electric Company. As a result of these meetings NHA announced that Tung-Sol's offices on the North Ward site would not be cleared and that a cleared area of adjacent land would be made available for expansion of its present offices. These meetings indicated Vieser's influence in the North Ward project at the time and his ability to bring Danzig closer to the local business community. The result was praised by NEDC as another sign that Danzig was something more than just a "housing man" and that he was willing to incorporate economic development goals in the slum clearance program.

When NHA received bids for redeveloping the North Ward site in May, 1957, Danzig discussed with Vieser the relative merits of these bids, and Vieser's opinion was influential in the final selection of a redeveloper. Several months later, when it became apparent that this redeveloper could not come to terms with FHA, Danzig and Vieser agreed that new redevelopers should be sought. In the ensuing months Vieser helped NHA through its worst crisis. He first encouraged Herbert Greenwald, a builder who had done some work for Mutual Benefit in Chicago, to take over North Ward redevelopment; then, through his access to FHA, Vieser helped secure mortgage insurance for the new proposal.

Despite his satisfactory arrangements with Vieser, Danzig proved unsuccessful in his attempt to attract local capital into the redevelopment program. During NEDC's first year Danzig spoke before several meetings, urged the Committee to endorse middle-income housing, described the North Ward project, and encouraged them to inspect the site. But the member corporations would not follow Danzig's lead. They were wary of any action that might be construed as a promise of subsequent capital investment in the program.

Early in 1956 a Subcommittee on Financing Enterprises was established by NEDC to encourage local investment in Newark's revival. Milford Vieser was named Chairman. Here the interests of Danzig and Vieser coincided, for the latter was anxious to see other corporations do their share and help revive the city. For a while Danzig slackened his own campaign and tried working through Vieser's subcommittee. Yet, Vieser eventually proved no more successful in encouraging local investment than Danzig had been. By 1957 Danzig had apparently abandoned all hope that a local firm would redevelop the North Ward or any other Title I site in Newark.

LIGHT INDUSTRIAL REDEVELOPMENT

The large commercial and financial institutions that made up NEDC were more interested in the downtown area than in the development of industry.[3] Perhaps the low priority of its work and the low visibility of its actions helped the Industrial Sites Subcommittee reach an accord with NHA. The result of this accord, a federally aided industrial redevelopment project, represents the apex of NHA's accommodation to the business bloc.

The purpose of the Subcommittee was to attract outside industries to Newark and to facilitate the expansion of local industrial firms by selecting sites suitable for new industrial construction. Albert Rachlin, a former president of the local real estate board, was named Chairman in 1955, and he, in turn, named a group of the city's leading industrial realtors as subcommittee advisors. For a while it seemed as if the question of whether vacant sites should be developed for industrial or residential use, an issue on which NHA and these same industrial realtors had clashed in 1952, would now be revived.

Yet, Danzig sought out the Subcommittee at its initial meeting and offered his services as consultant. While the offer surprised some of the Subcommittee members, they did not refuse. In fact, Danzig's suggestion that the Subcommittee focus on vacant sites in the meadows for heavy industry and on sites closer to the city for light industry was considered very sound by the realtors and was made the framework of all subsequent action. Heavy industry could be located in the meadows near Newark Airport, but light industry, which depended on the economies of concentration, required built-up areas nearer the center of the city.

The industrial realtors concluded that no suitable vacant sites for light industry existed and that some amount of clearance would be necessary. By summer, 1955, they had narrowed the choice of sites to three. The one favored by most realtors was a ninety-acre area in the Central Ward, immediately adjacent to NHA's sixty-block renewal project.

When the industrial realtors made their report at a meeting of the Subcommittee, Danzig informed them that these ninety acres had been part of NHA's original Central Ward application and part of the forty blocks eliminated by URA. Since NHA was planning to ask for a restoration of the forty blocks, Danzig offered to incorporate the realtors' proposal in this project. NHA would clear the ninety-acre site for new light industry, but the new forty-block project would have to be a package deal. URA would approve industrial redevelopment only as part of a larger, predominantly residential redevelopment project. If NEDC wanted new industry on the ninety-acre site, it would have to accept middle-income and public housing elsewhere in the forty-block renewal area. This offer involved only a slight change in NHA's plans, since the Authority had intended for several years to renew the area under question. Yet, this slight change represents one of the few cases in which NHA has accommodated a local group on the substance of policy.

Danzig's motion was tabled. Rachlin and the other realtors still believed that private enterprise, or at least local government, could achieve redevelopment without federal subsidies. They devised a plan in which NEDC would clear most of the ninety-acre area and would offer it at low cost to nearby industries if those industries would agree to share in the cost of acquisition and clearance. Rachlin, who assumed that local industries were cramped for space and would welcome an opportunity to expand at their present sites, was surprised to find his offer rejected. He next proposed that the

City float a $10-million bond, clear the area itself, and sell it to industrial firms at write-down values. The deficit would be made up by drawing on the City's surplus. The City Council, however, consistently opposed proposals involving redevelopment at local expense, and the Mayor gave such proposals only half-hearted support. By February, 1956, the Subcommittee recognized that it could not proceed without Title I. After a series of meetings with Carlin and Danzig, Rachlin recommended that NEDC adopt Danzig's proposal for a forty-block residential and light industrial redevelopment project.

After the formal designation of this area by NEDC the Industrial Sites Subcommittee receded into the background, leaving NHA to file an initial federal application, do the detailed planning, and attract industrial redevelopers. Yet, NHA officials have had some doubts about the project's eventual success. Projects that emerge through the process of local negotiation are generally considered less sound by the crucial nonlocal participants than projects planned by NHA's expert staff.

THE EARLY STAGES OF PENN PLAZA

During its first five years NEDC spent a great deal of its time and staked a great deal of its reputation on a proposal to clear the "Skid Row" area opposite Pennsylvania Station.[4] The idea of redeveloping this commercial fringe area for new office buildings originated with the giant retail firms of the central business district. BMR's Executive Director, Henry Conner, later became interested in this proposal but was unable to persuade either the local government or nearby businessmen to finance clearance operations. Early in the 1950s Conner became convinced that Pittsburgh's experiences with privately financed urban redevelopment might be the key to the success of Newark's Penn Plaza proposal. It was mainly through Conner's influence that the newly created NEDC showed an overriding interest in redeveloping Penn Plaza with private capital and that it voted, almost immediately after its formation, to visit the Golden Triangle in Pittsburgh.

If the purposes of the Pittsburgh trip were to buoy enthusiasm for a private renewal of Penn Plaza and to encourage business investment in a private redevelopment corporation, the net effect of this trip was just the opposite. NEDC members were despondent about the possibilities of a $15-million private renewal effort without the aid of an Andrew Mellon, and few indicated a willingness to risk their firm's capital on such a venture.

Within a few weeks of the Committee's return from Pittsburgh, Danzig began sounding out Conner and the recently formed Penn Station Subcommittee on a proposal to redevelop Penn Plaza under Title I. Once again Danzig indicated that he was willing to expand the program to accommodate economic development goals. At first his proposal was ignored. Though disillusioned by the Pittsburgh trip, most NEDC members retained an aversion to federal subsidy. Throughout the summer of 1955 Danzig continued to seek out the Subcommittee and to warn them that Penn Plaza would never get off the ground without federal aid. By September the Subcommittee and NEDC had agreed to let NHA initiate talks with URA. Thus far, the pattern of the light industrial project had been duplicated.

Having convinced NEDC that federal aid was indispensable, NHA then learned that such aid was unavailable. The 1949 Housing Act, according to URA, provided for aid to residential or nonresidential redevelopment on residential sites but not to nonresidential redevelopment on nonresidential sites. Penn Plaza was ineligible. Unwilling to let NEDC's commitment to Title I die, NHA's staff countered with a plan to divide the Penn Plaza area into five or six sections. Some of these sections would be eligible for federal aid because they involved nonresidential redevelopment on predominantly residential sites, whereas the others would have to be redeveloped by the City. At the same time, Danzig pointed out that the members of NEDC, through their contacts in the business world and in the Eisenhower administration, could lobby for amendments to the 1949 Act which would make projects like Penn Plaza eligible for aid.

NEDC's interest in redeveloping Penn Plaza through Title I proved difficult to sustain. In fall, 1955, the Committee voted to table the suggestion of its Penn Station Subcommittee that NEDC lobby for a liberalization of federal housing statutes. Instead, it urged the Subcommittee to explore the possibilities of state or local financing of the Penn Plaza proposal. But Danzig had been meeting with the Subcommittee for several months and now found some dedicated disciples among its members. He and the Subcommittee set out to convert the more conservative members of the full Committee.

In January, 1956, the Subcommittee reported out the same recommendation that NEDC once had tabled. Edward Curtis, Chairman of the Subcommittee and Vice-President of the New Jersey Bell Telephone Company, took this opportunity to deny charges that urban renewal meddled in local affairs or interfered with private enterprise. On this second vote NEDC agreed to support an expansion of federal aid; it thereafter lobbied for the necessary amendments until their passage in September, 1959. By this time, however, the amendments were no longer relevant to Penn Plaza.

Lobbying for liberalization, as far as NEDC was concerned, did not preclude continuing attempts to redevelop Penn Plaza without NHA or the federal government. The Committee repeatedly told NHA that, if some outside firm agreed to construct new office buildings on the site and if some local corporation agreed to underwrite clearance or to provide the mortgage funds, all plans for a federally aided project would be canceled. Whenever some prospect appeared on the horizon, NEDC would break off talks with NHA and enter negotiations with the outside firm and local fianciers. As one after another of these prospects failed to materialize, the project would resurface, and discussions between NHA and NEDC on federal aid would resume.

In 1957 URA rejected NHA's scheme for dividing Penn Plaza into several sections, and Congress again bypassed the liberalizing amendments. NEDC became pessimistic about the chances of federal aid and began reconsidering a rash of proposals for redeveloping Penn Plaza without NHA. At this point BMR urged the creation of two units: a new municipal redevelopment agency, which would clear the area entirely at City expense, and a business development corporation made up of local firms, which would provide the redevelopment capital. NEDC drafted a bill giving New Jersey municipalities the right to issue bonds for such purposes and piloted its bill through the New Jersey Legislature. But Danzig's prophecy that Penn Plaza could not be launched without federal aid proved to be an accurate interpretation of the local scene. The Mayor continued to be indifferent, and the City Council openly hostile, to locally financed redevelopment proposals; the important banks and insurance companies in Newark reiterated their reluctance to spark local redevelopment with their own capital. One product of NEDC's explorations was the decision to sponsor a land-use and planning survey of Penn Plaza and the central business district. After discussing it with Mayor Carlin, NEDC voted to postpone the survey until after the 1958 local elections.

From the creation of NEDC in 1955 to the local elections in 1958 there is a distinctive pattern to Danzig's relations with the members of NEDC. NHA's Executive Director made a major effort at conciliation during this period. He drafted several project proposals, sought out members of the Committee, and tried to sell them on the idea of commercial or industrial redevelopment through Title I. The only serious obstacles to their cooperation with NHA on clearance projects were their own objections to accepting "government handouts" and their reluctance to invest company funds in local redevelopment. Danzig eventually persuaded them that Title I was indispensable to economic development goals, but he did not succeed in persuading them to risk their own capital in these ventures.

During 1957 and 1958 Danzig felt obliged to abandon the idea that local business would invest in redevelopment. At the same time NEDC underwent some major changes in structure and purpose. As a result of these two developments, NHA's relations with NEDC entered a new phase.

THE "NEW NEWARK"

The frustrations of the Penn Plaza experience convinced some members of NEDC, like Chairman H. Bruce Palmer, that the Committee's interest in project building should be de-emphasized.[5] It would be wiser, he and others felt, to concentrate on attracting outside businesses and to let NHA handle site clearance

problems. Rather than focus on particular projects, NEDC should
launch an over-all campaign to sell Newark, to publicize its advan-
tages and achievements, and to interest outside firms in the possibility of moving to some site in the city.

Conner, Carberry, and other staff professionals supported this
shift toward public relations and publicity. Still disturbed by the
limited commitment of most members, they thought that the new
orientation would add some drama to NEDC's work and make it
more appealing to the local corporations. Under Palmer's and
Conner's guidance NEDC named an experienced and trained public relations man, Paul Busse, as the Committee's first Executive
Secretary.

As part of their campaign to sell Newark, NEDC's staff set out
to develop a publicly acceptable description of local renewal politics. In brochures, press releases, and magazine articles, they told
how the shift to mayor-council government had reawakened the
interest of local groups in revitalizing the city. According to this
account NEDC provided the initial spark for redevelopment projects by making recommendations to Mayor Carlin and by lining
up private redevelopers. After the Mayor had given his approval,
the projects were planned in detail by the Central Planning Board
and then referred to the Housing Authority for execution. The
core of local renewal organization was the bimonthly meeting
between Mayor Carlin and NEDC. The major reason for Newark's
success was the alliance between City Hall and the city's top business leaders. By 1958 these notions had become Newark's official
version of its renewal politics.

At the same time that NEDC's staff was formulating this doctrine, the Committee's importance in clearance decisions was on
the decline. This very preoccupation with public relations contributed to that decline by diverting NEDC's interests away from
project planning. NHA, at this time, had abandoned all hope of
persuading local business to redevelop sites and had begun the
search for out-of-town home builders. The two agencies, then,
edged away from the close interaction that had characterized their
relations since 1955. While the public relations men were propa-
gating a version of renewal politics that ascribed central impor-

tance to NEDC, the Committee actually was drifting away from the center of decision making.

Many local participants verbalize this doctrine, and some claim it to be an accurate description of the renewal program. It probably is more useful to view the "New Newark" notion as an attempt by participants to provide a normative version of their system. In this sense the doctrine can be viewed as a self-image, as a picture of what the participants think the system would look like if it were to adhere to widely held values. The normative version of a system, as expressed by its participants, sometimes coincides with the actual structure of the system. In Newark, however, the disparity between what the participants publicly allege they are doing and what they actually do is great. The more removed a local participant is from the center of policy making, the more likely he is to accept this doctrine as an accurate description of Newark's renewal politics. Those directly involved in clearance decisions are more apt to recognize both the shortcomings and the utility of this doctrine.

The creation of a professional staff had one other important effect on NEDC, in addition to a growing emphasis on public relations. The members of NEDC became increasingly reliant on the expertise of their staff, just as NHA, NCNCR, the City Council, and the City Planning Board had come to rely on their staffs. In recent years there has been less diffuseness in NEDC's structure, less subcommittee autonomy, and less exclusive reliance upon prominent businessmen acting as subcommittee chairmen. In their recent negotiations with NEDC, NHA officials have dealt primarily with Henry Conner, Paul Busse, Kenneth Carberry, and the other members of the professional staff.

NHA IN THE CENTRAL BUSINESS DISTRICT

Sometime during 1957 Danzig concluded that the future of the redevelopment program depended upon his ability to mobilize out-of-town investors.[6] Soon thereafter he began a campaign to attract professional home builders who had national reputations in the redevelopment field. The ambitious redevelopment proposals which NHA announced in 1958 and 1959 were the products of negotiation between Danzig and these out-of-town builders. NEDC members received little inkling of these projects until their formal announcement; nor are there any indications that NEDC members had a significant role in helping to attract these redevelopers to Newark. The Committee members had envisioned redevelopment of the downtown area by outside firms seeking new home offices; they had little contact with professional home builders like Parker, Turner, or Zeckendorf.

In January, 1960, members of NEDC and its staff said that they still had not had any communication with most of the new redevelopers. In a few cases, however, the redevelopers had asked local corporation executives about Danzig's reputation before committing themselves to a project. In such cases Danzig received unqualified endorsement from the members of NEDC.

The launching of the Penn Plaza project, though different in some respects from the beginning of other downtown proposals, serves to illustrate NEDC's role in the downtown program. It also summarizes the changing relationship between NHA and NEDC.

In summer, 1958, when Henry Conner and Paul Busse began discussing the central business district survey that had been delayed till after the elections, they were surprised by a new skepticism in Danzig's attitude toward the survey. NHA had begun formulating plans to redevelop major sections of the downtown area for middle-income housing. Danzig thought a survey geared to the problem of stimulating the local economy would urge the commercial redevelopment of downtown areas, including those slated by NHA for new housing. NEDC hoped that the survey would serve not only to provide more information on the district but to interest outside firms in potential downtown sites. This, too, conflicted with NHA's new housing program.

Although Danzig seemed opposed to any kind of survey, Mayor Carlin urged NHA and NEDC to negotiate their differences. The Mayor refused to take sides in the controversy, but he insisted that some study of the area be launched. Danzig eventually agreed to a compromise plan in which the study would be carried out by both economists and housing men and would be coordinated by an architect.

Oscar Stonorov was named architect and coordinator of the survey, largely because of his technical competence, but also because of his good contacts in the business world. It was hoped that he would draw outside firms to Penn Plaza or to some other site in the downtown area.

After surveying the local scene for several months, Stonorov quickly saw that NHA was the only local agency with adequate information on land uses in the city. It is not surprising, then, that Stonorov borrowed heavily from NHA's data and that his final report bore the unmistakable imprint of NHA's ideas. During this study Stonorov broached the subject of a redevelopment proposal for Penn Plaza to NHA's Executive Director. Danzig persuaded him to sound out some prominent home builders on the possibility of an FHA-insured Title I housing project in that area. Within a few months NHA and the Gilbane Construction Company of Providence, Rhode Island, had agreed upon a middle-income housing proposal for Penn Plaza, for which Stonorov would serve as architect.

The final recommendations of the central business district survey were in accord with NHA's plans for that area. The survey report argued that, due to changing technology and business practices, the total area needed for commercial usages in Newark was growing smaller. For this reason the city's central business district was contracting. This, in turn, explained the prevalence of half-deserted commercial slums on the district's outer fringe. The study concluded that the areas surrounding the district were no longer needed for commercial uses and that residential redevelopment of these sites was appropriate.

Although NEDC had received progress reports from Stonorov throughout 1959, his conclusions, followed by the announcement of Gilbane's redevelopment proposal for Penn Plaza, apparently took the Committee by surprise. In fact, during the same month that the report and the Gilbane proposal were announced, NEDC had been negotiating with a New York firm on the construction of a new home office in the Penn Plaza area. NEDC even had persuaded an important local firm to provide the mortgage funds. Despite these negotiations and their own earlier inclinations, the members of NEDC did not protest the conversion of Penn Plaza into a housing project. The Gilbane proposal, coming on the heels of Stonorov's recommendation, effectively settled the issue. Neither NEDC nor any other local bloc would consider standing in the way of a concrete redevelopment proposal.

In the ensuing months NHA continued its plans for the residential redevelopment of areas immediately surrounding the business district. NEDC's support for these plans also continued. The most significant facts about NEDC in summer, 1959, are the steps it did not take. It did not object to its limited participation in the initiation of these projects, to NHA's initiative in the redevelopment of the area, or to the subordination of economic development goals. The motives behind this acquiescence were several. Most NEDC members apparently were not sufficiently committed to economic development goals to think the issue worth fighting about. NEDC had no concrete proposals of its own in the summer of 1959 to present as alternatives to NHA's projects. If NHA's proposals will help the city, most members concluded, who are we to stand in their way?

This attitude was coupled with a general crisis in morale among Committee members and an overriding pessimism about the Committee's future. NEDC had few concrete achievements to show for its first five years of operation. In 1959 most members thought it highly unlikely that private initiative and local government by themselves could turn the tide of local economic decline. It also seemed unlikely that NEDC could do very much to attract new businesses to Newark without the help of NHA and federal aid. This crisis in morale had reinforced the Committee's drift toward greater emphasis on public relations. As one member of NEDC's staff said, in explaining the Committee's passivity during the summer of 1959: "Our job is to package the program. . . . We let Lou [Danzig] worry about particular sites and particular projects."

NEDC's staff placed great emphasis on maintaining good working relations with NHA. If the local economy could not be revived without Title I aid, then NHA's cooperation would be essential to NEDC's future. Throughout that summer the Committee's staff was careful to stress the "long-run point of view" and to maintain harmonious relations with Authority officials. NEDC also was anxious to avoid any disruption of NHA's continuing progress with the light industrial project.

THE FUTURE OF NHA-NEDC RELATIONS

In fall, 1959, NEDC's staff renewed its earlier interest in NHA's decision making.[7] During these months Busse and Conner began to draft proposals for commercial or industrial redevelopment projects to be executed under Title I. They also thought that they should have a voice in the detailed planning of NHA's recent downtown projects. Throughout that fall they sought out Danzig and presented project proposals to him. They also tried to elicit information from him on NHA's current activities and to keep economic development considerations before him.

When the Central Ward Urban Renewal Plan was completed late in 1959, NEDC's staff criticized the "excessive" amount of redevelopment planned for nontaxable, public uses. At about the same time, the staff urged NHA to revise its plans for the college expansion project by pushing the colleges back from Broad Street and permitting the construction of revenue-producing commercial frontage along Washington Park.

But latent conflicts between the housing goals of NHA and the economic development goals of NEDC's staff are not permitted to get out of hand. NEDC's criticisms are not submitted to the press. When asked about the resolution of these potentially explosive incidents, NEDC's staff members say: "We will have lunch with Lou and talk it out." Busse and Conner would rather concede a point than attempt to block activities that were generally beneficial to the city.

With the downtown program successfully launched, NEDC's staff found Danzig more relaxed and receptive. Recognizing that the downtown program would meet Newark's need for middle-income housing during the next decade, Danzig was prepared to move the Title I program in the direction of nonresidential redevelopment. He responded well to NEDC's proposal for an in-

dustrial park in the East Ward. He also proved receptive to the
idea of a light industrial project on North Broad Street, to be
sponsored by William Zeckendorf of Webb and Knapp, Inc. For
several years Danzig and Zeckendorf had discussed the possibility
of a middle-income housing project in Newark but had been unable to agree. In 1959 they finally broke off negotiations. A few
weeks later NEDC's staff sought out Zeckendorf and offered to
negotiate his differences with NHA. NEDC opted strongly for a
light industrial project. Late in 1959 Danzig indicated that, if
NEDC's staff and Zeckendorf's staff could agree on a suitable light
industrial proposal, NHA would give it serious consideration.

In addition, NHA officials apparently have been more amenable
to discussion of the details of clearance projects with NEDC's
staff than they were in the years preceding the downtown program.
Several local corporation executives, who are on the boards of
trustees of local colleges, have proved very helpful to NHA. They
have helped maintain the commitment of these schools to the college expansion project and have helped mediate differences among
the various participating colleges. Danzig, in turn, has shared information on the college project with NEDC and has given sympathetic attention to the suggestions of its staff. In January, 1960,
Conner and Busse were trying to secure the same advisory role in
some of the newer projects, but NHA officials seemed cool to the
idea.

Thus, NEDC has found it much easier to deal with NHA since
the launching of downtown redevelopment. These relations, however, bear little resemblance to Danzig's earlier efforts at conciliat-
ing local business. NEDC's support is valuable to NHA. Opposition from its members would make NHA's complex tasks more
difficult. Since discovering that a successful redevelopment program would have to be attained without the help of local capital,
however, NHA's staff has become less concerned about the question of NEDC's active participation and involvement in the program. Given the unavailability of local capital, Danzig will not
draft nonresidential redevelopment proposals and then try to sell
them to NEDC, as he did in 1955. If NEDC takes the initiative,

as it has in the East Ward industrial park and the Zeckendorf project, NHA will lend its cooperation. But, in dealing with NEDC, Danzig husbands the Authority's resources more carefully than he did in 1955.

The civic leaders' isolation from local politics during the 1940s helped NHA establish a firm footing at City Hall. After Carlin's election as mayor in 1953 the civic leaders, or at least some activists among them, re-entered local politics through the urban renewal program. This re-entry, however, failed to alter the prevailing renewal system. Despite their traditional aversion toward NHA, the civic leaders eventually reached a settlement with its Executive Director. The terms of this settlement, moreover, left untouched NHA's usual pattern of policy formation. The civic leaders settled for a role in renewal politics that excluded a dominant influence over the making of slum clearance policy.

The civic leaders were led to accept this role partly because of the weaknesses in their own position. Some of these weaknesses resulted from their late arrival on the renewal scene. NEDC and NCNCR, once created, found themselves effectively isolated by NHA's arrangements with City Hall. The Mayor was willing to create these committees but not to provide them with continuous support. Left to fend for themselves in renewal politics, the committees could choose either to become a part of the pre-existing pattern or to remain insignificant bystanders. In short, the political settlement of NHA with City Hall seems to have had a multiplier effect. The existence of a major settlement forces latecomers to participate in the system on the terms of that settlement or not to participate at all.

Cooperation with NHA also followed from the decision of the civic leaders to form quasi-official citizen committees and to turn these committees into operating agencies. The civic leaders' preoccupation with their own projects served to divert their attention from slum clearance and NHA's decision-making process. NHA and the citizen committees operated in different spheres, pursuing related but frequently compatible goals. It became possible for NHA and NCNCR to reach an agreement in which both could pursue their separate goals simultaneously.

Neither of these committees was able to build a staff on the basis of private contributions. Their inability to launch their projects without borrowing expertise and advice enabled Danzig to use as a source of influence the knowledge of his own staff.

The exercise of quasi-official responsibility also served to weaken the civic leaders' staunch conservatism on renewal and to erode their blanket opposition to federal aid in this field. Their experiences with the immensity of the renewal problem forced them to re-examine their earlier assertions that citizen participation and private enterprise could do the job alone. Without substantial federal aid NEDC proved unable to revive the local economy, and NCNCR proved unable to rehabilitate deteriorating neighborhoods. In grappling with these problems most members of the committees acquired the perspective of administrative officials. They proved less critical of municipal agencies than they had been as members of their civic groups and more responsive to bold governmental schemes in the area of urban renewal.

Finally, the civic leaders' growing involvement in renewal affairs and in negotiations with NHA made it difficult for their civic groups to continue their customary attack on the Authority or on the program generally. Participation in a quasi-official citizen committee seemed to preclude a continuation of traditional pressure group tactics, even though the civic leaders' experiences on these committees often proved frustrating.

There are two other characteristics of the civic leaders in Newark that hastened the drift toward settlement. First, most members of NEDC and NCNCR disliked political controversy, strove to keep "above politics," and sought to end any conflict as quickly as possible. This attitude, coupled with a lack of experience in political bargaining, often made agreement between NHA and the committees relatively easy to reach. For these same reasons the two committees rarely insisted upon radical changes in NHA plans and often accepted the settlement, as embodied in ordinance or tacit agreement, as the final solution of a question.

Second, it would be wrong to conclude that the civic leaders are dissatisfied with their present role in renewal politics. They do not stand at the center of renewal decision making, but there is no evidence to indicate that they want to. Most seem content with the prestige and information they receive as members of citizen committees and with the personal satisfaction they derive from civic participation.

CHAPTER VI

The Planners

For those who measure the progress of city governments by the development of their planning function, Newark in 1960 would be just emerging from the Dark Ages. In the 1920s and 1930s efforts to promote planned growth in Newark resulted only in a few study groups and abortive, temporary committees. Not until 1943, after almost "300 years of haphazard growth," did the City create a Central Planning Board (CPB) with some permanence, and not until 1955 did Newark hire a professional city planner. Thus, the professional planners and the laymen on CPB arrived late on the urban renewal scene and found a well-established renewal structure. Indeed, they arrived even later and found an even more imposing structure than the civic leaders had found. The planners' choice has been either to come to terms with the system and carve out some niche there for themselves or to denounce the system and seek a restructuring of renewal politics around a central planning office.

THE RISE AND FALL OF CENTRAL PLANNING

In June, 1943, the Board of City Commissioners, acting under the terms of the New Jersey Municipal Planning Act, created the Central Planning Board to prepare a master plan for Newark's future development.[1] Under the terms of the state act any body designated by a local government as its official planning agency was to consist of six lay citizens and three City officials serving ex officio.

After four years of study Harland Bartholomew and Associates submitted a Master Plan urging a twenty-five-year, $300-million capital expenditure program to reverse the pattern of encroaching blight, soaring tax rates, and departing businesses. Bartholomew and Associates warned, however, that the mere spending of public funds would not ensure a coordinated attack on urban decay. The report urged that CPB be empowered to "execute" the Master Plan by reviewing all proposals for public construction and judging whether they were in accordance with the Plan's recommendations. The proposed Master Plan was quickly approved by CPB and the city commissioners in summer, 1947.

This city planning movement, however, was the product of a "reform" alliance between Mayor Vincent Murphy and the civic leaders. When that alliance lost control of City Hall in 1949, the gains of the 1940s were all but canceled. The new Villani-Ellenstein-Moran coalition viewed central planning as one of Murphy's devices for wooing the "good government crowd." CPB was seen as a stronghold of Murphy appointees shielded from removal by the terms of the state Planning Act.

From 1949 to 1953 CPB's request for a professional planning staff to help implement the Master Plan was ignored. In addition, the Board's appropriations were cut to a point where its very survival was in doubt. The civic groups strongly protested this policy, arguing that it would make the Master Plan a mere scrap of paper and the CPB a useless appendix of city government.

NHA AND CPB: THE NORTH WARD

This, roughly, was the depressed status of central planning in fall, 1949, when NHA began its redevelopment program.[2] Despite the Board's lack of funds and its political isolation, CPB members still anticipated a major role in the planning of clearance projects. The fact was that CPB had key political resources which most other local renewal participants lacked. The New Jersey Redevelopment Agencies Act of 1949 gave local planning boards the powers to determine whether blight existed in all proposed redevelopment sites and to see that the urban redevelopment plan for each project was in accord with the local Master Plan. In short, CPB had an institutionalized role in redevelopment policy formation and a veto power over all projects. In addition, New Jersey statutes gave all local planning agencies the authority to approve subdivisions, the closing of streets, public housing sites, and amend-

ments to the zoning ordinance. In view of this institutional leverage, CPB members felt that NHA would have no choice but to
include them in the initial stages of project planning.

Danzig disagreed with CPB on this point and, throughout 1950–
51, clearly spelled out NHA's position. Redevelopment projects
would be submitted to CPB only after the negotiations with URA
had been completed and the formal announcement made. The
Master Plan would be consulted by NHA officials, but the major
decisions on project planning had to be made by those agencies
that had the staff to plan. The six laymen and three politicos on
CPB had no staff and little expertise of their own in urban redevelopment. A member of NHA's staff later said that, in 1949,
it would have made as much sense to abolish the Board and make
NHA the city's official planning agency as it would have to let
CPB help plan redevelopment projects.

NHA's reluctance to let local agencies like CPB interfere in
its internal procedures was reinforced, in this case, by the Authority's view of central planning as an unrealizable, utopian ideal.
Danzig also probably recognized CPB's political vulnerability at
City Hall and realized that central planning was not a popular program among the city commissioners. Another reason that NHA
kept its initial deliberations shielded from CPB was the Board's
ties to one of NHA's leading critics, Commissioner Leo Carlin.
In the reshuffling of agencies after the 1949 election Carlin had
acquired CPB as part of his Department of Public Works and
had named one of his long-time associates, Mariano Rinaldi, as
Executive Secretary. Although NHA officials knew that Carlin
did not control the Board, they were apparently wary of Rinaldi
and uncertain of exactly how far Carlin's influence did go.

NHA's position soon became apparent to most members of the
Board, as repeated attempts by its Executive Secretary to get information on NHA's plans failed. In January, 1952, when NHA
announced the North Ward project and urged an immediate declaration of blight by CPB, the Board criticized NHA's failure to
consult it earlier and implied that it would not give unquestion-
ing approval to the project. For several weeks there seemed to be

a real possibility that CPB would use its power of approval to block the project or to force changes in its substance.

Prior to 1952 CPB had approved all public housing sites without question, but there were no precedents to ensure that blight investigation would be handled in the same manner. State law, moreover, required the local planning agency to conduct a public hearing as part of its blight investigation. The North Ward residents, composed mainly of Italian-Americans, decided to focus their obstructive efforts on this hearing. Since the Chairman of CPB, the Executive Secretary of CPB, and the Mayor were all of Italian extraction, there was good reason to suspect that CPB would prove responsive to site resident demands, particularly at a public hearing.

Sensing the threat involved, NHA officials approached CPB soon after the formal announcement and attempted to impress their own version of a blight hearing on the Board members. Danzig and Nevin argued that CPB was not supposed to undertake an independent investigation of the area or to duplicate the surveying efforts of NHA. Instead, it was to examine the housing data compiled by NHA and to decide whether the existence of blight could be reasonably inferred from this information. It would be presumed that blight existed, since that was the major conclusion of the Authority's painstaking, house-by-house surveys. CPB would have to disprove blight by discovering errors in NHA's data or procedure.

In response to suggestions that CPB might find only part of the North Ward project area blighted, NHA warned that local planning agencies had no authority to change the boundaries of redevelopment projects. They could only grant or withhold approval of the area as defined by the official redevelopment agency. Danzig and Nevin also urged CPB to reach an informal decision on blight before the hearing started. CPB, they added, should make its formal announcement, not at the immediate conclusion of the hearing in the midst of a hostile audience, but at the next meeting of the Board. Nor could NHA's officials find anything in state law to justify the suggestions of some Board members that additional public hearings be held at subsequent stages of the project.

After some vacillation CPB accepted almost all of NHA's views on the blight hearing. The Board defined its role as that of a judicial tribune, which would make no independent investigations of its own. It would hear evidence presented by both NHA and the opposition and then would reach a decision on the existence of blight. This meant that the Housing Authority would have to prove the area to be blighted. There would be no presumption that blight existed simply because NHA had so designated. This also meant, however, that CPB would permit from the opposition only testimony refuting the evidence on blight presented by NHA. No random criticisms of the project, no demands for changes in policy, and no descriptions of personal hardships would be allowed.

Despite this claim of judicial impartiality, it soon became apparent that most Board members were already committed to finding blight in the North Ward. In the weeks immediately preceding the hearing CPB agreed that the blight hearing should be simply an opportunity for the opposition to air its grievances. CPB members discussed with NHA officials how to prevent site residents from disrupting the hearing and discrediting the project.

As it turned out, CPB could not silence the site residents, and the hearing was hastily adjourned in a furor of angry recriminations. Despite this intense opposition, CPB, at its next regular meeting, unanimously declared the project area blighted. The Board, moreover, had created distinct precedents, which would be followed in subsequent investigations of blight and which made it unlikely that either site residents or Board members would ever be able to use the hearings to force changes in NHA's plans. The blight investigation had been reduced to a ritual. It no longer constituted a significant threat to the Housing Authority's progress.

CPB's challenge to NHA's procedures never fully materialized for a number of reasons. Mayor Villani, as the following chapter shows, proved unresponsive to the site-resident opposition, even though this area was one of his electoral strongholds. Carlin and Rinaldi, while prepared to flirt with the neighborhood opposition in order to embarrass Villani, were actually in favor of the project and were careful to limit their attacks on NHA. Rinaldi eventually proved willing to negotiate with NHA on how to deal with the threat posed by a blight hearing.

The quick acquiescence of the planning bloc can also be explained by the structure and personnel of the Board. CPB is a citizen advisory committee and has inherited all the limitations of that form. The six private citizens on CPB generally lack knowledge of, or commitment to, the techniques and goals of professional planners. Many Board members seem interested primarily in the opportunities for "political" favors inherent in subdivisions and zoning variances. With the exception of occasional activists, most members have been indifferent to an expansion of planning in Newark and loath to donate much of their time to Board matters in the intervals between meetings. Thus, one reason that CPB failed to use the blight hearing as a vantage point from which to extract modifications in clearance policy was the over-all inertness of its lay members and the preoccupation of those members with other matters before the Board.

Even if the motive to assert greater control over NHA had been present, CPB still lacked any legitimate basis of opposition to the project. There was no central planning in Newark. CPB did not have any set of long-range planning goals by which to evaluate NHA's proposal. The Master Plan, the only criterion for such an evaluation, was based on 1940 census data and was badly in need of revision. The members of CPB, it is true, could have challenged NHA's finding of blight in the North Ward. But, since they lacked the resources to undertake an independent investigation of the area, they could hardly have backed up such a claim with evidence. The only recent, reliable information on the North Ward was NHA's.

If CPB had participated in the early stages of the North Ward project, it might have influenced NHA's planning decisions. But, after the Housing Authority staff had been working on the plans for two years, and after Danzig had secured federal backing for the project, the pressure on CPB to add its unqualified assent was irresistible. NHA had expertise on its side. CPB members were portrayed by the local press as obstructionists motivated by personal whim or "political" motives.

As the project progressed and the commitments to it multiplied, it became increasingly difficult for CPB to do anything else but approve NHA's actions. Thus, in April, 1953, CPB unanimously passed the North Ward Urban Redevelopment Plan without extended discussion or serious examination. In a similar manner, on three separate occasions the Board subsequently passed NHA's amendments to that Plan.

THE REVIVAL AND REBELLION OF CPB, 1954–56

The revival of a reform coalition between City Hall and the civic leaders during 1953–54 augured well for a revitalization of central planning.[3] Throughout the early days of the Carlin administration there were promises of a professional planning staff, a capital budget, a revision of the Master Plan, and other mechanisms through which CPB could oversee the activities of municipal agencies. The administration's first moves in this area were a reactivation of CPB, whose authority had lapsed with the charter revision, and the appointment of six new lay members to serve on the Board. Several of Carlin's new appointees, like Raymond Stabile, Joseph Zeller, and Joseph Cocuzza, promptly indicated that they were disappointed with CPB's role in the North Ward project. They said that they would press for a more active Board and for "closer cooperation" between CPB and the Housing Authority.

These promises and the expectations of an expanded role for central planning were quickly brought to a test. Just five months after the re-creation of CPB in January, 1955, Danzig unveiled the Central Ward renewal project and a proposal for the immediate construction of a public housing project within the renewal area. Since federal and state law required only that blight be declared sometime before the land acquisition stage, NHA could delay the request for a blight declaration. But federal and state law demanded planning board approval of public housing sites at the outset of such projects.

Danzig submitted his proposed public housing project for consideration at CPB's May 26 meeting. Speaking before the Board, Danzig indicated that the Public Housing Administration (PHA) had already given informal approval to the site. He urged the Board to add its endorsement before expiration of the annual public housing allotment on June 1. Ideally, Danzig argued, it would be better if CPB could consider NHA proposals leisurely, but this plan had been approved by PHA officials just a few days earlier. Now the only alternative for both NHA and CPB was to rush it through without prolonged discussion.

Most of Carlin's new appointees, however, felt that they were being stampeded into approving a site they knew nothing about. They denounced Danzig for not having discussed the site with CPB before formal announcement and accused him of deliberately delaying this announcement until the last possible moment. Danzig heatedly denied this and traced the delay to PHA's vacillations. CPB finally voted to examine the site further, to consult with City officials, and to dispose of the question at a special meeting on May 31—the eve of the federal deadline.

There was more to this rebellion, however, than pique at NHA's allegedly high-handed behavior. The Spruce Street merchants who would be displaced by the project had organized to block NHA's plan for the area. The lay members of CPB, a number of whom were themselves small, neighborhood businessmen, proved highly responsive to site-resident opposition. Most of the Board members favored a plan devised by the merchants' attorney, Sol Herships, whereby the proposed construction would be moved back from both sides of Spruce Street and the present commercial structures on Spruce Street left running through the center of the public housing project. The lay members of CPB felt encouraged in their rebellion by Mayor Carlin's apparent responsiveness to the merchants' proposal.

If CPB expected City officials to join their revolt against NHA at the May 31 meeting, those hopes proved groundless. Nevin had been in constant consultation with the Board of Education, the Department of Sewers, and several other relevant agencies since early in 1954. Before publicly announcing the project, NHA had secured from these agencies agreements to cooperate. At the May 31 meeting the heads of these and other agencies rose to endorse the project and to urge immediate approval.

At this same meeting Danzig countered with a compromise proposal. If CPB would give tentative approval to the site in order to secure PHA approval before the deadline, NHA would agree to restudy the site and to come up with something "better." But Danzig warned that CPB's letter to PHA, indicating approval of the site, would have to be "absolute and unequivocal," or PHA would not accept it as genuine approval. The agreement between NHA and CPB to negotiate further on the site would have to remain informal and unwritten. In order to maintain the flow of federal funds into Newark, CPB agreed.

In June PHA officials wrote CPB's Chairman to determine whether the Board's action on May 31 had been "final and conclusive as approval of site without qualifications." The PHA officials said that they would go ahead with the processing of NHA's application unless they heard otherwise from CPB. PHA was encouraged to take this position by NHA and by Mayor Carlin, who had told federal officials that this would be the final site.

Confused by the wording of PHA's question and reluctant to sabotage the project, CPB urged NHA to call an immediate meeting of federal and local officials. But Danzig thought that matters would become even more confused if he permitted other local agencies to deal directly with PHA. Fearful of jeopardizing the project, CPB decided to take no action. On June 27, 1955, the Housing Authority announced that PHA had approved the Spruce Street public housing application and that acquisition of properties soon would begin. It was not until October 27 that Danzig again appeared before CPB. He told the Board that PHA had informally rejected Herships's plan and had already earmarked funds for the project on its present site. Attempts by CPB or NHA to alter the boundaries of the site at this point would only mean a withdrawal of federal approval. Stabile, Cocuzza, and a new member of the Board, Samuel Kaphan, were incensed. They argued that CPB's tentative approval of the site on May 31 did not give NHA the authority to seek a final earmarking of federal funds and to freeze the site at its present boundaries. But there was little the Board could do, other than ratify NHA's action.

CPB, despite its more belligerent tactics, proved no more successful in the Central Ward public housing controversy than in the earlier North Ward incident. It failed in both cases to alter one word of NHA's proposal. The lack of expertise, funds, and legitimate or dramatic goals continued to hamper CPB's effectiveness. The activists never succeeded in stimulating the interest of other Board members in this issue. The activists also discovered that NHA had built good working relations with the important administrative agencies at City Hall and that CPB could expect little sympathy from that direction. More important was the fact that Mayor Carlin, while continuing to support the over-all goals of central planning, was not prepared to back CPB in a dispute with the Authority. Though he initially encouraged CPB to oppose the Spruce Street site, he subsequently undercut the Board's position by urging PHA officials to approve that site.

Throughout 1956 NHA officials continued to withhold their request for a determination of blight in the Central Ward renewal area. In June, however, CPB's activists seized upon NHA's controversy with NCNCR over state enabling legislation on neighborhood rehabilitation. Zeller, Stabile, and Cocuzza issued a condemnation of the Housing Authority's disregard for other municipal agencies. If NHA was to be given powers in the rehabilitation field, they warned, NCNCR, the Mayor, and the Council would have the same choice that faced CPB: to approve all NHA proposals or to be cast in the role of obstructionists. Whatever effectiveness this attack might have had was destroyed by their further proposal that neither NHA nor NCNCR but CPB be named the official rehabilitation agency, a proposal that no one took seriously and that seemed to discredit the entire line of argument.

THE PROFESSIONAL PLANNERS AND NHA, 1956–58

The creation of a professional planning staff had long been a major objective of the civic groups in Newark.[4] CPB's experiences with NHA on the Spruce Street site only accelerated demands for the appointment of professional planners to help bring the Housing Authority "in closer coordination" with the planning office.

Mayor Carlin agreed to create only one new position, a City Planning Officer. He delayed the introduction of an ordinance to this effect for several months and, after its passage, waited a full year before filling the newly created position. By summer, 1956, when Carlin named Robert Hoover as Newark's first City Planning Officer, the conservative groups that had long supported such an office were in the process of reaching a settlement with Danzig. They were, by this time, much less enthusiastic about the coordination of renewal functions. Thus, CPB acquired a professional staff only after the peak of enthusiasm for central planning had been passed.

The new City Planning Officer soon learned that central planning could not be achieved without prior disruption of established relations. Hoover's initial response was to play the "Young Turk," to ally with the activists on CPB, and to strengthen their rebellion against NHA. He attacked the Authority for failing to consult CPB at the initial phases of clearance projects, for adding to the high-density problem in Newark, and for ignoring the need for a greater number of open areas. In September, 1956, Hoover urged CPB to endorse an amendment to the New Jersey Municipal Planning Act which would authorize local planning agencies to approve all aspects of public housing proposals. The Board, long dissatisfied with its power to approve just the sites of such projects, quickly endorsed Hoover's proposed amendment. This proposal, however, never came to the floor of the Legislature.

In September, 1957, NHA sought to add five hundred units, specially designed for elderly persons, to five existing public housing projects. Before NHA could proceed, CPB would have to approve the sites and approve amendments to the zoning ordinance. Hoover and CPB's activists seized upon this opportunity to attack the high density in NHA's public housing projects and to insist that any such further increase in their density would be unwise. In this incident, as in earlier ones, the Board found little support for its self-assertion either with the Mayor or among the con-

servative groups. While Danzig was forced by CPB's intransigence
to make some minor changes in his "housing for the elderly" proposal, CPB's impact on NHA's final plans was small.

This clash convinced Hoover that urban redevelopment could
not be drawn within the ambit of central planning through CPB's
power of review and veto. CPB's ability to force minor changes
in NHA's finished products under threat of withholding Board
approval yielded little actual influence over clearance policy. Only
if the City Planning Officer helped prepare, as well as review,
NHA proposals, and only if NHA needed his approval at every
stage of a redevelopment project, could slum clearance be coordinated with other programs affecting the city's development.
Hoover's goal became an institutionalized role for the City Planning Officer in the initial stages of NHA's planning procedures.
Hoover believed that Danzig might be persuaded to make this concession. In 1957 he unveiled a new approach toward NHA and
convinced CPB's activists to quiet their attacks on Danzig. Hoover
also began de-emphasizing the role of the Board and relying more
heavily on his small staff of professional planners. Initiative within
the planning office shifted to the professional staff, as it had in
NEDC, NCNCR, and NHA.

Hoover also attempted to secure good working relations with
NCNCR and NEDC by lending them some of his expertise and
staff. In return he hoped to utilize their established access to NHA
officials, that is, to bargain with Danzig through Coleman, Conner,
and Busse.

Hoover's first move in this new direction was a suggestion that
NHA hire the City Planning Officer as a consultant in the formulation of the renewal plan for the Central Ward. At first Danzig
simply ignored the proposal. In October, 1957, when NCNCR
and NHA were discussing the terms of an ordinance on rehabilitation powers, Hoover saw an opportunity to press his claim. He
urged NCNCR to broaden its demands on NHA and to avoid
giving its endorsement lightly. He asked the Committee to demand
a consultative status for the City Planning Officer in Central Ward
planning as well as a foothold for itself in Central Ward rehabilitation. While advising NHA on Central Ward renewal, Hoover

said, he could also be looking out for the Committee's interests. It was Hoover, moreover, who convinced NCNCR that NHA's Executive Director had his back to the wall. If Danzig did not concede all of NCNCR's demands, Hoover said, URA would cut off funds for the Central Ward.

When Danzig presented the case for his ordinance at an NCNCR meeting on October 14, the Committee plied him with questions about Hoover's future role in the Central Ward project. Many on NCNCR seemed to view the City Planning Officer as their "executive director," more willing and better able to survey NHA's activities than they could themselves. To NCNCR's surprise Danzig quickly agreed to consultative status for Hoover. Danzig seemed anxious to eliminate this "extraneous issue" and to refocus attention on NHA's ordinance.

Hoover considered this his first major achievement as City Planning Officer and immediately pressed Danzig on the details of their arrangement. Their negotiations were abruptly terminated, however, when Hoover resigned to accept another position. Danzig let the matter drop, hoping, perhaps, that it would die with Hoover's resignation. But the new City Planning Officer, George Oberlander, had been Hoover's assistant during the battle for consultative status. He considered it just as important an achievement as Hoover had.

In resuming negotiations with the City Planning Officer, Danzig managed to whittle down the extent of his previous concession. He made it clear that the City Planning Officer would be consulted on specific planning questions but would not have the opportunity to help set over-all renewal policies. Oberlander seemed willing, at this point, to settle for marginal gains. In urging CPB to ratify this arrangement in March, 1958, he argued that it was at least a "foot in the door" and a great improvement over the dismal status of planning seven or eight years earlier.

This agreement on a consultative status for the City Planning Officer in the Central Ward seemed to create expectations of mutual support and to commit the parties to a nonpublic negotiation of their differences. NHA understandably assumed that, if Oberlander were consulted in the planning of a project, he would support the plan once it were announced. Battles lost at this initial planning stage would not be appealed to the press or to the public. As evidence of this new relationship the professional planners halted CPB's rebellion against NHA's proposals. Oberlander frequently warned CPB that consultative status was a major achievement, not to be jeopardized by "irresponsible attacks" on the Housing Authority. During 1958 CPB, with little debate or dissension, quickly approved a second public housing site and a school construction site within the Central Ward renewal area. After a perfunctory public hearing in July they also declared the entire sixty-block area blighted.

Oberlander hoped eventually to extend his consultative status from Central Ward renewal to all of NHA's projects. Meanwhile, he sought a voice in NHA's other projects by working through Busse, Conner, and NEDC. "When we have a meeting arranged with Lou Danzig," a member of the business bloc said, "we'll insist that George Oberlander be present. Danzig will gripe a little, but if we stick to our position George will be invited. . . . Sometimes we'll advise George that now is a good opportunity to press Lou on a particular point. At other times we'll tell George to stay away for awhile. . . . George is a junior partner in this arrangement, and he knows it. But he's a young fellow and has time." For reasons indicated earlier, Danzig has been willing in certain instances to share project decisions with the business bloc. But this concession to NEDC, as on the college expansion project, also proved to be an indirect concession to George Oberlander. If he failed to acquire consultative status in these projects, at least he had more contact with NHA officials and more information on their plans than ever before.

COORDINATION THROUGH BARGAINING

Consultative status and all it involved may be seen as a political settlement between the planners and NHA, similar to the arrangements Danzig had reached with other groups in the city.[5] The planners apparently decided to join the network of negotiations and settle for marginal gains. They decided to participate rather than to criticize, to seek influence rather than control. Rather than try to coordinate other renewal agencies, they settled for an attempt to keep central planning considerations before these bodies.

If Oberlander had been fully committed to this settlement and his position free of ambiguity, there would be little to add concerning the planners beyond this point. Yet, the planners still retained hopes of becoming the central renewal coordinators, of standing above the system rather than accommodating themselves to it, of overseeing other renewal agencies rather than negotiating with them.

Oberlander's attempt to expand his role in clearance projects by bargaining with NHA did not prevent him from also seeking further institutional controls over the Authority's activities. He continually sought to obtain information on NHA's plans through informal conversations with Nevin or Danzig. At the same time, Oberlander continued to press for ordinances or administrative rules that would compel NHA officials to confer with his office at various stages of their projects.

Throughout 1958 and 1959 the planners sifted a number of such rules and ordinances. Some privately urged an ordinance enabling CPB to review and pass all applications for survey and planning funds before their submission to URA. The planners eventually decided to press for a two-part program, placing their hopes for greater central planning in the institution of a five-year capital expenditure budget and in an updating of the Master Plan.

This retreat from their agreement with NHA can be explained by a growing disillusionment among the planners with their attempt to achieve central planning through persuasion and bargaining. Having secured consultative status in the Central Ward, Oberlander seemed incapable of cashing in on his settlement with NHA. The Authority's agreement with the planners did not include a role for Oberlander in setting general policy. At best, this settlement permitted the City Planning Officer to secure some information on NHA's Central Ward plans. Yet, even this information was forthcoming only in cases where the planners were prepared to seize the initiative and press their claims on NHA officials. In most cases, however, the understaffed planning office was harried by other matters and unable to keep after Danzig and

Nevin. NHA officials planned the Central Ward without them, consulting them only on specific planning problems. "They [NHA] call us up when they're in trouble," one planner noted. "They run into some snag and want us to straighten it out for them." But this type of coordination tended to diffuse the authority of the City Planning Officer in a maze of committee meetings, to tax his physical capacities, and to keep the initiative with the executing administrative agencies, while the planning office struggled frantically to keep abreast of these agencies' activities. After two years' experience with this exhaustive effort many planners were convinced of the need for a further institutionalization of the City Planning Officer's authority. New rules were needed, the planners privately concluded, which would require all renewal agencies to secure the Planning Officer's approval at the initial stages of their projects.

Dissatisfaction among the planners with the results of coordination through bargaining reached its peak in 1959, when NHA moved ahead with several ambitious proposals in the downtown area. As NHA launched its new program in the summer of that year, the planners were disheartened to learn that whatever concessions the Authority's staff may have made on Central Ward renewal would not be carried over into subsequent projects. Nevin may have discussed Central Ward renewal with Oberlander in the early part of 1959, but Oberlander received no inkling of the impending new program. "Every few weeks," one planner said in summer, 1959, "we open the newspaper and get hit with another clearance proposal for ten, twenty, or thirty blocks."

The professional planners, of whom there were now ten, began to criticize some substantive aspects of the downtown program, as well as their own exclusion from its initiation. They privately and informally accused NHA of ignoring the hard-core slum areas, of overemphasizing luxury apartments, and of surrendering many planning decisions to the private redevelopers. They also claimed that NHA was accumulating projects rather than planning the optimum, long-range development of the downtown area.

The planners failed to muster any significant support in 1958 or 1959 for their attempt to expand institutional controls over renewal agencies. NCNCR viewed Oberlander as a friend and backed him consistently in his dealings with Danzig, but it never approved making the City Planning Officer the central renewal co-ordinator. NEDC has been even more content to see Oberlander continue in the role of negotiant and junior partner. More important were the indications that neither the Mayor nor the Business Administrator would support Oberlander's claim, reorganize renewal functions, or intervene in renewal politics on a persistent basis. To Carlin and Rinaldi, the planning office was simply another renewal agency, with its own perspectives, programs, and ambitions.

In 1959, however, the planners did attain both of their major goals: the institution of a five-year capital budget and the formulation of a new ten-year urban renewal plan. Far from expanding the role of the City Planning Officer in urban renewal, these two devices again demonstrated the unwillingness of Carlin and Rinaldi to see the renewal system altered.

For several years the planners had encouraged City Hall to use its one-third contribution to the net costs of urban renewal projects as a means of exerting greater control over the Housing Authority. The capital budget, they argued, would now give City Hall the leverage to use that one-third contribution as a control mechanism. Under these initial capital budgeting procedures the Business Administrator and City Planning Officer would require all municipal agencies to estimate their capital needs for the next five years. After private budget hearings Rinaldi and Oberlander would relate over-all capital needs to estimates of the municipal government's future fiscal resources and then set priorities among the proposed projects. NHA would be expected to submit an estimate and itemization of the City's one-third contribution to redevelopment projects for the following five years. The planners hoped that Rinaldi would use the budget hearing to require explanations from NHA of its five-year estimates and to cross-examine Danzig on all aspects of clearance policy. City Hall thus would be able to secure information on NHA's future plans and to review redevelopment proposals which were still in their formative stages. The capital budget also would give City Hall a common frame of reference by which to judge NHA's claims on City funds in relation to the needs of other municipal agencies.

When closed hearings on the first capital budget were held, however, the Business Administrator showed little interest in extending City Hall control of NHA. Lacking the information or expertise to criticize NHA's estimates and anxious to avoid any action which might impede the flow of federal funds to Newark, Rinaldi accepted Danzig's statement without objection or cross-examination. The Business Administrator permitted the Authority a continued free hand in setting its own pace. He used the budget hearing largely to get some general idea of NHA's future plans.

Not only did the Business Administrator fail to bring NHA policies within the framework of more general priorities, he even instructed all other municipal agencies to adjust their own capital construction programs to that of NHA. To ensure that a maximum amount of local capital expenditure would be credited by URA as part of the City's one-third contribution, municipal agencies were told to place priority on public works directly related to NHA's clearance projects. A draft version of the first capital budget, prepared in January, 1960, revealed that NHA's pacing would be unaffected and that priority would be given to twenty-one local public works projects in or near the urban renewal areas. Said one planner: "Everything has turned out upside down; the tail is wagging the dog."

THE PLANNERS AND "THE SYSTEM"

The planners, then, were not on the verge of cashing in on their claim to be central renewal coordinators.[6] In the absence of any support for their claims, they were not yet prepared to precipitate an open break with NHA. While Carlin and Rinaldi remained indifferent to his demands, Oberlander was loath to rupture his bargaining relationship with Danzig. The reluctance of the planners to bring their claims for institutional control to the surface was demonstrated clearly in their drafting of a ten-year urban renewal plan in 1959.

The planners knew that an extension of control mechanisms like the capital budget would be pointless unless substantive, long-range goals by which to evaluate the activities of renewal agencies also were developed. For this reason they had urged an updating of the Master Plan or the drafting of a new plan. But Carlin and Rinaldi had set a ceiling on the size of the professional planning staff and consistently refused to raise it. In December, 1957, a member of NCNCR suggested that Oberlander take advantage of a recent amendment to federal housing legislation, which provided aid for local planning studies in urban renewal. The Mayor and Council agreed to contribute the necessary one-third, and URA soon added its approval. In May, 1958, the planning office began its Demonstration Grant Project to develop generally applicable criteria for delineating clearance, rehabilitation, and conservation areas and to apply these criteria by demarcating such areas in Newark. The survey would also try to ascertain the city's major renewal needs and set priorities for the next ten years.

While several members of NCNCR and some of the local press assumed that this project would yield a detailed ten-year renewal plan and would help bring NHA under greater central control, the planners took a more ambiguous position. At times the planning office referred to the project as a new master plan; at other times they seemed to view it as a good device for expanding their staff at federal expense.

The first and second interim reports issued in the summer and fall of 1959 were more significant for what they avoided saying than for what they did say. Outside of those parts dealing with the development of technical criteria for identifying various renewal areas, the two reports focused on methods of upgrading rehabilitation areas. Far from attempting to set out the guidelines for Newark's next decade in urban renewal, the reports carefully avoided any excursion into the domain of the Housing Authority. In drafting conclusions and recommendations the planners muted all the criticisms they had been leveling privately at NHA's downtown program. In its discussion of administrative organization, moreover, the report completely sidestepped the controversial question of reorganizing renewal functions. Instead, it merely catalogued the activities of the various renewal agencies and implied the existence of central coordination and direction.

In addition, the City Planning Officer set out to silence any criticisms of NHA's downtown program that might be inferred from his delineation of clearance and rehabilitation areas. In response to questions by newspapermen, Oberlander conceded that several of NHA's recent development proposals involved what the second interim report described as rehabilitation areas. But the planning office, Oberlander added, would approve a clearance project that encroached on rehabilitation areas, "as long as the project would benefit the city on an over-all basis. . . . The fact that any given area is marked [by the second interim report] for rehabilitation does not mean that we are trying to rule out slum clearance there."

The weaknesses of the planning bloc were much the same as those of the civic leaders. As latecomers, the members of CPB had to adjust to an existing system. The bloc was built around a semi-inert citizen committee and was slow to acquire a professional staff. A lack of experience in politics and an aversion toward conflict of any sort often made it possible for CPB to be outmaneuvered. The same lack of experience and the pressure of other business made it difficult for the professional planners to enforce their demands upon NHA.

To the extent that the planners are interested in restructuring the renewal system in order to attain an institutionalized coordinating role for themselves, their record of isolation and impotence will probably continue. While most local participants pay verbal homage to central planning, they are prepared to resist any attempts at disrupting their established relations with NHA. It cannot be said, however, that "coordination through bargaining" and "the strategy of marginal gains" have yielded any more impressive results. In this frustrating position, where the planners receive no support for their claim to a coordinating role and can participate in the network of informal negotiations only as junior partners, perhaps there is no alternative for the planners but to retain the ambiguities in their renewal goals. Perhaps there is no alternative but to vacillate between the roles of coordinator and negotiator, to continue the strategy of small gains while watching for some significant shift in the renewal structure.

In 1960 the planners were the most volatile of the renewal participants and the least committed to the present structure. They were the most receptive to proposals for change, and, at the same time, the least capable of effecting that change.

CHAPTER VII

The Grass Roots

Slum clearance projects directly touch the lives of many individuals and often provoke organized political action among those affected.[1] Those initially and most immediately affected are the site residents and businessmen who will be displaced and relocated. Perhaps the most common form of grass roots action in urban renewal is the ad hoc committee of residents and businessmen bent on blocking clearance in their neighborhood. The neighborhoods that surround a project and the neighborhoods that absorb displaced persons are also prone to organize, usually in opposition to the redevelopment agency's policies. Thus, the immediate popular responses that most clearance projects seem to engender are hostile. Most housing officials view grass roots movements with some trepidation.

The role of grass roots opposition in Newark's redevelopment program has been insignificant. Not once between 1949 and 1960 did a neighborhood committee succeed in altering or delaying NHA's plans for an area. The opposition of site residents, small businesses, and neighborhood associations may present a serious threat to some redevelopment agencies; to NHA such opposition is a minor irritant.

There are two aspects to the insignificance of grass roots opposition in Newark. Organized and sustained opposition at the grass roots level has seldom appeared. When it has appeared, moreover, it has lacked access to the key public officials and has been unable to penetrate the network of regular renewal participants. The following pages examine both of these aspects: the conditions under which organized opposition to a project does or does not appear, and the reasons that this opposition, even when present and well organized, has proved notably unsuccessful. This, then, is an account of the groups that are peripheral to the renewal system and a further description of how the system repels threats to its continuance.

NHA's decision to clear fifteen blocks in the North Ward provoked a classic case of site-resident opposition.[2] Ad hoc committees were formed to block NHA's plans; petitions, mass rallies, and marches on City Hall soon followed. The public hearing on a declaration of blight was attended by several thousand angry home owners and was adjourned amidst a furor of shouting and confusion. NHA's decision to renew sixty blocks in the Central Ward, on the other hand, failed to spur any organized neighborhood resistance. The political machine of Councilman Irvine Turner quickly endorsed the project, and various Negro civic associations followed suit. Only a handful of isolated individuals appeared at the blight hearing to criticize the project. The opposite responses of North Ward and Central Ward residents clearly imply that the emergence of neighborhood opposition must be explained, not presumed. A closer look at these two projects and the areas to be cleared may suggest some of the variables that determine whether or not organized opposition will appear.

The evidence concerning these projects suggests that intense opposition by site residents is a feature not of the hard-core slums but of areas peripheral to the slums. Organized opposition is more likely to appear in areas with a high percentage of home ownership, a predominance of one- or two-family houses, and a relatively stable population. It is less likely to appear in areas with a high degree of transiency and absentee ownership and a large number of tenements and rooming houses. While the former type of area tends to be a relatively integrated subcommunity with traditions of its own, the slums tend to be incapable of organized neighborhood action. The absentee landlords in such slum areas, moreover, are too politically vulnerable to press their opposition to clearance. Thus, NHA officials would probably meet little neighborhood opposition if they could restrict themselves to clearance in the hardcore slums and if concern over project feasibility did not force them into fringe areas like the North Ward.

Both the Central Ward and the North Ward projects involved the clearance of ethnically homogeneous areas, yet the response of the Italian groups in the North Ward was quite different from that of the Negro groups in the Central Ward. One was a status-preserving group, the other a status-seeking group. The Italians, standing high on the socio-economic ladder, were concerned with the threats to their property, status, and neighborhood posed by groups lower down on the ladder. On the other hand, several Central Ward leaders noted that the Negroes had no place to go but up and that any change had to be for the better. One other important factor was relevant: the Central Ward project would not change the ethnic characteristics of the project area, while the North Ward project would. Negroes might move into North Ward public housing, but whites probably would not move into housing in the Central Ward.

The ethnic leaders' perception of their groups' strength at City Hall also influenced the response to clearance. In personal interviews several Negro leaders emphasized how pointless any opposition would have been. On the other hand, at the time of the North Ward project the Mayor, the Chairman and the Executive Secretary of CPB, and the Chairman of the Housing Authority all were Italian-Americans from the North Ward.

The extent of neighborhood opposition to clearance also depends on the structure of ward politics. In the Central Ward, where Councilman Turner's machine was the dominant force since 1954, Turner endorsed the project, and that settled the matter. Provoking grass roots opposition beyond that point would have placed any political aspirant outside the Turner organization, and there is no future for insurgents in the Central Ward. In the factional politics of the North Ward, it is prudent strategy for some unknown to make a name for himself by stimulating opposition to clearance. Where the incumbents are insecure, newcomers are encouraged to try unseating them. Where the pretenders are numerous and all of the same ethnic group, an issue like opposition to clearance is necessary to distinguish an aspirant from the rest of the pack.

A closer look at the North Ward project reveals that Newark's lone case of overt rebellion by the site residents was far from spontaneous. It was stimulated and organized by those who hoped to make use of the issue.

The announcement of the project in banner headlines on January 20, 1952, did not provoke an immediate outcry from the clearance area. A few days later the *Italian Tribune* devoted most of its issue to the project but failed to make any editorial comment. For nearly two weeks there was no sign of neighborhood resistance. The North Ward announcement, however, was made eight months before a congressional election and fourteen months before a local election. Within a few weeks of the announcement a few political aspirants in the North Ward began their attempts to fan the embers of neighborhood discontent. Salvatore Bontempo, who had narrowly lost his 1949 bid for city commissioner, was reported to be highly critical of the project, although he made no formal statement to that effect. In addition, members of Alexander Matturi's electoral organization informally criticized the project. They placed the blame on Congressman Peter Rodino, Jr., since he had supported Title I legislation in Congress. Matturi was a Republican district leader in the North Ward, the Chairman of the Housing Authority, and the likely Republican choice to challenge Rodino in November. When the press publicized the activities of Matturi's organization, Rodino publicly pointed out that Matturi, as Chairman of NHA, was in no position to make accusations or to blame others for North Ward clearance. Matturi eventually repudiated his political lieutenants. Both he and Rodino restated their support for the project and agreed to keep it out of the congressional election.

The most active role in organizing the opposition was assumed by Joseph Melillo, a young attorney who had run for city commissioner in 1949 and lost. Aided by major property owners in the area, Melillo organized the Save Our Homes Council (SOHC). He eventually decided on a two-fold strategy: to join SOHC's cause with REBON's efforts to kill public housing in Newark, and to focus SOHC's pressure on Mayor Villani in the hope of weakening his ties to NHA. For several months SOHC maintained its pressure on City Hall through mass rallies, petitions, protest marches, and requests for audiences with the Mayor. These activities represented the first overt opposition to slum clearance and the first open attack on NHA that had appeared in Newark since the launching of redevelopment.

The North Ward case suggests that opposition to clearance tends to be greater in an area that has factional or fluid electoral politics. Almost every North Ward leader who held public office supported the clearance project. Grass roots opposition was organized largely by "outsiders" or aspirants who sought to up-end incumbents from that neighborhood.

THE FAILURE OF GRASS ROOTS OPPOSITION

Articulate site-resident opposition occurs only in a certain political and socio-economic environment. No other NHA project provoked the opposition that North Ward clearance did. Yet, even in this one case of well-organized neighborhood resistance, NHA's plans went off exactly according to schedule. Outwardly, the situation at City Hall in 1952 seemed highly receptive to the North Ward residents. As noted earlier, a number of leading City officials were Italian-Americans and drew strong electoral support from the area slated for clearance. Why, then, did the North Ward opposition prove so ineffective?

The weaknesses of the North Ward opposition are those of a sporadic political participant, one which intervenes only in response to a specific, adverse public decision and then only to delay, block, or divert the impact of that action. Crisis groups like SOHC are easy to form when the decision is announced, but they are difficult to sustain at high levels of interest or activity. Throughout its brief life, SOHC was starved for funds, information, and competence. Such groups tend to lose their vitality after a first setback. Because these groups do not participate regularly in renewal politics, moreover, they do not have an opportunity to build stable relations with NHA or with the other regular participants. Intervening in response to a public announcement means that the group acts only after the major commitments to support the project have been made. The group's strategy must be to press for a canceling of these commitments. The group must try to snap the network of stable relations by pressuring its more vulnerable points.

Here NHA's practice of securing the necessary commitments for a project before making it public seems to have yielded large dividends. Mayor Villani had been asked to give his backing for North Ward clearance at a time when the project had not yet been announced and when the degree of opposition to it was only a matter for speculation. In agreeing to support the project, Villani apparently underestimated the opposition that the venture would provoke. He may have noted that from 1938 to 1952 not one of NHA's public housing projects had met with significant neighborhood resistance. There was no precedent for a site-resident rebellion.

NHA did not have to sell the North Ward project to Villani; he received the news enthusiastically. The Mayor assumed that this area would be "for the Italians," a throwback from the 1940s, when public housing projects were parceled out among the city's major ethnic groups. This supposition probably stemmed more from Villani's unfamiliarity with Title I than from any explicit promise on Danzig's part. Whatever the origins of the assumption, it helped swing a number of North Ward leaders over to the project.

The North Ward opposition failed to find allies, either in the Italian community or in the city at large. Accepting Villani's notion that this would be an "Italian project," the Federation of Italian-American Societies, the *Italian Tribune,* and most City officials of Italian extraction supported clearance in the North Ward. Most civic leaders had little sympathy for neighborhood resistance movements. REBON supported SOHC, but that did not greatly improve SOHC's bargaining position at City Hall. Some Republican and Democratic district leaders opposed the project, but Newark's brand of nonpartisan politics made them strangers at City Hall. The Mayor's major loyalty was to that loosely integrated congeries of personal supporters from both parties known as the Villani organization. He apparently had few dealings with the North Ward district leaders and had little reason to save district leaders in the project area from extinction or embarrassment.

Of course, the Mayor was not oblivious to the feelings of North Ward residents or immune to their pressure. As opposition pressure began to mount, Villani found himself in the uncomfortable position of bearing political responsibility for decisions he had not made. Unwilling to renege his support for the project, Villani tried to alter some other elements in the equation. He urged NHA to amend its plans for the North Ward by raising income limits in the proposed public housing project, by guaranteeing to displaced businessmen a commercial site in the redevelopment area, and by reducing the number of stories planned for the public housing project from sixteen to twelve. The first two amendments were designed to ensure that the Italian community would be rebuilt on the cleared site; the third to lessen the resistance of residents of the surrounding area.

In response, Danzig pointed out that he lacked the legal authority to manipulate the income limits for public housing projects. Since NHA's staff had not yet begun planning land uses for the redevelopment area, moreover, Danzig could not make any rigid commitments on relocating displaced businessmen. NHA later reduced the number of stories planned for the public housing project, but it is not clear whether this was in response to Villani's request or to a demand by PHA.

If the site residents were responsible for the reduction in the number of stories, this was their only achievement. After CPB found the area blighted in July, 1952, and the Board of City Commissioners quickly confirmed the finding, SOHC dissolved, and the local opposition collapsed.

The most interesting aspect of this incident was the inability of site-resident opposition, emanating from the Mayor's own neighborhood and electoral stronghold, to shake either Villani's commitment to the project or his ties with NHA. None of the succeeding opposition groups ever had as good an opportunity to break through the renewal system as the North Ward residents had on that occasion. The North Ward clearance illustrates the failure of site-resident opposition acting even under optimal conditions.

THE FUTURE OF GRASS ROOTS OPPOSITION

The attempt by SOHC to stop North Ward clearance represents the high point of local opposition to, or mass interest of any kind in, NHA's renewal program.[3] At no time in the subsequent history of NHA's efforts did neighborhood opposition pose so substantial a threat. At no other point during the ensuing eight years did the Authority stir up such opposition, receive such front page press treatment, and operate in such an exposed fashion.

NHA's later projects tended to displace groups like the Negroes and Puerto Ricans, who are underorganized and lack influence at City Hall. These projects focused on abandoned, semi-commercial areas with small, ethnically heterogeneous, and highly transient populations. No significant opposition has emerged from these areas, and none seems likely to.

It is true that NHA is still in the early stages of most of its projects. If grass roots opposition has been either nonexistent or ineffectual at the initial stages, there is nothing to prevent its emergence at later stages in the projects. Perhaps low-income, low-education groups do not respond until concrete attempts at displacement are made. In attempting to gauge the future of site-resident opposition, therefore, it is necessary to know whether such opposition is more likely to occur at the execution stage of a project than at the announcement stage.

In answer to this, it should be noted that no new opposition emerged at the execution stage of either the North Ward or Central Ward projects. If anything, the site residents in these two areas became more reconciled to clearance as the projects progressed. Assuming, however, that local opposition might still emerge at the execution stages of NHA's downtown proposals, what would be its chances of breaking through the renewal system?

The story of neighborhood opposition to the North Ward project after 1952 suggests that grass roots opposition has its maximum chances of effectiveness at the outset of a project. As a project progresses and the commitments of various participants multiply, the opportunities for successful opposition diminish. If the site-resident opposition in Newark is to be effective, it must occur during a project's earliest stages, if possible even before the project is formally announced.

In 1954 a group of small businessmen from the area adjacent to North Ward clearance denounced NHA for trying to bring a suburban-type shopping center into the project. The Bloomfield Avenue merchants urged NHA to sell cleared land to them for a neighborhood parking lot. They also urged NHA to eliminate all commercial usages planned for the Broad Street boundary. At the same time, they asked the Mayor and Council to withdraw their approval of the project if NHA refused.

No one at City Hall or in NHA seriously considered altering the project at this point. To incorporate the merchants' objections in the project plans would have meant disrupting the finely balanced set of negotiations, jeopardizing federal support, and scaring away redevelopers. In addition, NHA officials felt that such a concession would have destroyed the rationale of the "no deal, project package" argument and would have exposed the project to intervention from other local sources.

If the cumulation of commitments precludes effective local opposition at all but the earliest stages of a project, any break in the project's momentum affords the opposition a new lease on life. When the first redeveloper in the North Ward withdrew and the site lay vacant for almost a year, the Bloomfield Avenue merchants revived their demands for amendments to the redevelopment plan. The longer the North Ward site lay empty, the stronger became the pressures to divert parts of the site away from its planned uses. A rash of proposals for the use of the vacant site were sent to the Authority in 1957. As soon as NHA re-established the project's momentum by coming to terms with a second redeveloper, all debate on the question was closed.

Future neighborhood oppositions may prove more formidable than the Bloomfield Avenue merchants. But the later in a project such oppositions appear, the less chance of success they will have.

THE ELECTORAL POLITICS OF SITE-RESIDENT OPPOSITION

Before closing the door on site-resident opposition and perhaps underestimating its effectiveness, one other aspect of this problem should be considered.[4] Is local opposition, though incapable of stopping a proposed clearance project, eventually expressed through the electoral process? Do redevelopment projects create strong, lasting sentiments among the residents of a neighborhood, and are these sentiments subsequently translated into electoral responses? Have NHA's clearance proposals altered the voting behavior of districts and affected the careers of elected officials involved in the project?

Some tentative answers may be suggested by looking at voting patterns in the North Ward, the scene of the most intense local opposition. It might prove particularly useful to trace the subsequent electoral fortunes of two persons who were intimately involved in this controversy—Ralph Villani and Joseph Melillo.

The data strongly suggest that Villani's support for the project did not diminish his electoral strength in the project area or in the surrounding neighborhood. Table 2 charts Villani's vote in 1949 and 1953 in the First Ward, an area that included the proposed clearance site. Although Villani lost his 1953 bid for re-election as city commissioner, his vote in this area remained constant. The First Ward, one of the largest Italian neighborhoods in the city, had traditionally given Villani his largest pluralities. In April,

TABLE 2

RALPH VILLANI'S VOTE IN THE FIRST WARD AS A
CANDIDATE FOR CITY COMMISSIONER, 1949 AND 1953

	Percentage of Vote		
Election Districts	1949	1953 [a]	Net Change in Percentage
1 [b]	72.0	76.4	+ 4.4
2 [b]	78.0	74.2	− 3.8
3 [b]	75.4	85.5	+10.1
4	80.0	71.2	− 8.8
5	80.3	76.1	− 4.2
6	72.7	66.9	− 5.8
7 [b]	78.5	82.4	+ 3.9
8 [b]	78.3	78.1	− .2
9	36.3	25.7	−10.6
10	44.0	54.1	+10.1
11	71.2	72.8	+ 1.6
12	83.8	83.2	− .6
13	74.4	65.3	− 9.1
14	80.4	73.0	− 7.4
Percent of First Ward vote	72.5	70.8	− 1.7
Percent of city-wide vote	46.0	33.2	−12.8

[a] Failed to gain re-election in 1953.
[b] Project area consists of Election Districts 1, 7, 8 (fully) and 2, 3 (in part).
SOURCE: Raw election data provided by the City Clerk of Newark.

1953, just fourteen months after the announcement of the project and just a few months before the start of clearance, this ward was still his electoral stronghold.

During the charter revision of 1953–54 the election districts were redrawn, and the First Ward was merged with several others into the large North Ward. For this reason a precise comparison between Villani's votes in 1953 and 1954 is not possible. Moreover, by April, 1954, NHA had completed the clearance and relocation process. Thus, it is difficult to know whether the former site residents continued to support Villani in 1954. An electoral map of the 1954 vote (Figure 3) indicates that Villani continued to draw his strongest vote from the area surrounding the project site. The

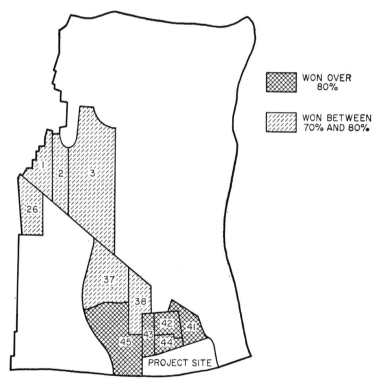

Figure 3. NEWARK'S NORTH WARD: ELECTION DISTRICTS WHERE RALPH VILLANI POLLED HIS LARGEST NUMBER OF VOTES AS A CANDIDATE FOR MAYOR, MAY, 1954 (FIRST BALLOT)
SOURCE OF MAP OUTLINE: Newark Central Planning Board

same pattern was apparent in 1958. If the people in the surrounding area were disgruntled over Villani's role in the North Ward project, they did not show it at the polls.

Whether the clearance project affected North Ward voting in Joseph Melillo's case is more difficult to say. Melillo ran for North Ward councilman in 1954 and narrowly lost. In 1958 he ran again and narrowly won. Some have said that his support of the North Ward opposition helped him gain the Council seat. In fact, Melillo drew support both in 1954 and 1958 from the area immediately adjacent to the project site (Figures 4 and 5). The correlation between the distribution of Melillo's 1954 and 1958 votes in the North Ward is relatively high (r = .62).

But the area adjacent to the project had also been among Villani's strongest districts in 1949, 1953, 1954, and 1958. While the correlation between Villani's vote and Melillo's vote throughout the North Ward is not high (r = .37), they did draw their strength from many of the same places (Figures 3, 4, and 5). Any attempt to call Melillo's vote an expression of site-resident opposition must explain why many Melillo supporters were also voting for Villani. One would have to explain why the correlation between their votes is not negative. If many North Ward voters viewed the project with bitterness, why did they vote for men who had been on opposite ends of the issue?

There is an alternative explanation of this voting pattern that places less emphasis on the expression of site-resident opposition. The 1954 race for North Ward councilman was a nonpartisan, highly unstructured election, in which nearly fifteen candidates, all of the same ethnic group, were contesting. Where no other cues are provided the voter, the familiarity of a candidate's name may prove decisive. It is likely that Melillo became well known in the North Ward, particularly in the districts noted in Figures 4 and 5, through his leadership of the neighborhood opposition. Thus, the residents of these districts may have voted for him largely because they recognized his name, not because they harbored grievances over North Ward redevelopment.

The same voters may have continued to support Villani in 1954 and 1958 because he was the only major Italian-American candi-

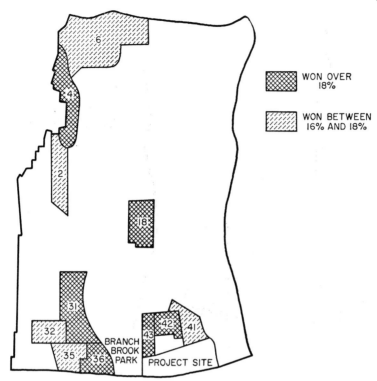

Figure 4. NEWARK'S NORTH WARD: ELECTION DISTRICTS WHERE
JOSEPH MELILLO POLLED HIS LARGEST NUMBER OF VOTES AS A
CANDIDATE FOR THE CITY COUNCIL, MAY, 1954 (FIRST BALLOT)
SOURCE OF MAP OUTLINE: Newark Central Planning Board

date for mayor. Several North Ward informants suggested that
resentment over the project was subordinated to the principle of
ethnic unity.

SLUM CLEARANCE AND THE POLITICS OF RACE

On the basis of the foregoing evidence, it would seem safe to
conclude that, other things being equal, grass roots opposition will
not disrupt NHA's arrangements with other government agencies
at least during the 1960s.[5] But, in a city experiencing such rapid
population shifts, the "other things" are decidedly not equal. A
massive tide of immigration from the South and a consequent
doubling of the city's Negro population in six years has served to

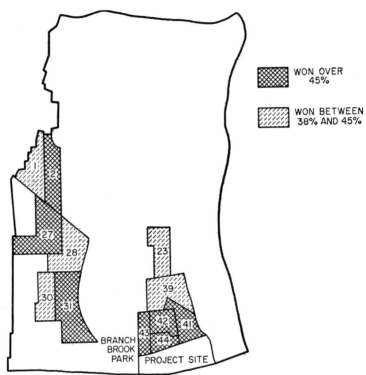

WON OVER
45%

WON BETWEEN
38% AND 45%

Figure 5. NEWARK'S NORTH WARD: ELECTION DISTRICTS WHERE
JOSEPH MELILLO POLLED HIS LARGEST NUMBER OF VOTES AS A
CANDIDATE FOR THE CITY COUNCIL, MAY, 1958 (FIRST BALLOT)
SOURCE OF MAP OUTLINE: Newark Central Planning Board

inject the race issue into almost all aspects of Newark politics. It
has provoked responses which, in the words of one NHA official,
"could blow the whole [renewal] program up in our faces."

In 1950, according to the U.S. Census, there were approximately
75,000 Negroes in Newark, comprising somewhat over 17 percent
of the city's total population; in 1960 federal census takers found
that 138,035 persons, or 34 percent of the city's population, were
Negro. As the migrants continued to flow into the Central Ward,
a breakup of the ghetto and a dispersion of Negroes throughout
the city became inevitable. A 1958 survey by the Mayor's Commission on Group Relations reported that almost every neighborhood
in the city had undergone rapid transformation during the previ-

ous six or seven years. Clinton Hill and the West Ward were the areas that had changed most drastically (see Tables 3 and 4 and Figure 6).

In recent years NHA's decisions have affected the Negroes more directly and persistently than any other group in Newark. NHA's constituency—those persons with whom the Authority deals on a

TABLE 3

THE NEGRO POPULATION EXPLOSION IN NEWARK, 1920–1960 [a]

Year	Total	Negroes [b]	Percentage of Negroes [b]
1930	442,300	39,000	8.9
1940	429,800	46,000	10.6
1950	438,800	75,000	17.1
1960	406,000	138,000	34.0

[a] All figures are rounded off.

[b] In 1960 there were approximately 13,000 Puerto Ricans in Newark. They are not included in the Negro total.

SOURCE: U.S. Census.

TABLE 4

DISPERSION OF THE NEGRO POPULATION IN NEWARK, 1950–1958

Neighborhood	Percentage Negro, 1950	Percentage Negro, 1958	Percentage Puerto Rican, 1958
North Ward			
Forest Hill	4	2	0 *
North Newark (site of North Ward project)	12	24	2
Roseville	4	17	0 *
East Ward			
Central Business District	35	46	33
Ironbound	7	14	6
Central Ward	63	85	2
West Ward: Vailsburg	10	43	0 *
South Ward			
South Broad	20	61	9
Clinton Hill	8	44	0 *
Weequahic	2	16	2

* Number too small to record.

SOURCE: Mayor's Commission on Group Relations.

daily, face-to-face basis—has become almost entirely nonwhite. NHA's policies materially benefit some individuals and directly inconvenience others. Negroes now comprise the major part of both categories.

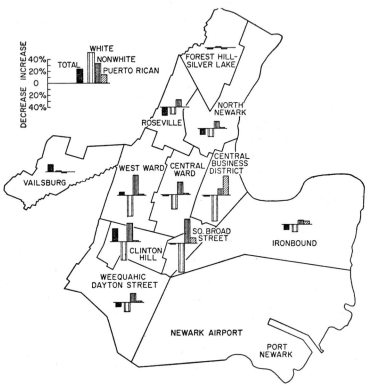

Figure 6. POPULATION CHANGES IN NEWARK'S NEIGHBORHOODS, 1950–1958
SOURCE: Market Planning Corporation and Newark Central Planning Board

Most Negroes leaders stress the benefits that NHA's policies bring to the Negro community rather than the inconvenience these policies cause particular Negro families. In the opinion of these leaders, NHA, through public housing and relocation, has taken major strides in expanding the supply of standard housing available to nonwhites. The Authority, they feel, has been more responsive to the needs of the nonwhite population than any other agency in the city. As a result, housing is not considered by Negro leaders as one of the major problems in Newark. The benefits Negroes derive from NHA policies have also been stressed by white informants. Many see NHA as an agency that "takes care of the Negroes" and helps their dispersion into white neighborhoods.

The change in NHA's constituency, then, has served to inject the race issue into urban renewal politics—a situation that constitutes the single most important threat to the future of the renewal system.

RACE POLITICS AND THE NORTH WARD

Perhaps the change in NHA's constituency began in 1949, when the Authority decided to integrate public housing and to focus a major part of its future public housing efforts in the Central Ward.[6] Before 1949 NHA had built segregated projects in outlying white areas and had filled them with people from the surrounding neighborhoods. As a result, the Negroes, who constituted something like 40 percent of those eligible for public housing in 1949, occupied only 7 or 8 percent of the units. After Danzig became Executive Director, NHA began constructing more public housing within the Central Ward, thus increasing the total number of units available to Negroes by increasing the number of "Negro projects." In addition, all-white projects throughout the city were opened to eligible Negro applicants.

Although NHA hoped to keep the latter projects racially balanced, no quotas were used in the selection of tenants. The result was a flight of white tenants from these projects and a substantial increase in the number of Negro tenants. In the three years between 1951 and 1954 the percentage of Negro public housing tenants in Newark tripled. By 1955 there were more Negroes than whites in public housing, and the flight of white tenants showed no signs of slackening. The number of Negro tenants continued to grow at an increasing rate.

The racial implications of urban redevelopment were first noted in 1952 by a group of North Ward leaders who were opposed to clearance in their area. The public housing phase of the North Ward project, they feared, would introduce a large number of

Negro families into the area and, eventually, serve as an opening wedge for a Negro invasion of North Newark. Villani thought he had a promise from Danzig that site residents would be given preference in tenanting and that the Italian community would be resurrected on the site. This implied that NHA would deliberately maintain a low ceiling on the number of Negroes in Columbus Homes, the North Ward public housing project. Some North Ward leaders later claimed that Danzig had agreed to keep the number of Negroes there below 10 percent.

It is unlikely that Danzig made any such commitment to Villani or the North Ward leaders, although he may have left his position ambiguous. Evidence indicates, however, that NHA did want to keep the number of Negroes in Columbus Homes at a relatively low level. If this is true, the Authority probably acted out of concern for the sale of adjacent redevelopment areas and not in accordance with any commitment to Villani. NHA began a campaign to seek out white tenants for Columbus Homes and agreed to give preference to all eligible families from the original site. But the Authority never intended this to be an "Italian project," nor did NHA have the power to make it one.

In November, 1955, when NHA opened Columbus Homes by moving in 300 white families, a score of Negro leaders descended on Danzig's office. Danzig denied that he had promised Villani to keep the project predominantly white and ridiculed the idea that he had to make such commitments to get NHA's projects approved. He argued that a proper racial balance in projects is best preserved when white families are moved in first; the next group moving into the project would be largely Negro.

Yet, Danzig would not commit himself to a strict open-occupancy policy in Columbus Homes. He was convinced that no private redeveloper would buy cleared land next to a predominantly Negro public housing project. In the ensuing years NHA's staff continued to accord a special status and a separate tenant selection policy to the Columbus Homes project. The percentage of Negro tenants in that project has in fact increased much more slowly than in any of the other NHA projects.

When NHA began moving Negro families into Columbus

Homes in January, 1956, Danzig was exposed to attacks from another direction. Some North Ward leaders now viewed NHA's
failure to give preference to Italian applicants and to keep Negroes
out of the project as a betrayal of Danzig's alleged agreement with
former Mayor Villani. Politicos and civic leaders from the North
Ward withdrew all support of the project and praised the earlier
efforts of SOHC. The *Italian Tribune* denounced NHA for oust-
ing people from the site area "under false pretenses" and for giving
greater consideration to "recent immigrants" than to "long-time
city residents."

This renewal of opposition in the North Ward came too late
in the execution of the project to be effective. Although NHA was
able to ignore these attacks and proceed with its plans, the tenanting of Columbus Homes had demonstrated just how disruptive
the race issue could be.

NHA AND THE NEGRO LEADERS

The growing number of Negroes in public housing generated
white opposition to NHA that otherwise might not have existed.[7]
On the other hand, what has been the response of Negro leaders?
To what extent do the beneficiaries of NHA's policies provide organized and effective support for those policies, and how important
is this support to NHA's over-all success?

Perhaps the most useful generalization that could be made about
Negro politics in Newark is that the schism in the community at
large between the politicos and the civic leaders is reproduced in a
somewhat altered version within the Negro community. The local
branches of the Urban League and of the National Association for
the Advancement of Colored People (NAACP) may differ in strategy, but they are run by the same people: middle-class, well-
educated Negroes, who have moved to the suburbs and have sev-
ered most of their ties to the Central Ward. Whatever differences
in style may exist among these "silk-stocking" leaders, they share
a common antagonism toward the Central Ward organization of
Councilman Irvine Turner. To the Negro silk-stocking leader
Turner is an erratic, unprincipled demagogue, who appeals to the
newly arrived, uneducated, southern Negroes in the Central Ward

with his "Vote Black" harangues but achieves little for the Negroes in the long run.

While the middle-class Negroes assail Councilman Turner for not cooperating with other Negro leaders, Turner dismisses them as "eggheads" who like to "study the problem" and ingratiate themselves with white leaders. He often asserts that it is they who are isolated from the great mass of Negroes in Newark, and not he. "If you mean by a 'Negro leader,' " one Negro informant said, "someone whom most of the Negroes in Newark know and turn to for help, there's only one 'Negro leader' in Newark, and that's Irvine Turner." The rest, Turner has implied, are self-designated leaders, serving as the "Negro representative" on citizen committees but better known at City Hall than in the Central Ward.

This schism extends into the fields of public housing and renewal. The result is a divided attitude toward most of NHA's policies. Councilman Turner has espoused a program of more public housing for the Negro in the Central Ward even at the price of continued residential segregation. Most silk-stocking leaders have shared the white conservatives' aversion to public housing per se and have shown more interest in expanding opportunities for Negroes in the home-buying market. On the question of Negroes in public housing, silk-stocking leaders have generally argued that integrated living is of higher value than just more housing for Negroes. Yet, when Turner has accused NHA of using racial quotas in public housing, the silk-stocking leaders have felt compelled to join him in support for open occupancy. They believe that their opposition to public housing and their emphasis on nonmaterial or "status" values are unpopular among the Negroes of the Central Ward. When major issues arise, these leaders have felt that they should accept Turner's position—the popular position—in order to maintain racial unity on the issue.

Turner received the news of an urban renewal project in the Central Ward with enthusiasm, interpreting it as a major victory for the Negro in Newark. Few whites could be induced to live in the Central Ward; anything built there would have to be Negro housing. The renewal project was also expected to remedy the municipal government's usual neglect of public facilities in the

Negro ghetto by drawing some badly needed public works to the area.

Many of the silk-stocking leaders had reservations about the Central Ward project, although they never voiced any objections publicly. They hoped that NHA would completely demolish the Negro ghetto and build a new "city within a city," integrating all classes and races. But many doubted the possibility of securing private development in the midst of a ghetto and feared that the end result would be just more all-Negro public housing within the Central Ward. Said one silk-stocking leader: "Fifteen years from now we'll be right back where we started from. Most of the Negroes will be living in overcrowded, no longer new, public housing projects within the Central Ward." To Negro leaders of this persuasion the ideal site for redevelopment and public housing was on the periphery of the ghetto, where white tenants could be attracted and truly integrated housing built. In the end, however, these leaders were not prepared to stand in the way of a project that would undoubtedly bring material gains to the Negro community.

There is one other criticism leveled at the Central Ward project by silk-stocking leaders that highlights their relationship to NHA officials. Several of the silk-stocking leaders criticized NHA's staff for not consulting them during the planning of the project. They argued that, since NHA decisions had such a persistent and direct effect on the Negro community, the Authority should establish a regular basis of discussion between its staff and Negro leaders.

NHA rejected this idea. If NHA's projects benefit the Negro community, Housing Authority officials argued, the function of the Negro leaders is to see that the project gains acceptance among the Central Ward residents. Negro leaders should have offered their assistance to NHA in carrying out the project, not asked indignantly why they were not consulted beforehand. The staff repeated the answer it had given other local interests: if those affected by clearance were consulted at every stage of planning and the plans tailored to meet their demands, renewal projects would never get off the ground.

Thus, there has not been any institutionalized or regular consultation between NHA and the spokesmen of its major clientele group. When interviewed in January, 1960, most Negro silk-stocking leaders still assumed that NHA was planning a racially integrated "city within a city" in the Central Ward.

THE YEAR OF "THE TROUBLE"

The year 1958 will be remembered by most Housing Authority officials as the year of "the trouble." [8] It was the year that a series of attacks on NHA policies, emanating from a variety of sources which shared a common interest in the Negro population explosion, reached their climax. NHA apparently rode out the storm without any damage to its program. Whether it succeeded in quieting the deep-seated concerns behind these attacks is more questionable.

"The trouble" stemmed from the widespread acceptance of two notions: that the large number of integrated public housing projects had attracted southern Negroes to Newark and that NHA's renewal of the Central Ward had helped disperse Negroes throughout the city. Added to these notions were a few igniting sparks. First, a survey by the Mayor's Commisson on Group Relations in 1957 documented the rapid increase in Newark's Negro population and its dispersion throughout the city's "better neighborhoods," trends which, until then, had been unsupported premonitions. Second, the 1958 local elections indicated the radical changes that had occurred in many electoral constituencies as a result of this dispersion. Finally, in 1957 and 1958 NHA issued public reports on its policies in relocating Negro families from the Central Ward renewal site.

In attempting to renew sixty blocks in the Central Ward, NHA was confronted with the monumental task of relocating more than 8,500 Negro families. Nearly 800 Negro families would be displaced immediately by the first stage of renewal, the Spruce Street public housing project. Relocation of these families in other public housing projects was only a partial solution, since vacancies were few and many of the displaced persons were ineligible. Despite this problem and NHA's reluctance to disrupt the racial balance of its projects, the Authority placed approximately 15 percent of the

800 Negro families in public housing. The fact remained, however, that between 80 and 90 percent of these families would have to be relocated in private housing.

NHA was loath to relocate many families elsewhere in the Central Ward, since this usually meant moving them into substandard dwelling units and into areas that might become subject to further renewal activity. The difficulty of finding homes for Negroes in white areas, however, forced NHA to resettle about 38 percent of the displaced persons within the Central Ward. Relocation of the remaining families might have delayed the project indefinitely, had it not been for the large number of vacancies opening up for Negroes in the "transitional areas" south and west of the ghetto. NHA eventually relocated almost 180 Negro families, about 23 percent of the total, in Clinton Hill and the West Ward, where racial invasion was already under way.

Several silk-stocking Negro leaders pointed out that this action simply reinforced the pattern of Negro dispersion through the invasion of a particular area, the flight of white residents, and the enlargement of the ghetto. But NHA officials insisted that, if Negroes were to be moved out of the Central Ward at all, it would have to be into transitional areas. Attempts to relocate Negroes in stable, all-white areas would create neighborhood disturbances that might seriously delay the project. The Authority's responsibility, its staff said, was to clear land and relocate residents, not to plan an even dispersion of the Negro population throughout the city.

The overt attack on NHA's relocation policies came from the Clinton Hill Neighborhood Council (CHNC), not from the Negro leaders. CHNC had been created in 1954 to stabilize the neighborhood and to stop the wholesale flight of white residents. Not until NHA's Director of Relocation, Samuel Warrence, spoke before the members of CHNC in May, 1958, did CHNC see a connection between NHA's policies and the rapid changes going on in their area. At this 1958 meeting Warrence provided detailed data on how many of the 800 Negro families had been relocated in Clinton Hill. He went on to inform CHNC members that their area should be prepared to receive between 40 and 50 percent of the

7,800 Negro families who would eventually be displaced by Central Ward renewal. According to one CHNC member who was present: "The audience was in an uproar." During the following months attacks on NHA's relocation policy became a regular part of the Clinton Hill group's program and of the statements issued by several other neighborhood councils.

Concurrent with this development was a growing opposition at City Hall to the construction of additional public housing. In view of the program's genuine popularity among the politicos throughout its almost twenty-year history, such a change in attitude was particularly significant. The first indication of this shift was a prolonged attack by city councilmen and neighborhood groups on high crime rates, mass destruction of public property, poor "tenant education," and inadequate maintenance policies in NHA's public housing projects. After months of public debate Danzig finally conceded that some of the criticisms, though not the motives of the critics, were just. He announced that NHA would create a Tenant Relations Division, screen problem families at the tenant selection stage, step up social work within the projects, and consider a private police force to patrol the projects.

But the City Council's attacks on public housing continued and, after the 1958 election, even increased. Soon after the election a number of councilmen called for an end to all public housing. Resolutions requiring NHA to sell existing projects to private enterprise were introduced and seriously discussed by the Council. As one informant on the Council put it: "Today, Lou Danzig couldn't get another public housing proposal through this Council if he stood on his head."

Most of the Councilmen remained convinced that public housing, along with the public welfare program, was sustaining the massive migration of nonwhites to Newark. They expressed concern over falling revenues and rising relief payments, over the increase in crime rates, and over the flight of businesses reliant on a middle-class clientele. It is also likely that many councilmen were responding to changes they had noticed in their constituencies during the 1958 election and to the possibility that they would be unable to hold their seats if such population shifts continued. Some spoke of the likelihood that the Negroes would gain two additional Council seats in 1962. Many of the councilmen, moreover, had long-standing "political" grievances against NHA that may have reinforced their concern about their own political future.

Neither the City Council nor the neighborhood groups, however, seemed capable of disrupting the renewal system on these public housing and relocation issues. NHA probably could have ridden out the storm indefinitely, had it not been for an additional development. Concern over the political implications of this massive migration apparently spread to the Mayor's office during 1958 and led Carlin to re-evaluate his stand on public housing. The climax to NHA's "trouble"—and the first serious note in the controversy—came in October, 1958. At that time Mayor Carlin, approving the Mercer Street project as part of Central Ward renewal, said that it would be the city's last public housing project. Newark, he added, had "no immediate plans for further public housing projects."

Carlin seemed to share the City Council's concern over growing crime rates and growing fiscal problems. In addition, the Mayor voiced all the criticisms that the civic leaders had been leveling at public housing since 1938. It is likely that Carlin, like the councilmen, was responding to the problems of political survival created by recent population shifts.

Although Mayor Carlin won re-election in 1958, there were two disturbing lessons implicit in the electoral data. First, Carlin seemed unable to come to terms with the Turner organization or to generate any support of his own within the Negro community. Outside of Villani's "home districts" in the North Ward, Carlin's poorest showing was in the most heavily Negro parts of the city. The only ward that Carlin lost was the Central Ward. (See shaded areas in Figure 7.) Second, Carlin's greatest losses between 1954 and 1958 came in the transitional areas within and adjacent to the Central Ward. Of the twenty election districts in which Carlin lost more than 10 percent of his 1954 vote, eight are on the outskirts of the Central Ward, ten are in the South Ward, and two are in the West Ward. (See hatched areas in Figure 7.)

The largest block of contiguous districts where Carlin lost heavily
is in and around the Clinton Hill Rehabilitation Area. These
dramatic losses may reflect the growing number of Negro voters
in these districts. It is also reasonable to posit an antiadministra-
tion shift by disgruntled white residents.

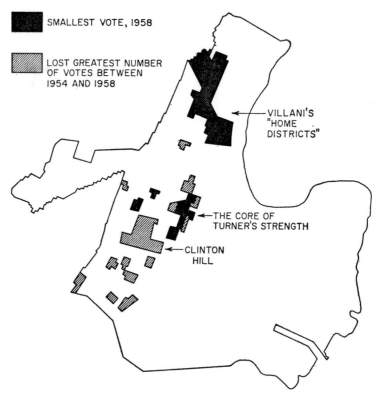

Figure 7. ELECTION DISTRICTS WHERE LEO CARLIN POLLED HIS
WEAKEST VOTES AS A CANDIDATE FOR MAYOR, 1954 AND 1958
(FIRST BALLOTS)
SOURCE OF MAP OUTLINE: Newark Central Planning Board

In short, Carlin seemed to be losing support among those white
voters threatened by Negro invasion, while failing to improve his
poor showing in the Negro wards. He apparently lost votes on both
sides of the fence. He was labeled both "pro-Negro" and "anti-
Negro." Wherever the racial issue was relevant, Carlin suffered.

The Mayor's strongest support, and the votes that returned him to office, came from outlying neighborhoods where racial problems were matters of hypothetical debate, but not of pressing concern. The question that concerned Carlin in 1958–59 was whether these areas would still be untouched by the racial issue when he sought re-election in 1962.

RACE AND THE URBAN RENEWAL SYSTEM

It is difficult to determine from these events alone how disruptive the race question might eventually prove to the urban renewal system.[9] The attacks on NHA were never anything more than a potential opposition. "The trouble" that NHA encountered in 1958 consisted of shifts in attitude and predisposition, of declarations by several local actors that they would oppose NHA should the Authority make certain proposals. These declarations were not brought to a test because NHA did not initiate any new public housing after the Mercer Street project in 1958.

The attacks on NHA subsided in 1959. After the Mayor's statement in October, 1958, most of NHA's critics assumed that the issue had been resolved in their favor. But NHA officials did not concede the death of their public housing program.

The Authority's top staff has tended to minimize the importance of the racial issue as a threat to the renewal program. In personal interviews NHA officials expressed faith in the ability of their good relations with the mayor's office to withstand stronger shocks than this. One official said: "We could get a public housing proposal through tomorrow if we wanted to."

As partial justification for their optimism, NHA officials have noted that at no time during the agitation, from its inception in 1956 until January, 1960, did the Authority trim its sails in response to the attacks. NHA did not abandon its plans for a second public housing project in the Central Ward renewal area and did not hesitate to announce this proposal in the midst of the agitation. The Mayor and Council did indeed warn that this would be the last public housing project they would approve. But the fact remains that Mercer Street public housing was ratified without incident or delay.

Furthermore, in relocating the 2,400 families displaced by
Mercer Street clearance, 91 percent of whom were Negro, NHA
continued the same policies it had used in the Spruce Street
project. In January, 1960, when relocation from the Mercer Street
project was half completed, NHA officials estimated that 50 percent of the displaced persons would be relocated elsewhere in the
Central Ward, about 20 percent (480 families) in Clinton Hill,
and about 10 percent (240 families) in the West Ward.

Thus, except for the creation of a Tenants Relations Division—
which may have been sparked by local attacks but which had been
germinating in NHA's offices for some time—"the trouble" apparently had no impact on the substance of NHA's policies.

There were a few additional indications in fall, 1959, that
NHA's stable arrangements with City Hall would withstand the
pressures engendered by the race issue. In November, 1959, the
second interim report of the City Planning Office's Demonstration
Grant Project declared that Newark would need a massive public
housing program over the next ten years to help relocate the more
than 11,000 families who would be displaced by renewal activities.
This incident indicated the emergence of fresh support among the
planners for NHA's public housing program. It also demonstrated
the unwillingness of the civic leaders to join NHA's newer critics.
The civic leaders had always viewed public housing as damaging
to the city's economy, but they had no sympathy or rapport with
the 1958 opposition and considered much of this opposition to be
"politically inspired." Overt opposition to NHA's public housing
efforts, moreover, might disrupt the renewal program and impair
the civic leaders' good relations with Danzig. The city councilmen
and many neighborhood groups eventually denounced this part of
the report; NEDC, NCNCR, and the civic groups remained con-
spicuously silent.

When the planners made their recommendation in October,
1959, they and the civic leaders assumed that the Mayor was still
opposed to additional public housing in Newark. Just days before
the publication of the planners' report, Corporation Counsel
Vincent Torppey, a close advisor of the Mayor's, had issued a
statement opposing additional public housing and urging that the

existing projects be sold. Yet, in January, 1960, Carlin, as Chairman of the Metropolitan Regional Council's committee on housing and renewal, presented a report urging substantial public housing for the New York metropolitan area. When questioned by reporters on the seeming inconsistency in his position, the Mayor said that he had never intended to rule out the possibility of more public housing construction in Newark. His statement in October, 1958, had meant only that NHA had not yet submitted to him any additional plans for public housing. Asked whether he would approve plans for more public housing, should NHA submit them, Mayor Carlin said that he would decide when a specific proposal was presented.

Thus, the Housing Authority's optimism has had some basis in fact. NHA's policies during the first decade of urban renewal were in no way altered or delayed by the race issue. The Mayor's statement and other events in fall, 1959, implied that the public housing program was not dead. In the long run, racial issues might disrupt the present urban renewal system. The race issue is still a relatively new one; the political ramifications of Negro migration to Newark are just beginning. In 1960, however, no break in the present system seemed imminent. The pattern of renewal politics described in this study seemed likely to continue well into the new decade.

THE GRASS ROOTS

Citizen participation is frequently alleged to be a basic condition of renewal success.[10] The federal government, among others, has urged local redevelopment agencies to educate the public, to create a broad, popular basis of support, and to consult periodically with those affected by clearance policies. Without such widespread participation, the program will presumably founder on popular apathy, suspicion, or misunderstanding. Citizen participation is one of the seven requirements in the workable program that the federal government imposes on all local communities engaging in renewal.

The evidence in this study implies that such citizen participation is not always necessary to renewal achievement. The active support of persons affected by renewal may be vital in the rehabilitation phases of the program, but nothing more than the acquiescence of those affected is necessary to clearance. Widespread participation in the program may be desirable, but it is probably not indispensable. This may be one reason the citizen participation requirement of the workable program, like the central planning requirement, has been more honored in the breach.

Far from being indispensable, citizen participation, in many cases, may even prove detrimental to the program's progress. Slum clearance in Newark, and probably in most other cities, generates more hostile than favorable responses at the grass roots level. It is easier to organize site residents than to organize those who will ultimately benefit from new middle-income housing. The major beneficiaries of NHA's public housing policies, the Negroes, have been underorganized and powerless. Nor, since the collapse of the Citizens' Housing Council, have there been any broadly based associations or committees of local notables to provide active, articulate support for NHA's policies.

Given this type of grass roots response, NHA's attitudes toward the question of citizen participation are understandable. The Authority has not generally relied on the use of public relations or on the generation of mass support. It has attempted instead to delimit the boundaries of renewal politics and to come to terms with persons inside these limits. NHA's arrangements with City officials and civic leaders are sufficient means to achieving clearance goals. The Authority has had no need for an expansion of the renewal public and of the system's boundaries. In view of the grass roots response to clearance, such an expansion probably would hurt NHA more than it would help.

In addition, NHA officials realize that extensive publicity and more widespread involvement could destroy the routine, low-temperature aspects of the renewal process. This would be true even if the grass roots were less hostile to clearance. A sudden increase of mass interest in the renewal program might turn routine proposals into controversial issues and strain relations among the members of the renewal system. Limited participation and low visibility seem to be necessary to the system's survival.

CHAPTER VIII

The Urban Renewal System
in Newark

A number of recent inquiries into the politics of large cities have yielded remarkably similar images of urban power structure.[1] Instead of revealing a single, integrated structure for the entire city, these studies show a set of loosely integrated, semi-autonomous subsystems clustering around centers of significant decision making. Most political actors in the city specialize in one or two of these policy areas. Even if they are so inclined, few actors prove capable of spreading their influence across three or more areas. The decisions in one subsystem are largely unaffected by the demands of other subsystems; the policy products of the various subsystems are uncoordinated.

These subsystems are occasionally bridged by a political machine, as in Chicago, or by a strong mayor, as in New Haven. But city-wide politics is generally so loosely integrated that it may be more accurate to speak of a city's "power structures" than of its "power structure." The autonomy of Newark's urban renewal system and the apparent absence of any city-wide coordinating structure suggests that the plural term may be highly applicable to Newark.

There are two methodological implications in such a model of uncoordinated power structures. First, the model suggests that one useful approach to community power structure is through an analysis of the community's major policy areas. Since these areas form well-integrated systems, they may be treated as the basic units of the community-wide structure. Except for a city-wide consensus on a relatively small number of political norms, the total power structure of a community may be nothing more than the aggregate of the smaller structures that form around centers of significant choice. Second, the model implies that the politics of a particular policy area may be viewed as a social system and may be usefully analyzed in those terms.

This chapter attempts to summarize and recast Newark's urban renewal politics in the terms frequently used to describe social systems. It focuses on the system's level of integration, its internal structure, and the prerequisites for its emergence. The major advantage of such a recasting is that it facilitates comparison with other studies.

LEVEL OF INTEGRATION

One factor by which various social systems may be characterized is the degree of integration.[2] An aggregate of actors constitutes an integrated social system when there exist a common set of norms, a high degree of interaction among the actors, clearly defined and stable roles, role differentiation, resistance to deviation from the norms, and socialization of new members. Actual systems may be characterized and compared by their approximation to this abstract model of integration. In these terms the aforementioned studies of urban power structure found the politics of particular policy areas to be more highly integrated than the politics of the entire city. The power structure of a city may be so loosely integrated that it meets only a few of the basic requirements of a social system. In the same terms, one can compare the degree of integration among various subsystems, either in the same city or in the same policy area across the nation.

Newark's urban renewal politics may be characterized as a relatively well-integrated system. Newark renewal seems to be more highly integrated than most other policy areas in Newark and perhaps more highly integrated than renewal systems in many other cities.

The foregoing account has suggested that there is a relatively small number of persistent renewal participants who interact with each other on a daily basis. The inner core of renewal politics can be defined in interactional terms. NHA, the mayor, certain administrative agencies, NCNCR, NEDC, and the planners interact more closely with each other than with any other individuals or groups in the city. Persistent interaction with a central actor like NHA is a test of membership in the system and a way of distinguishing "insiders" from "outsiders."

The behavior of the regular participants toward each other, moreover, is highly structured and predictable. The launching and execution of clearance decisions occur in a routine fashion. The behavior of most actors is circumscribed by a previously defined pattern of roles, and the role of an actor in a clearance decision varies little from one project to another. The staff of NHA has little difficulty in anticipating the responses of relevant local actors to a clearance decision.

The resistance of the regular renewal participants to a disruption of their normal relations has been described throughout the study. In personal interviews these actors testified to their satisfaction with present arrangements. Some recognized that there was a distinctive "way of doing things" in Newark, which bore directly on that city's renewal achievements. Others simply stressed the importance of reciprocity and of maintaining good working relations with other renewal actors.

The major norm of the system seems to be a procedural one, concerning the way in which conflicts are to be resolved rather than the substance of the settlement. This norm requires that conflicts be settled through informal bargaining, not through overt attacks or public agitation. It may be that such a tacit agreement on the informal resolution of internal differences is a normative concomitant of all stable social systems. The norm is more a prohibition than an obligation. It states that participants should not take their claims to the press or to elements outside the system. In private negotiations with other members claims should not be pressed to the point where they strain working relations. NHA's major demand of local participants, with the exception of the mayor, has been acquiescence or neutrality rather than active support or cooperation.

There also is a common commitment among the participants to any action that will bring private or federal capital into Newark. They view Newark as a competitor for this capital with all other cities in the nation. A unified front and the submergence of local conflict gives Newark a good name and helps attract capital. This norm also implies a common acceptance of renewal activity in any form, of activism per se. Any concrete proposal that would help the city and attract capital is supported, even though other participants in the system might have ideally preferred some other form of action.

Any stable social system must minimize internal conflict by providing a division of tasks or a differentiation of roles. This process has occurred in Newark renewal. Each of the major participants has developed a role which leaves undisturbed NHA's initiative in clearance policy. Thus, NEDC has played the role of publicist and legitimizer, the mayor has served as catalyst and broker, and NCNCR has focused on code enforcement and Clinton Hill rehabilitation.

The various renewal participants had different types of interests and goals, which operated in different spheres and seldom came into conflict. Thus, reciprocal relations could be formed in which both role-partners pursued their separate goals simultaneously. Another subsidiary norm of this system is noninterference in the distinctive domains of other renewal participants.

No system fits the model of perfect integration. Every system has a permissive area, an area of legitimate conflict in which the norms and established roles do not apply. In addition, there are always disagreements over the meaning of roles, the terms of exchange, and the application of norms to particular or new situations. In a relatively well-integrated system, however, these differences will be settled without disrupting the over-all accord. "Bargaining is perpetual," Sayre and Kaufman have noted of New York City politics.[3] But bargaining within an integrated system is more highly structured and narrower in scope than bargaining in a fluid situation. The big questions are settled and are not to be reopened. In settling outstanding questions participants are not to push their claims to the point where established relations are threatened.

Although no system attains perfect integration, Newark renewal probably falls short of the level attained by most bureaucracies, voluntary associations, and small groups. The scope of consensus and the area of normative action in Newark renewal do not extend much beyond the commitment to quantitative achievement and nonpublic resolution of differences. The same dissensions over renewal goals that existed in 1949 are still apparent, although the range of disagreement has been reduced.

Similarly, the roles that comprise this system are narrow in scope and make relatively few demands of the participants. Such roles are restricted to the activities involved in local approval of project plans. Moreover, the content of most roles, as noted earlier, is more prohibitive than obligatory. NHA's inability to bring neighborhood rehabilitation within its orbit or to have the City launch Penn Plaza under the "three-fourths" arrangement demonstrate the outer limits of the established roles of the participants in Newark. The Authority can count on little beyond the acquiescence of local actors in a specific clearance proposal.

In summary, the Newark system represents a structuring of behavior in a few specific areas among actors of different viewpoints. The structuring of behavior serves to suppress, but not to obliterate, these differences. No strong expressive sentiments or emotional attachments develop. It is too early to say, moreover, whether the system will develop the techniques of recruitment and socialization necessary if it is to outlast its present personnel. The Newark renewal system probably represents a lesser degree of integration than most formal organizations but a higher degree of integration than many other policy areas.

INTEGRATION: SOME IMPLICATIONS

All social systems are built around a productive and allocative mechanism.[4] The relative integration of a social system seems to be one determinant of the system's output or productivity. Of course, integration may occur around counter-productive norms, but integration provides a potential for high output that is absent in more fluid systems. If the success of a system is measured by its output or ability to alter its environment, then success is a by-product of structural integration.

The chances for any successful, planned innovation at the local level depend upon the appearance of an integrated system capable of sustaining that innovation. Martin and Munger, in *Decisions in Syracuse,* have stressed the importance of the Onondaga County Republican organization in achieving metropolitan-wide reform. In explaining similar cases of political innovation elsewhere, Banfield has emphasized the role of the Cook County Democratic party in Chicago, and Dahl has emphasized the executive-centered coalition built by Mayor Richard Lee in New Haven.

Success in urban renewal also may be seen as the output of an integrated system. The more fluid the politics of urban renewal, the less active the renewal program will be. The degree to which Newark's renewal politics is structured is one explanation of the city's renewal success. Newark's renewal participants have succeeded in institutionalizing the process of innovation.

To clarify the above argument, it might be useful to define "fluid politics" more fully and to distinguish Newark renewal from another type of political system which will be called "open-ended pluralism."

The basic features of open-ended pluralism include overt conflict over a public policy decision, occurring among a wide variety of affected interests. Entrance into the system is relatively open. The behavior of participants and the outcome of the issue is relatively unpredictable. Ad hoc coalitions are formed on a particular issue, but the coalitions rarely outlast the issue. Initiative generally lies with private interests, who often reach a settlement before bringing the issue to the public officials. The resulting policy tends to reflect the balance of power among the contending interests at that particular time. The final decision resolves nothing more than the issue at hand; it may not even resolve that issue. Moderation, compromise, delay, and inertia seem to be built into this system. It is always easier to block action under such conditions than to achieve it.

Described in these terms, open-ended pluralism may be seen as a model of a weakly integrated political system. Actual political systems may be placed along a continuum, with open-ended pluralism at one end and perfect integration at the other. Among the crucial variables are the degree of normative consensus, patterned activity, and division of labor. Newark renewal is closer to the integration end of the continuum. The success of a renewal program may well depend on its ability to overcome the conditions of open-ended pluralism and to move toward the other end of the continuum.

A central problem in the analysis of any policy area, then, is the degree to which behavior in this area is structured and the level of integration that it has attained. This statement has several methodological implications. Studies which focus on the resolution of a single issue or decision are probably most useful in the analysis of highly unstructured situations, when generalizations about persistent roles or norms would be hazardous. This approach would not be quite so useful in examining more highly integrated systems, in which the continuities in behavior and the broader structural context are more important than the particular issue. In addition, a "single issue" approach runs the risk of overemphasizing the complexity and uniqueness of each issue and of overstating either the fluidity or the open-ended pluralism of the system under study.

There are similar risks in defining politics solely in terms of overt conflict and in focusing on cases where such conflict appears. One virtue of the integration model is that it helps define the incidence and ambit of overt conflict. Open conflict is most likely to occur in an area of decision where no stable structure exists, where a structure is just being formed, where a structure has just broken down, or where two structures are involved with no higher structure to coordinate them.[5] An approach which seeks out overt conflict may tend to overemphasize stalemate and inertia in local politics and to neglect cases of achievement and planned innovation. In fact, the best indices to the presence of an integrated system in many areas of public policy making are the absence of overt conflict and the success or high output of the system.

Like the focus on a single issue, the study of individual decision making and the application of calculative models to political behavior are most useful in the analysis of highly fluid situations. Their utility declines as a larger area of behavior falls under the prescriptions of roles and norms, as the area of routine behavior expands and the area of special problem-solving behavior contracts. As Karl Mannheim has noted, conscious reflection on one's course of action occurs when systems break down. It also occurs in the permissive areas where stable expectations and duties do not exist.[6]

STRUCTURE OF THE SYSTEM

The structure of a system can be described in terms of the flow of interaction, the sources of initiating action, the size and permeability of the system, the characteristics of the personnel, and the terms of exchange.[7]

Described in sociometric terms, the urban renewal system in Newark would assume a starlike or spokelike appearance, with NHA at the center. The lines of most frequent interaction run between NHA and each of the major renewal participants; much less interaction occurs around the outer rims of the structure. The fact that the renewal participants have different types of goals and act in different policy spheres may have discouraged extensive cooperation among them. But NHA, as a major center of funds, legal authority, expertise, and initiative, has served as a magnet for the attention of most renewal participants.

The system is starlike in another sense. Initiative in this structure rests with the public officials, or core group—those immediately and officially responsible for clearance decisions.

There is a rough correlation between a participant's rate of interaction with NHA, his influence over certain aspects of NHA's activities, and his personal commitment to the system. The participants, ranked according to their interaction with NHA, their influence, and their commitment, are: the mayor, certain administrative agencies, NEDC, NCNCR, and the planners.

There is one other significant center of interaction—the mayor's office. In a certain sense, Newark urban renewal is a dual system or, more accurately, a system within a system. NHA became the major center of interaction in part because Mayor Carlin refused to make his own office the major center. The quiescence of the executive-centered system permitted, and perhaps required, NHA to construct an alternative system.

Mayor Carlin's role in the NHA-centered system was, in effect, a judicial one. In contrast to NHA's staff, Mayor Carlin rarely initiated interaction. He was the court of last appeals for those who did not receive satisfaction from NHA. He generally intervened in renewal politics only after he had been urged to do so by one of the regular participants. He also intervened, on his own initiative, to help break deadlocks in negotiation.

The pattern of the division of labor between Danzig and Carlin corresponds to the instrumental and expressive aspects of social systems. Danzig pressed the system toward its goals, while Carlin kept the system from flying apart. Danzig was goal-oriented; Carlin was more interested in smoothing ruffled feelings and urging disgruntled participants back to the bargaining table. The mayor's office is more firmly committed to preserving the system's harmony and high productivity than to attaining any particular version of policy.

The size and permeability of the system have been defined largely by NHA and largely in accordance with the nature of the renewal function and with the requirements of local approval contained in state and federal statutes.[8] The Authority has consciously sought good working relations with the mayor's office, whose support is obviously indispensable to the local approval of a project. The legal endorsement of the City Council and CPB is also required, but NHA has assumed that they would follow the mayor's lead. The Authority has also sought to accommodate the local corporations, who can contribute a great deal to the program's ultimate success in terms of prestige, funds, and business contacts.

Other local interests, like NCNCR and the city planners, have had to pry their way into the system, first acquiring some form of leverage over NHA. Carlin's insistence that NHA clear rehabilitation legislation with NCNCR, for instance, provided the Committee with such leverage. Interests that could not acquire this leverage—site residents, for example—have had to try to weaken the system by pressuring its more responsive participants. Overt attack and denunciation have been the weapons of the outsider and have been largely unsuccessful.

Newark's urban renewal system, then, is a relatively small and closed circle. In part this reflects the nature of the system's central activity—slum clearance—and the kind of legal requirements that surround it. In urban renewal the major inputs come from outside the local system, that is, from the federal government and the private redevelopers. The active cooperation of only a few public officials is absolutely essential to the success of a clearance project. All that NHA requires of other local groups is their nonintervention. Widespread participation in slum clearance politics, far from being necessary, often proves disastrous. In this respect clearance might well be distinguished from rehabilitation, which requires the active cooperation of site residents and neighborhood groups.

There is also reason to believe that limited membership and relative impermeability are aspects of all well-integrated systems. Interrelated and stable roles probably cannot develop in an aggregate of independent actors that is too large. Newark's renewal politics would probably become less stable if additional interests, like the City Council or the county Democratic party, were included in the renewal system. Stable social systems also require a clear distinction between members and nonmembers and some barriers to separate the two categories. Entrance into a stable system cannot be too easy, or the system will be subject to constant disruptions from without.

The urban renewal system in Newark may be viewed as a small circle of urban renewal professionals, who devote most of the working day to housing and renewal affairs. Most members are staff men, like Danzig, Conner, Oberlander, and Busse—men for whom participation in urban renewal is part of the job. Most participants, moreover, have official or quasi-official responsibilities for some aspect of the renewal problem. In a sense, they are all administrators. The renewal system exists almost entirely within the formal governmental structure. All the members, consequently, have a degree of expert knowledge in renewal matters and share a common technical vocabulary. If they do not agree on all aspects of the renewal program, they do at least have similar administrative problems, a common interest in the policies of federal housing agencies, and a common concern over "obstructionists" and grass roots opposition.

If any interest groups are represented in the system, they are groups like the realtors, the downtown corporations, and the planners, whose stake in renewal is professional and long-range. The site residents, small businessmen, neighborhood associations, and others more immediately affected by renewal decisions tend to be "obstructionists" and "outsiders." Yet, even the spokesmen of the represented groups are relatively insulated from the demands of their constituents and are able to bargain freely with other spokesmen. Most of them agree that quasi-official status has given them more discretion and less visibility than they had as staff members of interest groups.

The nature of the system's membership strongly influences the kinds of claims made on NHA and the terms of exchange between NHA and each of the participants. What debate there is within the system tends to center around long-range and relatively abstract goals like central planning, reviving downtown, and containing the slums. This often is reduced to a debate over procedure: whether the city planners, or NCNCR, or NEDC will have an institutionalized part in NHA's policy process, thus permitting them to impress their long-range values on the renewal program. If a specific NHA decision is informally challenged by a member of the system, it is apt to be because of the way in which that decision was made. Only the politicos have been more interested in the specific content of NHA decisions than in the decision-making process.

The resulting settlements between NHA and the other participants did not involve any change in NHA's policy-making procedures or any marked intervention in the work of its staff. Instead, additional renewal committees were formed, permitting the realtors and the corporation executives to pursue their renewal goals separately. These settlements may have preserved NHA's internal procedures, but they also drew boundaries around NHA's influence in urban renewal. NHA could continue to make its own decisions and secure local approval of them, but it could not prevent some renewal plans from being formulated elsewhere. To an extent, initiative had been diffused.

The diffusion of the system, however, is less than a formal organization chart would imply. The renewal committees soon learned that they could not attain their respective goals without applying to NHA for help on staff, funds, expertise, and access to federal agencies. Thus, NHA has remained the major center of interaction and initiative.

In a sense, the civic leaders were co-opted into the renewal system. Instead of achieving an institutionalized role in NHA's procedures, they attained quasi-official status to pursue their goals separately. The urban renewal system in Newark is largely an intra-bureaucratic one. This helps explain why much of the internal debate has focused on the process of decision making and the jurisdiction of various renewal agencies.

Despite this limited diffusion of initiative, NHA has largely attained the kind of local political structure it initially sought. From Mayor Carlin NHA attained what amounted to a promise of active cooperation in pressing renewal plans through the Council and CPB. From each of the other major participants NHA in effect secured an agreement to refrain from interfering in the Authority's policy process and to go along with the final decisions.

The stable relations that make up a social system generally involve reciprocity or an exchange of values. In return for the above commitments, NHA had to make certain commitments of its own. Yet, none of the Authority's commitments impaired its control of clearance policy or altered the substance of its policies. NHA spent resources unrelated to clearance policy in order to improve its control of that policy. For example, NHA could lend some of the drama and prestige of urban renewal to other participants without jeopardizing the success of the program. It could also fortify the insulation of its policy-making processes by lending others its expertise, its staff, and its access to federal officials.

Sayre and Kaufman speak of environmental accommodations that imprison an administrative agency and those that liberate it.[9] By reaching an accommodation with its environment on terms unrelated to the substance of policy, NHA has liberated its policy-making processes from intervention and direct pressure.

An emphasis on the *quid pro quo* in political relations, however, has its limitations. It fails to explain, for example, why actors who derive negligible benefits from the Newark system still remain committed to that system.

Norms or common values, like the widespread commitment to reviving Newark, are important in holding the system together. While the system must provide benefits to its members in order to endure, the rewards need not be tangible, extensive, or unfailing. Moreover, established relations have a certain inertia, which only the repeated frustration of a participant's interests can disrupt. Finally, the kind and amount of rewards a system must provide are commensurate with the demands that a system makes of its participants. In instances like Newark renewal, where the scope of the roles is relatively narrow and the content of the roles more prohibitive than obligatory, fewer rewards are needed to maintain the system.

There is another reason that the terms "rewards" and "*quid pro quo*" should not be overemphasized, and that is the low temperature and intensity of Newark's renewal politics.[10] Most participants, outside of NHA, have proved relatively listless in the pursuit of their goals. Many reiterate their support for a goal and then easily accept NHA's alternative or compromise proposal. Many seem to back off at a crucial moment in some controversy, permitting NHA to win by default. Most participants could probably expand their own role in the system and shrink NHA's, but few are prepared to make the effort. The model of alert interests, strongly committed to their goals and prepared to press these goals at every occasion, does not apply to Newark renewal. The slackness of the Newark system has enabled NHA, the major value-dispensing agency, to manage with minimal concessions.

The low intensity of Newark's renewal politics can be explained partly by the political inexperience of most participants. The civic leaders and their spokesmen generally found political conflict highly distasteful and sought harmony on almost any terms. They were unfamiliar with the bargaining process in politics and proved to be poor negotiators. They were often willing to settle for symbolic or statutory gains, for the form rather than the substance of power. Added to these factors was the uncertain commitment of most civic leaders to Newark's future and their penchant for periodic withdrawals from local politics.

In addition, many of the participants seem more strongly committed to participation of politics per se than to the attainment of any substantive goals. Political participation may give an individual the satisfaction of knowing he is helping the city, a certain amount of prestige and a reputation for being powerful, access to information or an ability to be "in the know," and a possible steppingstone to higher political office. The publicity value of urban renewal was particularly important to Mayor Carlin when he began making renewal the hallmark of his administration.

As noted earlier, NHA can freely lend to others the prestige and drama of urban renewal without damaging the program. The "New Newark" doctrine, by thrusting NHA into the background and emphasizing the role of other participants, does just this. It spreads the prestige of civic participation and the reputation for power to all members of the system.

If there have been no overwhelming incentives for cooperating with NHA, neither have there been any for obstructionism. As the conservatism of the civic leaders steadily weakened, the only major division in the system over ideology or substantive policy disappeared. For most local actors there has been no reason not to support NHA's proposals. The realization that opposition to NHA's proposals would jeopardize the continuance of federal aid has usually been sufficient to override any mild dissension.

NHA's accommodative problem, then, was greatly lessened because the Authority and the various participants wanted different things of the program. Their renewal goals were not in conflict; satisfying one demand did not mean sacrificing another. Many participants, for example, had little interest in helping shape NHA's decisions on general clearance policy. Under these conditions reciprocal relations built on a division of labor and mutual noninterference proved possible.

PRECONDITIONS

This study has been largely concerned with the way in which the urban renewal system emerged. The origins of the stable relations that make up Newark's renewal system have been traced to the political settlements reached by NHA and each of the major participants. The term "settlement" has frequently been used to describe any resolution of a controversial question. Some settlements, however, may succeed in structuring the future behavior of those involved. The scope of a settlement can be defined by the area of participant behavior that it reduces to predictability.

Settlements of a somewhat broad scope, as evidenced in Newark renewal, tend to be cumulative. Once the mayor's office and the administrative agencies had settled with NHA, the other local participants had little choice but to seek similar settlements with the Authority. As the number of settlements grew, the system became better integrated and better able to accommodate or withstand new actors.[11]

Why this system emerged in Newark and what the preconditions for its emergence were are highly important questions, not fully dealt with in this study. Another study might treat the system described above as a dependent variable and would try to relate its existence to broader environmental factors. Such a study might begin with the following hypothesis.

One precondition of the emergence of the urban renewal system in Newark was the presence of skilled political entrepreneurs who undertook to build major portions of that system. NHA officials have always stressed the superiority of stable working relations to the ad hoc coalition. In addition, these officials have mustered the initiative and political skills necessary to secure stable relations. This point is reinforced by the similarity of the Newark system to the supportive systems that form around other alert, skilled agencies. The Port of New York Authority, New York's Triborough Bridge and Tunnel Authority, the U.S. Army Corps of Engineers, and the Tennessee Valley Authority would be cases in point. The comparison goes further. At the core of most of these systems are skilled political entrepreneurs like Robert Moses, Austin Tobin, or Louis Danzig.

These similarities suggest another hypothesis: that such systems are more likely to form around public construction activities, around local activities receiving federal aid, and around the activities of independent government corporations.[12]

Public construction activities may be more conducive to such systems because, as suggested earlier, they do not require the active cooperation of very many interests. They do not, for example, require the active support of the agency's clientele as much as neighborhood rehabilitation and regulatory activities do. Approval by the local governing body is sufficient; all other interests need only acquiesce or remain inert. This is particularly true when nonlocal agents provide most of the funds for such construction.

In addition, new highways, housing, or public buildings have a certain drama and popularity with which the construction agency can easily identify itself. Such agencies often have the benefit of a good press and a favorable climate of mass opinion. Public construction units also have the advantage, which regulatory bodies lack, of being significant spending agencies. Such expenditures, and the staff and expertise these agencies accumulate, are important political resources. Because of these resources construction agencies, unlike regulatory agencies, can reach an accommodation with their environment without sacrificing the substance of their policies.

The vesting of redevelopment powers in Newark's public housing authority was a crucial step toward renewal success. It permitted NHA to transfer to redevelopment the staff, expertise, influence at City Hall, and access to federal officials that it had amassed in public housing. Legal independence also gave the renewal entrepreneurs the flexibility they needed in negotiating with other participants.

No element in this equation is more important than an agency's access to large amounts of federal aid. Such access releases the agency from direct financial dependence on the local government and insulates it from local budgetary controls. Federal aid enables NHA to build the staff resources it needs to facilitate local approval of projects. Because NHA's policies are synonymous with federal aid, moreover, NHA's critics tend to smother their criticisms rather than jeopardize the influx of aid.

NHA's success in the local system depends upon its success in another system, a system circumscribed by the demands of URA, FHA, and the private redevelopers. NHA's top staff men also have to maintain an integrated system within NHA, that is, to prove successful in their dealings with the NHA commissioners and the

Authority's lesser staff. Success in any one of these systems (the internal, the local, and the nonlocal) breeds success in the others. There is also a cycle of failure. Success or failure in any aspect of the agency's activities tends to be cumulative.

There are other preconditions of the urban renewal system that relate to certain aspects of Newark's governmental structure and electoral politics and certain aspects of the broader socio-economic environment.

To a large extent the system rests on the mayor's ability to secure City Hall approval of NHA's plans and on the mayor's willingness to give NHA a free hand in policy formation. The "strong mayor" charter adopted in 1954 helped stabilize the renewal system by concentrating power at City Hall. This charter, plus the City Council's own willingness to approve almost all of the mayor's proposals, relieved NHA of the necessity of dealing directly with the Council. It is true that NHA was able to originate and maintain good relations with City Hall under the city-commission form of government, but NHA officials have much preferred dealing with a single center of authority at City Hall.

Danzig's insistence on a free hand in policy questions and Carlin's willingness to grant this can be explained, at least in part, in terms of personalities. It is also likely that Newark's particular brand of nonpartisan politics increased the elected officials' preoccupation with "political considerations" and made such an agreement between Carlin and Danzig more feasible. In the absence of overt or covert activity by the regular party organizations, each candidate must build his own electoral organization. The turnover at City Hall tends to be high. In such a fluid situation the help of a major agency like NHA with small "political considerations" and favors can be crucial to a politico. Nonpartisan politics has also impeded the rise of a city-wide party machine which would serve as a counterweight to NHA's influence.

The importance of NHA's cooperation on "political" matters was enhanced by Mayor Carlin's economy drive, including his policy of not filling governmental positions that became vacant. With the City's payroll declining, most politicos channeled their requests to independent agencies like the Board of Education and

NHA. In addition, this freeze on new personnel curbed the activities of the planning office, NCNCR, and NEDC, and encouraged these agencies to turn to NHA for advice and staff assistance.

The renewal system in Newark is subject to little pressure from the larger political community. One explanation is that the Newark public is "underorganized," or less prone to form politically oriented groups, than the publics of other cities. If this is true, the low temperature of Newark's renewal politics would reflect the low temperature of Newark politics in general.

"Joining" and civic participation are often alleged to be most characteristic of the middle and upper-middle class.[13] Low political involvement and low participation are associated with low-income, low-education, nonwhite, and mobile or transient groups. If these assertions are correct, the underorganization of Newark politics can be explained, at least in part, by the flight of its middle and upper classes to the suburbs and by the great influx of nonwhites. The very mobility of Newark's population, regardless of which groups are leaving and arriving, may also help explain the dearth of politically oriented interest groups.

There is another aspect to the passivity of the system's broader environment. In Newark, as in many other cities, there is a gap between the electoral system and the policy-making system. The former focuses on the filling of elective and appointive positions; the latter focuses on broad issues and the substance of policy. One is concerned with favors, considerations, and the detailed application of policy; the other is interested in policy at its most general level. There tends to be a different set of actors in each of the two systems, with little interaction occurring between the two sets.[14]

Most of the groups remaining in Newark or recently arriving there have focused their demands on the electoral system. The demand of most labor unions and Negro leaders has been "fair representation" on the City Council and in appointive offices and a "fair share" in the distribution of favors and considerations. They have had little influence in the broad policy-making areas. Those groups who traditionally had favored participation in policy making and had disdained any involvement in electoral politics were the very groups who fled to the suburbs. Their departure, and the political vacuum this departure created, may explain why some municipal agencies, like NHA, have had great discretion in forming policy.

Eventually, some of these former residents—namely, the realtors and corporation executives—reluctantly agreed to a limited form of participation in policy areas like urban renewal. But the basic outline of the urban renewal system had already been solidified in their absence.

SOURCES OF CHANGE AND INSTABILITY

Many of the prerequisites described in the preceding section are unlikely to change during the 1960s. Others are more volatile and may be viewed as the system's major instabilities.

The mayor, as the only elected official in the renewal system, represents that system's most vulnerable point. There are always dangers accompanying the election of a new mayor, even though NHA has bridged such transitions before. More threatening is the possibility of a growing fractionalization of power at City Hall. Whether the business administrator and members of the City Council could be incorporated in the system without damaging its cohesion is questionable.

The regular participation of the Essex County Democratic organization in Newark's politics would have sweeping, but not entirely predictable, consequences. It probably would reduce the value most politicos place on NHA's "political considerations." It might require NHA to bring the county chairman into the network of negotiations. Beyond this, however, its effects are speculative.

Finally, there is a possibility that the broader political environment will become more vocal as the program matures, as population movements stabilize, and as the Negroes become better organized.

CHAPTER IX

Postscript: 1963

The research for this study was completed in the summer of 1960. During the subsequent process of writing and revision it was tempting, at various points in the text, to allude to events that have occurred since then. But, since no systematic study of the 1960–63 period proved possible, it was considered more prudent to let this study stand as a survey of the first eleven years in Newark renewal and to add a short postscript. This chapter notes briefly some of the major events of 1960–63 that concerned NHA's program. To reinterview the major participants was not feasible. Thus, in contrast to the preceding chapters, the following comments are based entirely on written records and newspaper accounts. The chapter deals largely with overt events rather than with the status of NHA's informal relations with the other renewal participants.[1]

The 1960–63 period was one of continued progress for NHA and saw the realization of many of its plans. One new project was initiated—a new, expanded center for the United Hospital Foundation in the downtown area. Most of the ambitious downtown proposals initiated in 1959 proceeded to the execution stage. Clearance began on the college expansion project and on Phase One of the South Broad Street project. Clearance was completed on the Hill Street site. In the other three downtown proposals—Penn Plaza (renamed Newark Plaza), Seton Hall, and Essex Heights—blight was declared by CPB, and NHA is awaiting final local and federal approval of the renewal plans.

Of NHA's three earliest projects the North Ward project alone is completed. Its middle-income housing was fully tenanted by the beginning of 1961. In the Central Ward renewal area the two public housing projects are open for occupancy, and clearance has begun on the redevelopment portions. A seven-block area was cleared and turned over to the Board of Education. Four other blocks were also demolished. On the Jeliffe Avenue project, now called Newark Industrial Park, NHA is awaiting final local and federal approval of its renewal plan. Clearance should begin early in 1964.

Many of NHA's projects have expanded in size since their original conception. The Parker site has grown, and the federal government increased the grant reserved for it to $6.6 million. St. Michael's Hospital decided to expand its facilities as part of the college expansion project. The federal commitment on this project is now $7.7 million. The Jeliffe Avenue proposal also has grown in size and cost since 1960. As of April, 1963, URA had reserved but not yet spent approximately $65 million for Newark clearance.

NHA officials, encouraged by expressions of interest by redevelopers in the possibilities of building in the Central Ward, revised their original pessimism about the prospects of Title I in the Negro area. They revised the Central Ward Urban Renewal Plan to provide for more clearance and less rehabilitation in that area. This interest on the part of redevelopers probably attests to the cumulative nature of renewal success. Title I in the Central Ward probably would not be possible had it not been for the wholesale redevelopment of adjacent areas.

Table 5 indicates that Newark still ranks high among the nation's leading urban renewal cities.

Though proud of their achievements, NHA officials remain keenly aware of the shortcomings of their program. NHA has recognized from the outset that the apartments planned for the downtown area will not be true middle-income housing. For close to a decade NHA's staff has argued that apartments at moderate rents were not possible in a high-tax, high-wage area like Newark without prior changes in federal or state housing legislation. During 1960–63 NHA, working through NJAHRO, pressed for new state legislation which would permit the redevelopers in NHA's downtown projects to lower their proposed rentals. At the same time NHA sought state legislation that would empower local housing authorities to construct and operate middle-income housing projects, just as they were already operating low-rent housing.

NHA also sought FHA's cooperation in an attempt to lower the interest rate charged on loans to redevelopers.

In 1961 the New Jersey Legislature passed the Fox-Lance-Crane bill, giving tax relief to developers and redevelopers who agreed to limited dividends and moderate rentals. NHA soon announced that this legislation would be applied to four downtown proposals

TABLE 5

FEDERAL FUNDS SPENT IN THE FIFTEEN LEADING
URBAN RENEWAL CITIES, 1949–1962

City	Total Federal Funds Spent (in millions of dollars) [a]
New York	143.3
Chicago	108.0
Philadelphia	79.6
Baltimore	54.6
Washington, D.C.	52.4
Pittsburgh	43.8
Cleveland	40.8
New Haven	38.6
St. Louis	35.4
Newark	34.5 [b]
Detroit	34.4
Norfolk	33.9
Cincinnati	29.1
Memphis	23.2
Minneapolis	19.5

[a] Includes grants for both clearance and rehabilitation.
[b] Includes grants for Clinton Hill rehabilitation project.
SOURCE: URA, *Urban Renewal Project Characteristics* (Washington, D.C., 1962).

—South Broad, Hill Street, Essex Heights, and Newark Plaza—and might serve to lower the rentals planned for these projects. The bill permitting housing authorities to construct middle-income housing twice passed the Assembly but twice failed in the state Senate.

In 1961 NHA received a firm proposal from a redeveloper interested in building an industrial park on the Jeliffe Avenue site. The redeveloper apparently wanted a slightly larger site than NHA had originally planned. With URA approval NHA agreed to expand the project area by adding several blocks to the south of the original site. This decision provoked the first overt controversy over NHA since the North Ward incident in 1952. The residents of Clinton Hill, CHNC, and Councilwoman Sophie Cooper of the South Ward felt that NHA's proposal introduced light industry into heretofore residential areas and further contributed to the decline of the Clinton Hill neighborhood. Enlarging the project also provoked concern among many Negro leaders in the Central Ward over the increased number of Negroes who would be displaced. The fact that a larger project meant additional displaced Negro families was also apparent to the Clinton Hill leaders. They knew that NHA would relocate most of these Negro families in Clinton Hill; they charged NHA with deliberately upsetting their attempt to create a balanced, integrated neighborhood.

Other than calling for a humane relocation policy that would avoid the creation of new ghettos, the Negro leaders did not openly oppose the project. The Clinton Hill leaders, on the other hand, made a major effort to prevent City Council approval of the renewal plan or, as an alternative, to force NHA to move the boundaries northward. Despite this opposition, in 1962 CPB officially declared the area blighted, the City Council ratified the declaration, and URA gave final federal approval to the expanded project. A suit to have the blight declaration reversed is still pending; a similar suit involving the North Ward was dismissed by the courts in 1953.

It now appears that public housing in Newark is far from dead and that NHA will gain local approval of additional projects. In recent years NHA has continued to move very cautiously on this question. After the 1957 announcement of a 1,680-unit project—now called Edward Scudder Homes—as part of Central Ward renewal, NHA did not make any major public housing proposal for six years. During that period it did, however, add 746 new units designed for elderly persons onto existing projects. Some of these units were approved by CPB and the City Council over the objections of the City Planning Officer.

Throughout this six-year period NHA remained convinced that the dimensions of the relocation problem would all but compel

City officials to accept more public housing. In March, 1963, after the election of Hugh Addonizio as Mayor, Danzig asked local approval of 2,500 new public housing units, 2,000 of which would be designed for elderly persons and 500 for large families. Although the City Council has delayed NHA's application and raised several questions about it, the chances are good that it will be approved.

The other renewal agencies have continued to play peripheral roles in the clearance program. NCNCR and the City Planning Office now feel that the amount of clearance planned for the Clinton Hill project is so great that the project might best be turned over to NHA. NCNCR probably sympathized with CHNC's objections to the southward expansion of the light industrial project but made no public comment on this issue. The final report of CPB's Demonstration Grant Project, like the earlier reports, focused on nonclearance activities. It said that NHA's clearance program should have major priority in the renewal program for the next four or five years and urged the municipal government to cooperate with NHA in speeding up the execution of its projects. NEDC dissolved after Leo Carlin's defeat in the 1962 mayoralty election. In 1963 Mayor Addonizio created the Newark Industrial Development Commission to focus on heavy industry in the outlying meadows. The City Council took a somewhat recalcitrant stand on a number of NHA's applications. The councilmen continued their campaign for an amendment to the City Charter which would vest the appointment of NHA commissioners in the City Council. Their campaign was not successful, and, in the end, the Council passed all of NHA's proposals.

There have been no apparent changes in the internal organization of NHA or in the NHA Board of Commissioners' firm support of their Executive Director. Commissioner Spatola continued his attack on Danzig's "high-handed practices" and on the Board's quiescence. The other NHA commissioners continued to denounce Spatola's attacks and to reiterate their high opinion of Danzig. In 1961 the NHA Board voted full discretion to its staff members in all matters not involving the expenditure of funds. In submitting applications to URA and resolutions to CPB or the City Council,

Danzig may now act first and ask for ratification at the next meeting of the Board.

Along with all the other NHA commissioners, Spatola voted in favor of full discretion. A few weeks later, however, he tried unsuccessfully to have his vote reversed. In September, 1961, Spatola introduced a resolution which would have permitted NHA commissioners to caucus without Danzig before each meeting. It was defeated by a five-to-one vote. When Spatola's term ended in 1962, Carlin refused to reappoint him on the grounds that he had created unnecessary dissension in the Housing Authority.

In 1960 Joseph Nevin retired as Director of Redevelopment, and Albert Walker was named in his place. Nevin has continued to serve NHA in an advisory capacity.

The major events of 1962 were the decision of Congressman Hugh Addonizio to challenge Leo Carlin's bid for a third term as mayor and Addonizio's overwhelming victory on May 8. As a Congressman and member of the Housing Subcommittee of the House Banking and Currency Committee, Addonizio had been a leading supporter of the urban renewal program and one of NHA's important contacts in Washington. During the mayoralty campaign Addonizio attacked Carlin for not moving fast enough on urban renewal and for not being sufficiently in command of the program. Addonizio criticized the new boundaries of the Jeliffe Avenue project and promised Clinton Hill residents that he would review this decision. On the whole, however, he praised NHA's projects and promised faster action on all phases of urban renewal.

The election of Addonizio was followed by one of the most radical change-overs in government personnel Newark had witnessed in many years. Almost all of the leading City Hall officials, including civil servants with tenure, resigned, and their positions were filled with a crop of new men. The Carlin era, which had lasted almost ten years, was over. Some observers added that the era of Irish dominance of Newark politics was also over.

In view of the radical change-over at City Hall, NHA's personnel remained remarkably stable. It is possible, although not certain, that changes in personnel occurred at the secretarial and clerical level of NHA's staff; it is likely that this would be part of Danzig's accommodation to the new regime. But none of NHA's leading staff officials left in the year following Addonizio's inauguration. Danzig seems to have stuck to his policy of keeping appointments outside of City Hall "politics."

A more important question is whether Addonizio's election will alter NHA's dominant position in the urban renewal system. Two highly tentative answers can be given. It seems likely that Addonizio will do nothing to disrupt the complicated network of relations that NHA has built over the last fifteen years. To do so would be to disrupt the entire renewal program after Addonizio had promised a speeding up of renewal progress. At the same time, Addonizio seems eager to secure a larger role in renewal politics than Carlin sought. He probably will be more in command of the program than his predecessor was and less willing to give NHA a completely free hand. Exactly what kind of role the new Mayor will play in renewal and whether his intervention will impede NHA's dealings with redevelopers and federal agencies by curtailing its discretion are still unanswered questions. There are only a few clues, which, inadequate as they are, should be noted.

Shortly after his inauguration, Addonizio asked Danzig to a conference on urban renewal and urged Danzig to reconsider certain aspects of the Jeliffe Avenue project. The Mayor urged some changes in the renewal plan to provide for more housing and neighborhood rehabilitation and for somewhat less industry. This apparently was the Mayor's, or NHA's, solution to the problem of Clinton Hill opposition and Addonizio's campaign promises. Rather than cut back the size of the project, NHA would eliminate industry from the southern section. In the following months NHA did in fact revise its renewal plan along these lines.

If NHA's discretion may be curbed somewhat by the new Mayor's activism, the Authority may also benefit from that activism. In March, 1963, Mayor Addonizio called a meeting of NHA, URA, and FHA officials in order to speed up renewal progress and to explore ways of lowering the rentals planned in the new projects. Addonizio seemed to accept Danzig's argument that FHA's extreme caution in insuring mortgages and its high interest rates on loans to redevelopers were at the root of Newark's renewal problems. The new Mayor invited Newark's three Congressmen and New Jersey's two Senators to this meeting to support his plea for a more expeditious and sympathetic policy at FHA. Addonizio's long stay in Washington and the network of relations he built there may help NHA in its bargaining with the federal housing agencies.

Notes

Between January and May, 1960, approximately sixty personal interviews were held with approximately forty-five local participants. Most of the central actors discussed in this study were interviewed, and some were later interviewed for a second time. The guarantees of anonymity given to these participants preclude any citation of specific interviews; the Notes summarize only the written sources of information. It should be kept in mind, however, that a large part of this study rests on personal interviews and that interviews have supplemented the written sources in almost all of the Notes. Specific Notes indicate the places in which the written evidence has been particularly scanty and the reliance on interviews particularly great.

ABBREVIATIONS

In addition to those abbreviations used in the text, the following abbreviations appear in the Notes:

CC   Chamber of Commerce
Newark *News*   No distinction has been made between the Newark *Evening News* (six days a week) and the Newark *Sunday News*. Most agencies keep some kind of file of *News* clippings. In addition, the *News* has its own file room, and the Newark Public Library has the complete *News* on microfilm.
NHA-Redevel.   Newark Housing Authority sitting as the Newark Redevelopment Agency.

The location of unpublished sources of information is abbreviated and placed in parentheses:

(BMR)   Bureau of Municipal Research, Inc., 605 Broad Street, Newark, N.J.
(CC)   Chamber of Commerce, library now at the offices of the Commerce and Industry Association of Newark, 9 Clinton Street, Newark, N.J.
(CPB)   Newark Central Planning Board, City Hall, Newark, N.J.

(NCNCR)   Newark Commission on Neighborhood Conservation and Re-
             habilitation, City Hall, Newark, N.J.
(NHA)   Newark Housing Authority, 57 Sussex Avenue and 222
             Market Street, Newark, N.J.
(NPL)   New Jersey Room of the Newark Public Library (main
             branch), 5 Washington Avenue, Newark, N.J.
(REBON)   Real Estate Board of Newark, 901 Broad Street, Newark, N.J.

CHAPTER I. INTRODUCTION

1. A description of the urban renewal program and a good formula-
tion of the problems of renewal achievement can be found in Reuel
Hemdahl, *Urban Renewal* (New York, Scarecrow Press, 1959), es-
pecially pp. 280 ff., and in George Duggar's various articles, includ-
ing "Local Organization for Urban Renewal," *Public Management*,
XL, No. 7 (July, 1958), 158–63, and "Relation of Local Government
Structure to Urban Renewal," *Law and Contemporary Problems*,
XXVI (Winter, 1961), 49–69.

2. This chapter and the entire essay owe a major debt to the works
listed below.

For material on urban renewal as a political problem: Robert A.
Dahl, *Who Governs? Democracy and Power in an American City* (New
Haven, Yale University Press, 1961); Martin Meyerson and Edward
Banfield, *Politics, Planning, and the Public Interest* (Glencoe, Ill., Free
Press, 1955).

For material on agency and environment: Herbert Simon, Donald
Smithburg, and Victor Thompson, *Public Administration* (New York,
Knopf, 1950), especially Chapters 18 and 19; David B. Truman, *The
Governmental Process* (New York, Knopf, 1951), especially Chapter
14; Wallace S. Sayre and Herbert Kaufman, *Governing New York City:
Politics in the Metropolis* (New York, Russell Sage Foundation, 1960),
especially Chapters 8–10, 19.

CHAPTER II. NHA: THE STRATEGY OF SLUM CLEARANCE

1. The following account relies heavily on personal interviews and
NHA documents. NHA officials kindly permitted the author free access
to their files. They also proved most generous with their time. It should
not be concluded, however, that they agree with the final product.

The best written sources on NHA are its own documents: NHA
Minutes; NHA-Redevel. Minutes; *From the Ground Up* (1958); *Redevelopment Sites in Downtown Newark* (1959); *Construction Report*
(1956); *Rebuilding Newark* (1952); *Public Housing in Newark* (1944).
In addition: *New Jersey Revised Statutes*, Cum. Supp., 55:14A-3, 4,
6; New Jersey Department of Conservation and Economic Develop-

ment, Division of Planning and Development, *Directory of Local Housing Authorities and Redevelopment Agencies* (Trenton, N.J., 1959); New Jersey Legislature, *Report of the Legislative Middle Income Housing Study Commission* (Trenton, N.J., 1956).

2. *"Getting the Jump"*: NHA-Redevel. Minutes, April 12, June 14, Oct. 11, 1950; Newark *News*, Feb. 1, 4, April 27, 1950; City Commissioners' Minutes, July 27, Aug. 10, 24, Sept. 7, 21, 1949, Jan. 11, April 4, May 3, Nov. 8, 1950.

3. *The North Ward: Adjustments in Purpose:* NHA-Redevel. Minutes, Dec. 13, 1950, May 16, Sept. 19, Nov. 14, Dec. 12, 1951, Jan. 19, March 14, 1952; NHA Minutes, Jan. 7, 16, Feb. 7, Sept. 19, Nov. 14, 1951; NHA, Redevelopment Plan for the Branch Brook Park and Broad Street Redevelopment Projects (NJ UR 3–1, 3–2), approved Feb., 1953; other NHA publications cited in Note 1. See also: Newark *News*, Jan. 20, 1952; CC, The Practical Aspects of Middle Income Housing, 1959.

4. *The Central Ward: Redevelopment in the Ghetto:* NHA, Urban Renewal Plan: Old Third Ward Urban Renewal Project, tentative version, Jan., 1960; NHA publications cited in Note 1; NHA-Redevel. Minutes, April 13, June 1, 1955, Jan. 14, April 18, 1959, Jan. 13, 1960; Newark *News*, Dec. 19, 1954, March 13, 18, April 6, 10, 14, May 27, June 5, 19, 1955, Jan. 19, 27, 1956, Jan. 31, March 6, Aug. 16, 1957, Jan. 30, 1958.

5. *Industrial Redevelopment: All Rules Have Exceptions:* NEDC Minutes, March 23, May 4, June 1, 29, Sept. 28, Oct. 19, Dec. 21, 1955, Feb. 8, March 14, April 11, Oct. 10, Nov. 14, Dec. 12, 1956, March 13, June 12, Sept. 11, 1957; Newark *News*, March 21, Sept. 20, 1956, Nov. 13, 14, 19, Dec. 19, 1957, July 8, 13, Aug. 24, 1958.

6. *Rutgers and Seton Hall: Redevelopment for Institutional Use:* NHA-Redevel. Minutes, Oct. 8, 1958, April 8, July 8, Nov. 11, 1959; Newark *News*, Sept. 28, Oct. 9, 16, Nov. 16, 1958, Jan. 26, March 10, June 19, 23, July 2, 8, 9, 19, Sept. 28, 1959, Jan. 10, 1960.

7. *Reappraisal and Departure:* For the North Ward crisis see: NHA-Redevel. Minutes, May 16, Sept. 12, 1956, May 15, July 10, Oct. 16, 1957, Feb. 26, May 14, Oct. 31, 1958; Newark *News*, Nov. 16, 1958, Aug. 23, Oct. 11, 1959. The new strategy is described in: Louis Danzig, Housing and Urban Renewal Guides in the Development of Our City, June, 1959; Newark *News*, Oct. 5, 1959.

8. *The Downtown Program:* NHA-Redevel. Minutes, April 8, May 21, June 10, July 8, Oct. 14, Nov. 11, 1959; Newark *News*, Dec. 23, 1958, Jan. 9, March 8, May 23, June 14, 24, July 2, 8, 9, 10, 19, Oct. 4, 8, 15, 16, Nov. 5, Dec. 12, 17, 20, 1959, Jan. 10, 14, 1960.

9. *Staging a Project:* Since the statements in this and the following subsections are the author's own synthesis of personal interviews and

of a large body of written data, the sources of these statements cannot be precisely pinpointed. The generalizations are, to a large extent, documented and illustrated throughout the remainder of the study.

10. *Maintaining the Pace:* For the pyramiding of resources see Robert A. Dahl, *Who Governs? Democracy and Power in an American City* (New Haven, Yale University Press, 1961), Chapter 19; for the strategy of activism as practiced by independent authorities see Wallace S. Sayre and Herbert Kaufman, *Governing New York City: Politics in the Metropolis* (New York, Russell Sage Foundation, 1960), pp. 337–43.

CHAPTER III. THE POLITICOS

1. *Taking NHA out of "Politics":* This account of NHA in the 1940s and of the events in 1948 is based largely on interviews but can be glimpsed in the publications of NHA cited in Chapter II, Note 1. In addition, see: review articles in Newark *News,* Aug. 22, 1952, June 7, 1953, and Sept. 15, 1957; *The Realtor,* 1949, *passim.*

2. *The "Political" and the "Nonpolitical":* Statements in this section rely largely on personal interviews. The relevant NHA documents are: Personnel Report (presented by Executive Director at every Board meeting); Annual Report of the Tenant Selection and Relocation Division; Tenancy Report (periodically submitted to the Board), *passim.* The Newark *News* has carefully covered NHA's policies on the hiring of personnel, the awarding of contracts, and the selection and treatment of public housing tenants. Coverage during the 1953–54 change-over in government was particularly good. See: May 6, 10, June 7, 11, 30, July 5, 9, 16, 19, Aug. 2, 25, Sept. 23, Oct. 9, 23, 1953, Jan. 21, 30, March 5, 11, April 17, 31, May 13, 20, June 15, 17, 24, 25, July 22, Aug. 7, 9, 17, 18, 19, 22, 29, Sept. 16, 23, Oct. 21, 1954, Jan. 7, March 2, April 7, May 24, June 2, Sept. 22, Oct. 5, 11, 1955, Jan. 15, June 8, Aug. 9, Nov. 15, Dec. 13, 1956, Jan. 9, 10, March 1, 3, 15, 28, April 11, 26, May 3, 10, 11, 16, 24, June 13, Dec. 19, 1957, April 25, May 9, 31, June 19, July 11, Aug. 6, Sept. 28, Nov. 23, 1958.

3. *NHA and City Hall Politics:* Newark *News,* May 11, 1949, Feb. 12, 25, 1950; Newark *Star Ledger,* April 27, Dec. 14, 1950, Jan. 12, 1951, June 26, 1952, Jan. 16, 1953; City Commissioners' Minutes, Jan. 11, April 5, May 3, Nov. 8, 11, 1950, May 16, 23, June 13, Dec. 12, 1951, Jan. 9, June 25, July 9, 23, 1952, Jan. 21, April 29, June 10, 1953. For a general discussion of the period see Herbert Rosenbaum, Labor Unions and Their Leaders in Politics and Government of Newark and Essex County, New Jersey (Master's Essay, Columbia University, May, 1951). On the 1953–54 change-over see: Newark *News,* April 26, May 14, Nov. 4, 1953, March 6, May 5, 11, June 2, 16, 29, 30, 1954, March 29, June 2, 24, 1955, May 4, 1958; Charter Commission of Newark, *Final Report,* Sept., 1953; Stephen Decter, The Politics of

Municipal Charter Revision: Newark, New Jersey, 1947–1953 (senior thesis, Princeton University, 1959); "Home Rule Pays Dividends," *National Municipal Review*, XLIV (April, 1955), 176.

4. *NHA Commissioners and Their Staff:* NHA Minutes, especially June 14, Oct. 11, Dec. 13, 1950, Nov. 14, 1951, Oct. 8, 1953, May 12, 1954, May 15, 1956, June 11, 1958, April 8, Nov. 11, Dec. 9, 1959; NHA-Redevel. Minutes, especially April 13, 1950, Jan. 19, 1952, June 23, 1955, May 15, Oct. 31, Dec. 27, 1957, April 8, May 21, Oct. 14, Nov. 11, 1959, Jan. 13, 1960. Most of the generalizations in this section are nicely illustrated in the revolt of Commissioner Gerald Spatola: NHA Minutes, March 13, Aug. 8, Dec. 10, 1958, Jan. 14, 28, 1959; Newark *News*, June 13, 1957, Dec. 11, 17, 1958, Jan. 10, 15, 19, 20, 1959.

5. *NHA Commissioners and City Hall:* Newark *News*, May 28, June 6, Sept. 17, Nov. 5, 1953, April 15, May 13, 1954, March 2, April 24, June 2, 24, 1955, March 18, April 5, 1956, March 31, May 2, 1957, Feb. 2, 1958, March 5, 1959; NHA Minutes, Dec. 13, 1950, Nov. 14, 1951, July 16, 1952, Jan. 7, March 11, 1953, June 8, Oct. 28, Dec. 14, 1955, May 16, 1956, April 10, May 15, June 12, 1957, April 8, Nov. 11, 1959.

6. *The Politics of Acquiescence:* Newark Municipal Council, Annual Reports, 1955–1958; *City Administrative Code*, Sects. 2.20–2.29; City Council Minutes, June 15, July 5, Nov. 3, 1954, July 2, Sept. 20, 1955, May 15, June 15, 1957, Jan. 15, March 5, May 7, July 23, Aug. 20, 1958; Leo P. Carlin, "Progress for Newark," *National Municipal Review*, XLVI (Feb., 1957), 77; Leo P. Carlin, "Letter on Mayor-Council Relations," *National Municipal Review*, XLVII (Oct., 1958), 456; NHA-Redevel. Minutes, June 23, 1955, Sept. 12, 1956, May 14, 1958; Newark *News*, July 8, Oct. 14, 1954, Jan. 19, 22, 23, March 26, 29, May 20, 28, June 16, July 8, Aug. 18, Sept. 22, 1955, Nov. 18, 1956, June 16, Aug. 10, 1957, June 16, 28, 1958.

7. *NHA and the 1958 Elections:* The material for this and the following section are drawn from: Newark *News*, March 15, April 9, 26, May 3, 9, 14, 15, 17, 18, 20, 22, 23, 24, 31, June 2, 4, 14, 18, 19, 22, 28, July 2, Aug. 9, Nov. 29, Dec. 12, 21, 1958, Jan. 28, March 13, 21, April 19, July 8, 9, 10, 19, 23, Sept. 6, 12, 13, 26, Oct. 4, 5, 8, 15, 16, 19, Nov. 5, 12, 13, 17, 19, 24, Dec. 2, 3, 7, 8, 10, 12, 17, 20, 1959, Jan. 3, 7, 8, 14, 15, 20, 1960.
Some of the controversy surrounding the office of business administrator is covered in: Newark *Star Ledger*, June 18, 1954, Jan. 20, 1955, June 19, 22, July 2, 1958.

CHAPTER IV. THE CIVIC LEADERS: NEIGHBORHOOD REHABILITATION

1. The description of the role of the civic elite in Newark politics during the 1940s has been culled largely from personal interviews and from the files and publications of BMR, REBON, CC, and the Na-

tional Municipal League. The most useful publications have been: *The Realtor,* a monthly publication of REBON; *Memo,* periodically issued by BMR; *Pru News,* issued by the Prudential Life Insurance Company of America; *Newark Commerce,* published by CC; and the Newark *News.*

The isolation of the civic elite is evident in other cities as well: Robert O. Schulze, "The Bifurcation of Power in a Satellite City," in Morris Janowitz, ed., *Community Political Systems* (Glencoe, Ill., Free Press, 1961); Robert H. Salisbury, "St. Louis Politics: Relationships among Interests, Parties, and Governmental Structure," *Western Political Quarterly,* XIII (June, 1960), 498–507; Robert A. Dahl, *Who Governs? Democracy and Power in an American City* (New Haven, Yale University Press, 1961), Chapter 6.

2. *The Civic Elite and Public Housing: The Realtor,* March–Dec., 1949, April, Dec., 1950; CC, 82nd Annual Report of the Board of Directors, 1950; BMR, Annual Report, 1950; and miscellaneous material in the files of BMR and CC. In addition, see Chapter III, Note 1.

3. *The Civic Leaders and the Grass Roots:* The publications and records of CHC can be found in NPL and in the files of BMR and CC. CHC's history is covered in the Newark *News,* Nov. 8–12, 17, Dec. 3, 8, 10, 15, 28, 1949, Jan. 2, 17, Feb. 10, 21, March 8, Oct. 30, Nov. 1, 1950, Jan. 9, April 27, Oct. 24, 25, 30, 1951, June 8, 14, Aug. 10, Oct. 16, 1952, Jan. 22, May 10, June 7, 14, Aug. 11, Sept. 16, 17, Oct. 9, Nov. 17, 1953, March 31, May 23, Sept. 21, Dec. 9, 1954, Sept. 25, 1955.

4. *The Civic Elite and Urban Redevelopment:* For NHA's relations with local business see: Minutes of meeting of Board of Directors of Chamber of Commerce, Dec. 20, 1949; "Urban Redevelopment in Newark," an address by Louis Danzig, Dec. 20, 1949; letter from Charles Watts to Board of Directors of Chamber of Commerce, Dec. 8, 1949; BMR *Memo,* March 6, 1950; letter from President of Chamber of Commerce to its members, May 8, 1950; other material in CC's files.

For NHA's relations with REBON see: *The Realtor,* Jan., Feb., March, 1950, June, Sept., Oct., Dec., 1951, March, May, July, Aug., Oct., 1952, Jan., Feb., March, April, 1953; Newark *News,* Jan. 27, Feb. 3, 1950, Jan. 24, 30, Feb. 18, 25, March 2, 27, Aug. 22, 1952, April 16, Sept. 27, 1953; and material in files of NHA and CC.

5. *Re-emergence of the Elite: The Realtor,* Jan., June, Sept., 1951, April, 1952, Jan.–Dec., 1953; Newark *News,* June 14, 1953, Sept. 17, 21–29, 1953, May 17, 18, 1954, Feb. 18, 19, 23, March 9, 1955; NAREB, Blueprint for Neighborhood Conservation, 1954; BMR *Memo,* 1953–1955; CC, Annual Reports, 1951–1955; Henry Conner and Clayton Cronkwright, Some Suggestions for City Development (CC).

6. *The Citizen Advisory Committee:* The statements in this section

are the author's own conclusions. Information on the internal structure and operations of the two committees is found in: NEDC Minutes, *passim;* NCNCR Minutes, *passim;* NCNCR, Annual Reports, *passim;* NCNCR, Budget Reports, *passim; Neighborhood Conservation Newsletter,* a publication of NCNCR, 1956–1960; *Neighborhood News,* a monthly publication of CHNC, 1956–1960; Office of the Mayor, Annual Reports on the Strengthening of the Workable Program, *passim;* and material in NCNCR's files and the personal files of some NEDC members. In addition, see Note 1 in this chapter.

7. *NHA and NCNCR: Round One:* Newark *News,* Sept. 18, 29, Oct. 5, 1953, March 19, 20, 24, April 6, Oct. 6, 11, 27, Dec. 28, 29, 1954, April 21, Jan. 4, April 7, 21, May 4, 1955; BMR *Memo,* May, July, Dec., 1955. The record of NCNCR's activities since 1955 is available in: NCNCR Minutes, May 3, 17, June 7, Sept. 15, Nov. 1, 15, Dec. 7, 1955; Reports of Subcommittee on Code Enforcement, *passim;* NCNCR Policies and Procedures, Nov., 1955.

8. *Round Two: State Enabling Legislation:* NCNCR Minutes, Dec. 7, 1955, March 6, May 1, 8, 15, June 12, July 10, Sept. 11, Nov. 7, 27, Dec. 12, 1956, Jan. 8, 1957; Newark *News,* March 25, Nov. 2, 1955, March 7, April 11, May 1, 3, 6, 16, June 7, 10, 13, 20, July 7, 1956, Jan. 10, Oct. 17, 1957; BMR, Proposed Supplements to the Housing and Redevelopment Laws, April, 1956 (BMR).

9. *Round Three: Local Ordinance and Settlement:* NCNCR Minutes, April 11, Dec. 6, 1955, March 6, April 3, Oct. 9, Nov. 27, Dec. 11, 1956, Jan. 8, 27, May 28, July 18, 23, Aug. 7, 20, Oct. 1, 8, 15, 1957, Jan. 8, 1959; Newark *News,* May 3, Sept. 12, 26, 28, Oct. 10, 21, 23, 1956; NHA-Redevel. Minutes, Oct. 16, 1957; and material in NCNCR's files.

10. *The Settlement in Force:* Newark *News,* June 12, 13, 1955, Dec. 13, 1956, Feb. 24, March 14, 24, 29, April 9, May 1, 15, June 19, Aug. 7, 8, 22, Sept. 5, 11, 19, Oct. 2, 1957, Jan. 14, 18, 22, Feb. 5, 8, April 7, 23, May 19, July 7, 9, Aug. 15, Sept. 30, Oct. 2, 13, 16, 24, Dec. 12, 1958, Jan. 7, 10, Oct. 7, 26, 1959; NCNCR Minutes, Aug. 7, Oct. 10, 1957, June 16, Nov. 17, 1959; and material in files of NCNCR and CC.

11. *Political Settlement and Administrative Coordination:* On the values of administrative pluralism see: Samuel P. Huntington, *The Common Defense: Strategic Programs in National Politics* (New York, Columbia University Press, 1961), pp. 146–74, 378–81.

CHAPTER V. THE CIVIC LEADERS: ECONOMIC DEVELOPMENT

1. The general sources on NEDC are reviewed in Chapter IV, Note 1. For NEDC's first half-year see: NEDC Minutes, Feb. 18, March 9, 23, April 19, May 4, June 1, 15, Sept. 28, Oct. 19, 1955; Reports of NEDC's Subcommittee on Parking and Subcommittee on Highways,

passim; Newark *News,* Feb. 19, March 9, 13, April 14, May 5, 1955.

2. *NHA and NEDC: The Beginning of Negotiations:* NEDC Minutes, May 4, Dec. 7, 21, 1955, March 14, April 11, Nov. 14, 1956; Reports of NEDC's Subcommittee on the Financing of Enterprises, *passim;* Newark *News,* Sept. 13, 14, 16, 20, 1956. The account of Vieser's role in the North Ward project is based largely on interviews. For more information on North Ward see Chapter II, Note 3.

3. *Light Industrial Redevelopment:* For sources see Chapter II, Note 5.

4. *The Early Stages of Penn Plaza:* NEDC Minutes, Feb. 18, March 9, 23, April 19, May 4, June 15, Aug. 10, 24, Nov. 9, 23, 1955, Jan. 12, Nov. 14, Dec. 12, 1956, Jan. 9, Feb. 13, May 8, July 10, Sept. 11, 1957, Jan. 14, Feb. 5, 1958; Minutes and Reports of NEDC's Penn Station Subcommittee (later the Central Business District Subcommittee), *passim;* Annual Reports of the President of the Newark Downtown Association, *passim,* (NPL, CC); "Implementing Redevelopment in Newark," BMR *Memo,* July, 1957; Newark *News,* March 8–15, April 14, 1955, Jan. 8, Feb. 7, Nov. 30, 1956, June 25, Oct. 9, 10, 11, 13, 15, 1957, March 7, April 18, June 6, Aug. 15, Dec. 11, 1958.

5. *The "New Newark":* This doctrine can be found in any official City publication, e.g., Office of the Mayor, Annual Reports on the Strengthening of the Workable Program, *passim.* It is also contained in articles on Newark in periodicals such as *Time, Business Week, Architectural Forum,* and *The Nation.* See also: H. Bruce Palmer, "National Programs Affecting Local Economic Growth," in *The Little Economies* (New York, Committee for Economic Development, 1958). For NEDC's movement toward public relations activities see: Newark *News,* Jan. 11, March 21, 1957, Sept. 12, Oct. 20, Dec. 10, 1958, May 3, 4, 7, 1959; Paul Busse, A Public Relations Program for Newark (1958?) (BMR). For analogous cases see: Edward Banfield, *Political Influence* (New York, Free Press of Glencoe, 1962), Chapter 10; Robert A. Dahl, *Who Governs? Democracy and Power in an American City* (New Haven, Yale University Press, 1961), pp. 130–37.

6. *NHA in the Central Business District:* NEDC Minutes, Sept. 10, Oct. 15, Nov. 12, 1958, Oct. 14, 1959; Minutes and Reports of NEDC's Central Business District Subcommittee, Sept., 1958–June, 1959; Oscar Stonorov *et al., A Study of the Downtown Area, Newark, New Jersey* (Newark, Office of the Mayor, 1959); Newark *News,* June 27, July 13, Aug. 2, Oct. 7, 8, Dec. 16, 18, 23, 29, 1958, Aug. 19, 23, Sept. 13, 14, Oct. 4, 1959.

7. *The Future of NHA-NEDC Relations:* On the East Ward industrial park see NEDC Minutes, Nov. 12, 1958; on the Zeckendorf proposal see Newark *News,* Nov. 2, 1959.

CHAPTER VI. THE PLANNERS

1. *The Rise and Fall of Central Planning:* Office of the City Clerk, *Newark, City of Opportunity: The Municipal Yearbook* (published until 1949), *passim;* New Jersey, *Revised Statutes,* Cum. Supp., 40:44-1 to 40:55-21; CPB, *Official Master Plan for the City of Newark, New Jersey* (1947) and accompanying studies; CPB, Annual Reports beginning in 1947 and appearing annually thereafter, *passim; The Realtor,* 1949 *passim;* CC, 81st Annual Report of the Board of Directors, 1949; Newark *News,* May 11, June 24, 1949.

2. *NHA and CPB: The North Ward:* CPB Minutes, June 23, Nov. 25, 1949, Dec. 28, 1950, Jan. 24, Feb. 28, May 22, 1952, March 26, April 23, 1953; CPB, Annual Reports, 1949–1953; CPB, Transcript of Hearing on the First Ward Redevelopment Project, May, 1952; NHA-Redevel. Minutes, Jan. 16, Nov. 14, 1951, Jan. 19, 1952; Newark *Star Ledger,* Dec. 14, 26, 29, 1950, Jan. 22, 24, March 10, 28, May 1, June 25, 1952. For more information on the site residents see Chapter VII.

3. *The Revival and Rebellion of CPB:* CPB Minutes, Feb. 24, March 24, May 26, 31, June 23, Oct. 27, 1955, June 28, 1956; Office of the Mayor, First Annual Report of the Mayor to the Municipal Council, 1955 (NPL); NHA Minutes, June 1, 15, Oct. 26, 1955; NHA-Redevel. Minutes, April 13, 1955; Newark *News,* March 9, 13, 18, April 6, 10, 14, May 27, June 1, 5, 19, 24, 27, 28, Oct. 13, Nov. 1, 10, 1955, June 29, July 1, 1956.

4. *The Professional Planners and NHA:* CPB Minutes, Sept. 27, 1956, Jan. 24, Sept. 19, Nov. 12, 20, Dec. 9, 1957, Jan. 23, Feb. 28, March 27, May 29, June 26, Aug. 14, Sept. 17, 25, 1958; CPB, Transcript of Blight Hearing in the Central Ward, July, 1958; City Council Minutes, June 15, Aug. 17, 1955, Dec. 4, 18, 1957; NCNCR Minutes, Oct. 8, 15, 1957; Newark *News,* Oct. 23, Nov. 11, 1955, May 9, Sept. 27, 29, Oct. 10, 1956, Dec. 13, 19, 1957, July 11, 1958; *The Realtor,* June, 1955, May, Oct., 1956.

5. *Coordination Through Bargaining:* Personal interviews have been more important in this and the next section than in preceding sections. For written sources on the first capital budget see: Newark *News,* Sept. 14, Nov. 18, 1959; Newark *Star Ledger,* Jan. 20, 1960; Office of the Mayor, Annual Report on the Workable Program, Dec., 1959.

6. *The Planners and "the System":* On the Demonstration Grant Project see: CPB Minutes, Jan. 13, 18, 1958; CPB, Application for an Urban Renewal Demonstration Grant, Feb., 1958; CPB, Newark Urban Renewal Plan: A Demonstration Grant Project, First Interim Report, April, 1959; CPB, Newark Urban Renewal Plan: A Demonstration Grant Project, Second Interim Report, Oct., 1959; BMR, Descrip-

tion of Demonstration Project for City of Newark, (1958?); Newark *News,* May 1, Dec. 19, 1957, Jan. 24, Feb. 6, 10, May 23, July 13, 24, Oct. 2, Dec. 10, 1958, May 10, Nov. 20, 1959.

CHAPTER VII. THE GRASS ROOTS

1. For the role of grass roots organization in other cities see: Martin Meyerson and Edward Banfield, *Politics, Planning, and the Public Interest* (Glencoe, Ill., Free Press, 1955), Chapter 4 and *passim;* Reuel Hemdahl, *Urban Renewal* (New York, Scarecrow Press, 1959), pp. 207–22, 235–38; the "metal houses" case in Robert A. Dahl, *Who Governs? Democracy and Power in an American City* (New Haven, Yale University Press, 1961), Chapter 16.

2. *The Incidence of Opposition:* This and the succeeding section rely on the following sources:

North Ward Opposition: *Italian Tribune,* Jan. 25, Feb. 1, 8, 15, 22, 29, March 7, 28, April 6, July 4, Oct. 31, 1952, Jan. 9, Feb. 1, Dec. 18, 1953, July 29, 1955; Newark *Star Ledger,* Dec. 15, 1950, Jan. 21, 22, 24, Feb. 4, 5, 6, 9, 19, 25, March 1, 2, 28, May 2, 23, June 26, 1952; Newark *News,* April 27, Dec. 14, 1950, Jan. 24, 26, March 14, April 6, 9, July 22, 1952, Feb. 24, March 6, 1953, June 20, 1954; NHA Minutes, Feb. 6, 14, April 19, June 11, July 16, 1952.

Central Ward Opposition: Newark *News,* Jan. 23, March 18, April 6, 7, 10, 14, May 27, 1955, Jan. 19, 22, 1956, Aug. 21, 1958.

The distinction between fluid factionalism and machine politics is drawn from V. O. Key, Jr., *Southern Politics* (New York, Knopf, 1949). Statements about ward politics and about the role of the regular party's district leaders in nonpartisan elections are based on personal interviews and an examination of the 1958 election. See: Newark *News,* Aug. 10, 1957, March 15, 29, April 26, May 14, 15, 18, June 14, 18, 1958.

3. *The Future of Grass Roots Opposition:* On the Broadway–Bloomfield Avenue merchants and small business opposition see: Newark *News,* Sept. 2, 16, 1954, Feb. 9, Nov. 15, 1956, Jan. 25, April 29, May 11, 1957; NHA-Redevel. Minutes, Sept. 1, 15, 1954, Nov. 14, 1956, May 10, 1957.

4. *The Electoral Politics of Site-Resident Opposition:* Acknowledgments are due to Philip Parilli, Junior Planner in the City Planning Office, who urged the author to examine the impact of North Ward clearance on voting behavior in that area, and to Harry Reichenstein, City Clerk, and Joseph Quinn, of the City Clerk's staff, who made the electoral data readily available.

Councilmanic elections in the North Ward resemble direct primaries in Alabama, Florida, or Arkansas. See Key, *Southern Politics,* Chapters 3, 5, and 9.

5. *Slum Clearance and the Politics of Race:* On the Negro in Newark

see: Mayor's Commission on Group Relations, Group Relations in Newark, 1957, Newark, A City in Transition, 1959, and *Human Relations News, passim;* Annual Reports of the Urban League of Essex County, 1950–1960; Brief on the City of Newark, prepared by James A. Pawley, Executive Secretary of the Urban League of Essex County, April, 1956; Records of Newark Committee for Fair Housing Practices (in Urban League's files).

On the integration of Newark's public housing projects see: NHA Minutes, Aug. 9, Oct. 11, 1950, Feb. 7, 1951, March 10, May 12, 1954; Reports of Division of Tenant Selection and Relocation, *passim* (NHA); NHA publications cited in Chapter II, Note 1; Newark *News,* Sept. 25, 1949, Aug. 31, 1950, June 12, 1952, Feb. 18, 1953, Jan. 26, June 6, 1954, Dec. 13, 1955, Aug. 9, 1956, June 2, Sept. 15–19, 1957; miscellaneous material in the files of NHA and of the Urban League; Morton Deutsch and Mary Evans Collins, *Interracial Housing. A Psychological Evaluation of a Social Experiment* (Minneapolis, University of Minnesota Press, 1951), especially Appendix by Louis Danzig, pp. 130–31.

6. *Race Politics and the North Ward:* NHA Minutes, Jan. 6, Feb. 2, June 8, Oct. 26, Dec. 14, 1955; Newark *News,* Oct. 26, Nov. 18, Dec. 14, 1956; Urban League of Essex County, Report to the Public, 1958; *Italian Tribune,* Jan. 14, July 22, 29, Aug. 12, 26, Sept. 23, Oct. 14, 1955, Aug. 10, Oct. 19, 1956.

7. *NHA and the Negro Leaders:* This section is based largely on personal interviews. Councilman Turner is best studied during the 1954 and 1958 City elections. The activities of the silk-stocking groups, like the Urban League, are covered in the publications of these groups and of the Mayor's Commission on Group Relations (see Note 5 above). See also: records and publications of the Central Newark Community Council; Newark *News,* Dec. 19, 1954, June 16, 24, Nov. 18, 1955, Nov. 17, 1957, March 2, Dec. 2, 1958, Jan. 9, July 26, Oct. 15, 18, 30, Nov. 22, Dec. 11, 13, 1959.

8. *The Year of "the Trouble":* For relocation policies and CHNC see: NHA, Administration of the Relocation Plan, 1953, Your Next Move, 1957, Final Relocation Report on NJ 2–15, Oct., 1958, Relocation Plan for the Central Ward Renewal Area, 1959; Annual Report by Officers and Leaders of the Clinton Hill Neighborhood Council, Jan., 1958 (NCNCR); *Neighborhood News,* a monthly publication of CHNC, *passim;* Associated Community Councils of Newark, Report of Community Councils Workshops, June, 1953; Newark *News,* April 3, 9, May 15, 19, 20, Nov. 12, 17, 1957, Feb. 3, March 7, 12, 14, April 15, 20, July 7, Aug. 1, 24, Sept. 24, 30, Oct. 2, 12, 13, Nov. 7, Dec. 5, 11, 1958, Jan. 7, 10, Feb. 3, March 19, 1959. For City Hall's attack on public housing see: Newark *News,* July 10, 11, 16, Aug. 8, 11, 18, 20, 30, Oct.

17, 23, 1957, March 4, 6, 20, June 30, July 3, 11, 19, 25, Oct. 9, 16, 21, Nov. 13, 23, Dec. 11, 1958, March 21, Aug. 6, 1959; Louis Danzig, "Reorganization of Local Housing Authority to Meet Needs of Troubled Families," an address delivered at the NAHRO meetings, Oct. 22, 1957.

9. *Race and the Urban Renewal System:* Newark *News,* July 20, 1958, June 14, Nov. 17, 20, 1959, Jan. 21, 22, 1960; NHA, Housing Survey of the Site NJ 2–19, June, 1958. Personal interviews have been more important in this section than in the preceding one.

10. *The Grass Roots:* The official position can be found in the Housing and Home Finance Agency's publications, among other places: *The Workable Program—What It Is* (Washington, D.C., 1957); *How Localities Can Develop a Workable Program for Urban Renewal* (Washington, D.C., 1955). Citizen participation in urban renewal is critically examined in: Peter H. Rossi and Robert A. Dentler, *The Politics of Urban Renewal: The Chicago Findings* (New York, Free Press of Glencoe, 1961), and Webb S. Fiser, *Mastery of the Metropolis* (Englewood Cliffs, N.J., Prentice-Hall, 1962), especially Chapters 5 and 7. See also Samuel P. Huntington, *The Common Defense: Strategic Programs in National Politics* (New York, Columbia University Press, 1961), pp. 174–78, 248–51, 391–94.

CHAPTER VIII. THE URBAN RENEWAL SYSTEM IN NEWARK

1. See Wallace S. Sayre and Herbert Kaufman, *Governing New York City: Politics in the Metropolis* (New York, Russell Sage Foundation, 1960), especially Chapters 13 and 14; Robert A. Dahl, *Who Governs? Democracy and Power in an American City* (New Haven, Yale University Press, 1961), Chapter 19; Edward Banfield, *Political Influence* (New York, Free Press of Glencoe, 1962); Norton Long, "The Local Community as an Ecology of Games," *American Journal of Sociology,* LXIV (Nov., 1958), 251–61. For a description of state party organization in similar terms see: David B. Truman, "Federalism and the Party System," in Arthur Macmahon, ed., *Federalism: Mature and Emergent* (New York, Doubleday, 1955), especially pp. 124–25.

2. *Level of Integration:* The word "integration" has a variety of meanings in the social sciences. As used in this study, it is synonymous with institutionalization or equilibrium. See Talcott Parsons and Edward Shils, *Toward a General Theory of Action* (Cambridge, Harvard University Press, 1951), especially pp. 159–234; Harry Johnson, *Sociology: A Systematic Introduction* (New York, Harcourt Brace and World, 1960), pp. 15–79; David B. Truman, *The Governmental Process* (New York, Knopf, 1951), pp. 26–33, 156–87, 264–70. For an attempt to apply these notions to a congressional committee see Richard F. Fenno, Jr., "The House Appropriations Committee as a Political System: The

Problem of Integration," *American Political Science Review,* LVI (June, 1962), 310–24.

3. Sayre and Kaufman, *Governing New York City,* p. 713.

4. *Integration: Some Implications:* On integration and output see: Parsons and Shils, *Toward a General Theory of Action,* pp. 210–11, 232; Amitai Etzioni, *A Comparative Analysis of Complex Organizations* (New York, Free Press of Glencoe, 1961), pp. 175–82; Chester Barnard, *The Function of the Executive* (Cambridge, Harvard University Press, 1938), pp. 55–59, 92–95. On the references to Chicago, Syracuse, and New Haven see: Banfield, *Political Influence,* pp. 307–23; Roscoe Martin and Frank Munger, *Decisions in Syracuse* (Bloomington, University of Indiana Press, 1961), pp. 305–28; Dahl, *Who Governs?,* pp. 119–30, 200–14. Models that approximate open-ended pluralism are described in: Harold Stein, ed., *Public Administration and Policy Development* (New York, Harcourt Brace, 1952), Introduction; Avery Leiserson, *Administrative Regulation: A Study in Representation of Interests* (Chicago, University of Chicago Press, 1942), Chapter 1; Martin Meyerson and Edward Banfield, *Politics, Planning, and the Public Interest* (Glencoe, Ill., Free Press, 1955), pp. 304–12. In the study of political parties the notion of integration can be used to distinguish "factional" organizations from "machines"; see V. O. Key, Jr., *Southern Politics* (New York, Knopf, 1949), especially Chapters 2, 3, and 14.

5. As Meyerson and Banfield point out in *Politics, Planning, and the Public Interest* (pp. 258, 267), overt conflict over public housing occurred largely because the stable structure built by Mayor Edward Kelly in Chicago was not maintained by his successor. Political scientists' lack of interest in structure is noted in C. Wright Mills, *The Power Elite* (New York, Oxford University Press, 1956), pp. 242–48.

6. Karl Mannheim, *Ideology and Utopia* (Harvest Books ed.; New York, Harcourt Brace, 1936), pp. 1–13. For routine, problem solving, and the related problem of programming see: James March and Herbert Simon, *Organizations* (New York, Wiley, 1958), especially pp. 136–50.

7. *Structure of the System:* The sources cited in Note 2 have also been of use in this discussion of structure. The term "core" or "core decision makers" will be applied to NHA; the term "participants" means those in the renewal system but outside the core. For the public official as a core actor see: Sayre and Kaufman, *Governing New York City,* pp. 710 ff.; Dahl, *Who Governs?,* pp. 187–89.

8. The views stated in this and the following paragraphs are discussed in: Barnard, *The Function of the Executive,* Chapter 11 and pp. 106–10; March and Simon, *Organizations,* Chapter 4.

9. Sayre and Kaufman, *Governing New York City,* p. 713; Banfield, *Political Influence,* p. 315.

10. For low-pressure, slack systems see: Banfield, *Political Influence,* Chapter 10; Dahl, *Who Governs?,* pp. 271–75, 305–10; Harold Lasswell and Abraham Kaplan, *Power and Society* (New Haven, Yale University Press, 1950), pp. 6–7. See also Note 8.

11. The notion "settlement" is discussed in: Meyerson and Banfield, *Politics, Planning, and the Public Interest,* pp. 304–12; Truman, *The Governmental Process,* pp. 439–46; Parsons and Shils, *Toward a General Theory of Action,* pp. 220 ff.

12. For TVA, the Army Corps, Moses, and Tobin see: Philip Selznick, *TVA and the Grass Roots* (Berkeley and Los Angeles, University of California Press, 1949); Arthur Maas, *Muddy Waters: The Army Engineers and the Nation's Rivers* (Cambridge, Harvard University Press, 1951); Robert Wood, *1400 Governments* (Cambridge, Harvard University Press, 1961), Chapter 4; Sayre and Kaufman, *Governing New York City,* Chapters 9 and 10. For the tendency of government corporations to produce such structures see: Sayre and Kaufman, *Governing New York City,* Chapter 9; Charles Abrams, *The Future of Housing* (New York, Harper, 1946), Chapter 21. On the role of federal aid in such a system see: William Anderson, *The Nation and the States: Rivals or Partners?* (Minneapolis, University of Minnesota Press, 1955), Chapters 11–13. On the drama of public works see: Herbert Simon, Donald Smithburg, and Victor Thompson, *Public Administration* (New York, Knopf, 1950), p. 420.

13. On political participation see Robert Lane, *Political Life* (Glencoe, Ill., Free Press, 1959), pp. 220–72.

14. See: Dahl, *Who Governs?,* Chapter 26; Robert Salisbury, "St. Louis Politics: Relationships Among Interests, Parties, and Governmental Structure," *Western Political Quarterly,* XIII (June, 1960), 498–507; William Form and Delbert Miller, *Industry, Labor, and Community* (New York, Harper, 1960), pp. 572–86.

CHAPTER IX. POSTSCRIPT: 1963

1. See: Newark *News,* April 14, July 8, 21, Aug. 4, 1960, July 13, Sept. 20, Oct. 18, Dec. 6, 1962, Feb. 22, March 7, 17, 1963; NHA, *Newark: A City of Progress,* 1962.

Index

Access, *see* Relations, established

Activism, strategy of: and NHA, 34-36; and the citizen committees, 74-75, 93, 111-12; and the Mayor, 91, 172-73; as a norm of the urban renewal system, 167-68

Addonizio, Hugh, 6, 188-91

Administration of urban renewal, *see* Urban renewal agencies in Newark

Administrative agencies, and their political environment, 4-5, 179-80

Administrative agencies in Newark: as urban renewal participants, 30-32, 121-23, 166, 172, 179; and the planning office, 129-31; and "political" considerations, 181-82

Army Corps of Engineers, 179

Associations, *see* Interest groups

Authorities, public, *see* Independent boards and authorities

Baltimore, 3, 186

Banfield, Edward, 170

Bargaining, *see* Negotiations

Bartholomew, Harland, 114-15

Baxter Terrace (public housing project), 76

Behavior: structured, 5-6, 59-60, 87, 111, 164-72, 174, 176-77; models of, 169-72

Bisgaier, Murray, 6, 79-80, 82

Bloomfield Avenue merchants, 142-43

Bontempo, Michael, 6, 52, 54

Bontempo, Salvatore, 6; as City Commissioner, 43-44; and NCNCR, 72, 76; and the North Ward opposition, 138

Boston, 3

Boys' Club of Newark, 19

"Bridging" of political systems, 165

Broad Street and Merchants Association, 64

Buffalo, 3

Bureau of Municipal Research, role of staff in citizen committees, 63-64, 73-74, 77, 100

Business administrator, office of, 51, 59, 130-31, 183

Business corporations: local firms serving as redevelopers or financiers in urban renewal, 4-5, 20, 24-25, 66-67, 70, 94, 96-98, 102-5, 107, 110, 173; and city politics, 61-62, 73-74; as members of NEDC, 70-75, 100, 107, 110, 174-75; *see also* Economic development; Redevelopers

Businesses displaced by clearance, 89, 121, 135, 141-43, 175

Businessmen as political actors, 6; corporation executives, 20-21, 61-67, 70-75, 79, 91-113, 177-78, 182-83; small businessmen, 61, 71, 142-43; *see also* Newark Economic Development Committee; Realtors

Busse, Paul, 6, 174; role in NEDC, 104; and NHA, 106, 109-10, 125, 127; and the planners, 125, 127

Callaghan, James, 6, 54, 57-58

Capital budget, 120, 128, 130-32

Carberry, Kenneth, 6, 67, 71, 73, 104-5

Carey, Dennis, 6, 54-55, 59

Carlin, Leo, 6; and the urban renewal program, 30, 58-59, 91, 104, 130, 190; and the administrative agencies, 32; dealings with Danzig, 32, 43-46, 52, 54-59; as City Commissioner, 43-44; and the NHA commissioners, 48-50, 189; and the City Council, 51-58; and the *1958* election, 53-56, 159-61; and the Essex County Democratic Party, 54; and NCNCR, 78-80, 87, 111; and the planners, 88, 116, 120-24, 130; and NEDC, 94-95, 100, 103-4, 106, 111; and the grass roots opposition, 118-19, 143; and public housing, 120-25, 159-61,

Carlin, Leo (*Continued*)
  163; and the Negroes, 159-61; role in
  the urban renewal system summarized,
  168, 172-73, 176, 178, 181; defeated in
  1962 election, 189
Catholic Church, 48, 61
Census Bureau, 148-49
Central business district: NHA's downtown program, 25, 56, 89-90, 105-10,
  129, 132-33, 142, 184-86; retailers as political actors, 71, 98; revival of, 93-96,
  98, 175; survey of, 103, 106-8; racial
  composition of residents, 149-50
Central Planning Board, 9, 95, 150; approval of NHA's renewal plans, 34,
  118-20, 122-23, 127, 173, 176; and
  NCNCR, 86, 123, 188; role in planning
  renewal projects, 104, 115-16, 119-20,
  123, 125; and its staff, 105, 117, 123-25,
  127; and the politicos, 112-13, 117-20,
  123, 176; declarations of blight, 115-
  20, 123, 127, 136-37, 141, 184, 188; political success evaluated, 116, 119-20,
  125, 133-34; structure and personnel,
  119-20, 123; rebellion of, 120-25, 127;
  approval of public housing sites, 120-
  25, 127; role in urban renewal system
  summarized, 166, 172-73, 175-76; recent
  role, 187-88; *see also* Planning, central
Central Ward: feasibility of renewal in,
  16-20, 185; public housing in, 41, 151,
  155; leadership and politics, 136-37,
  153-56, 159-60; and Negro population
  movements, 148-50, 153; relocation
  within, 157, 162
Central Ward Renewal Project, 8, 14;
  Wright Homes (Spruce Street public
  housing project), 8, 18-20, 95, 120-23,
  156-58, 162, 184; Scudder Homes (Mercer Street public housing project), 8,
  18-20, 127, 159, 161-62, 184; origins,
  16-20; Urban Renewal Plan, 19-20,
  109; and the South Broad Street project, 26; staging of, 32; local approval
  of, 46, 120-25, 127, 161; rehabilitation
  phases, 79-87, 89-91; relocation, 89, 91,
  156-58, 162; and NEDC, 95, 99, 109;
  Planning Officer's role in, 125-29; and
  grass roots opposition, 136-37, 142; and
  the Negro leaders, 136-37, 154-55; recent progress, 184-85
Chamber of Commerce, 61, 63-64, 67-68
Charter revision, *see* City Charter of *1954*

Chicago: urban renewal program, 1, 3,
  186; Banfield's study of, 165, 170
Cincinnati, 1, 3
Cities: renewal programs, 1-3, 185-86;
  power structure, 165-66; as rivals for
  capital, 167-68
Citizen committees: origins, 64-65, 67-68,
  70-72; and NHA, 70, 73, 75; problems
  of structure and personnel, 71-75, 182;
  problem of apathy, 73-74, 87, 90, 104,
  108, 119; Negro representation on, 74,
  154; alter behavior of the civic leaders,
  88, 175; CPB as an example of, 119,
  133; *see also* Newark Commission on
  Neighborhood Conservation and Rehabilitation; Newark Economic Development Committee
Citizen participation: as a goal of the
  civic leaders, 84, 88, 112; role in renewal success, 163-64, 173-75, 182-83;
  and city politics, 182-83; *see also* Public opinion and participation
Citizens' Housing Council, 65-68, 164
City Charter of *1954*, 120, 145; effect on
  NHA, 32, 44-46, 49; and the City
  Council, 51, 58, 188; and strong mayor,
  51, 181; and the civic leaders, 65, 71-72
City Clerk's office, 51-53, 56-57, 144
City Commissioners, Board of: and urban renewal, 30, 39-44, 141, 181; and
  public housing, 39-43, 55-56; and the
  NHA commissioners, 48-49; and the
  civic leaders, 64-65; and the planners,
  114-17
City-commission government, 58, 181
City Council: and urban renewal politics, 33-34, 51-59, 123, 187-88; and the
  Faulkner Act, 44-46, 51, 58, 188; and
  the NHA commissioners, 49; and its
  staff, 52-53, 105; and electoral politics,
  53-56, 182; and the citizen committees,
  75, 81-82; ordinance on neighborhood
  rehabilitation, 82-83, 86; oppose locally
  financed clearance, 100, 103; and the
  Demonstration Grant Project, 132, 162;
  and the grass roots opposition, 143,
  187; opposed to public housing, 158-
  59, 161-62, 188; role in urban renewal
  system summarized, 173-74, 176, 181-82
City government: one-third share of
  project costs, 31, 130-31; City Charter
  of *1954*, 44-46, 51, 58, 181; requirements on local approval of projects,

52-53, 115, 117-18, 120, 173-74, 180; the future of City Hall politics, 58-59; personnel, 65, 181-82, 189; city officials as "core group," 172-74

City-manager government, 51, 65

City Planning Officer, see Planners, professional

Civic leaders: and charter revision, 45, 51; role in city politics, 61-62, 111, 115, 120, 153; and NHA, 63-65, 68-70, 73, 75, 159, 162, 164; and the citizen committees, 64-65, 70-75, 112; and the grass roots, 65-67, 140; distaste for "politics," 72, 75, 80, 82, 90-91; role in the urban renewal system summarized, 111-13, 172-78; and the planners, 115, 120, 129-30

Civic leaders' professional staff, 63-64, 66-75, 174-75

Civil service, Newark, 62, 181-82, 189

Class: middle class in city politics, 61-62, 153, 182-83; and political participation, 136-37, 142, 182-83; Negro middle class leaders, 153-56

Clearance, see Slum clearance and redevelopment

Cleveland, 186

Clientele groups, see Constituency groups

Clinton Hill neighborhood, 74-75, 79; racial invasion of, 88-89, 149-50, 157-58; and NHA's relocation policies, 157-58, 162, 187; voting behavior, 160-61

Clinton Hill Neighborhood Council, 89, 157-58, 160, 187-89

Clinton Hill Renewal Project, 9, 14, 168; early stages, 74-75, 79, 82-83; NHA's role in project, 83-87; later evolution, 88-89, 188; impact of NHA's relocation policies on, 89, 157-58, 187; see also Neighborhood rehabilitation and conservation

Cocuzza, Joseph, 6, 120, 122-23

Code enforcement: as a goal of the civic leaders, 66, 168; and "containment policy," 77-78; and the building inspection agency, 86, 89; in Clinton Hill, 88-89

Coleman, Agnes, 6, 70-73, 77-79, 84, 86-88, 125

Colleges Expansion Project, 9, 14; origins, 21-24, 96; and NEDC, 109-10; and the Planning Officer, 127; recent progress, 184-85

Columbus Homes (public housing project), see North Ward Redevelopment Project

Commercial redevelopment, see Penn Plaza Redevelopment Project; Slum clearance and redevelopment

Conflict: civic leaders find distasteful, 80, 87, 112, 133, 177; and structure of urban renewal system, 92; and public visibility of urban renewal system, 164; and integrated political systems, 167-68, 170-71; overt and covert, 170-71, 177

Congress: and 1949 Housing Act, 1-2, 5, 11, 98; Addonizio as member, 189

Conner, Henry, 6; initial role in renewal politics, 63-64, 67-69; and the citizen committees, 70-74, 83, 94, 100, 104; and NHA, 104-6, 109-10, 125, 127; and the Planning Officer, 125, 127

Conservatism: of the civic leaders, 65, 112, 178; of NCNCR, 87-88; of NEDC, 100-3; of Negro silk stocking leaders, 154; see also Private enterprise

Constituency groups: of NHA, 149-51, 153-56, 164; of public works agencies, 180

"Containment policy," see Code enforcement

Cook County Democratic Party (Chicago), 170

Cooper, Samuel, 82

Cooper, Sophie, 187

Cooperative housing, 96

Corporation Counsel, 82, 162

Crime: in public housing, 158; and Negro immigration, 158-59

Cronheim, Dorothy, 90

Curtis, Edward, 102

Dahl, Robert, 170

Danzig, Louis, 6; importance in the urban renewal system, 11, 37-38, 173-74, 179, 181; and redevelopers, 15-29, 32, 34-37, 96-97, 107, 110-11; and the civic leaders, 20, 66-70; and the city commissioners, 40-44, 140; and Mayor Carlin, 43-46, 52, 54-59, 173, 181; and the NHA commissioners, 44-51, 188-89; and the City Council, 49, 52-53; and NCNCR, 75-77, 79-87, 125-26; and NEDC, 94-103, 105-11; and the planning bloc, 116-17, 119, 121-22, 125-31;

Danzig, Louis (*Continued*)
and the public housing opposition, 140, 152-53, 158; and Mayor Addonizio, 189-91
Democratic Party of Essex County, 54-55, 59, 174, 183
Demonstration Grant Project, 9, 131-33, 162, 188
Detroit, 3, 186
Displaced persons, *see* Site residents; Small business
Downtown, *see* Central business district
Downtown Association, 61
Driscoll, Alfred, 22

East-West Freeway, 95
Economic development: attraction of new business, 63, 67, 70-71; reviving the central business district, 94-95, 105-8; federal aid needed, 99-100, 102-3, 108, 112; and public housing, 159; *see also* Newark Economic Development Committee
Education, Board of, 11, 86, 181; as redeveloper, 19, 185; coordinates construction program with NHA's, 31-32, 121
Eisenhower Administration, 101
Elections, city: *1949*, 115-16, 138, 144; *1953*, 138, 144-45; *1954*, 145-47; *1958*, 53-56, 103, 146-48, 156, 158-62; *1962*, 159, 162, 188-90
Elections, congressional: *1952*, 138
Electoral politics: role of party leaders, 54-55, 137-38, 140, 182-83; and the civic leaders, 61-62, 182-83; and opposition to clearance, 137-41, 143-48; and Negro immigration, 158-61; and the urban renewal system, 181-83
Elite, *see* Civic leaders
Ellenstein, Meyer, 6, 43-44, 115
Entrepreneurial function in urban renewal, 4, 37-38, 179
Essex County Democratic Chairman, 54-55, 59, 174, 183
Essex County Prosecutor, 40
Essex Heights Renewal Project, 9, 26-27, 184-86
Ethnic groups: as public housing tenants, 40, 140-41; rise to political importance, 61-62, 182; as project opposition, 136-37, 142; voting behavior, 143-

48, 159-61; *see also* Irish; Italians; Jews; Negroes; Puerto Ricans
Executive-centered coalition, 170, 172

Farco, Mario, 54
Faulkner Act (New Jersey Optional Municipal Charter Act), 44-47, 58
Federal aid for urban renewal: defined in federal law, 1, 4-5; as an index of local success, 2-3, 185-86; the three-fourths program, 56; civic leaders' views on, 67-69, 95, 99-103, 108-9; local participants reluctant to jeopardize, 87, 122-23, 132-33, 143, 167-68, 178, 180; for nonresidential redevelopment, 101-3; for long-range planning surveys, 132; as a political resource for local agencies, 180-81; *see also* Urban Renewal Administration
Federal Housing Act of *1937*, 11
Federal Housing Act of *1949* (as amended), 138; definition of urban redevelopment, 1, 15; need for amendments, 101-2, 185; requirements on local approval of projects, 120, 173; *see also* Federal aid for urban renewal
Federal Housing Act of *1954*, 18, 77
Federal Housing Administration: as a major participant in urban renewal programs, 2, 4; role in NHA's program, 15-18, 23, 28-30, 180; and the North Ward crisis, 23, 97; and neighborhood rehabilitation, 80, 88; and Penn Plaza, 107; impact of policies on rentals in new housing, 186, 190-91
Federation of Italian-American Societies, 140
Finance, public, *see* Tax rates
Financing of urban renewal projects: City's one-third share, 1, 31, 130-31; mortgages for redevelopers, 2, 4, 78, 96-97, 102, 107, 186, 190-91; clearance without federal aid, 95, 99-103, 108-9, 112; *see also* Federal aid for urban renewal
First Ward, 8, 144-45; *see also* Central Ward
Forest Hill neighborhood, 149
Fox-Lance-Crane Act (New Jersey Limited Dividends Housing Act), 185-86

Gallagher, Michael, 54

Gilbane Construction Company, 26, 107-8

Goals: lack of consensus in urban renewal, 4-5; of the civic leaders, 109, 112-13, 174-78; of the planning bloc, 119, 123, 128-34; of the urban renewal participants summarized, 168, 173-78; of the Mayor and the politicos, 173, 175

Golden Triangle (Pittsburgh), 100

Gordon, Philip, 54

Grass roots in urban renewal, 6, 135-36, 163-64, 174

Greenwald, Herbert, 6, 97

Groups, see Interest groups; Systems, social and political

Hagios, J. Anton, 94

Harper, Donald, 97

Herships, Sol, 121-22

Highway construction, 94-95

Hill Street Redevelopment Project, 6, 9, 25, 89, 184, 186

Hoover, Robert, 6; and the citizen committees, 85-88; as City Planning Officer, 124-27

Housing and Home Finance Agency, as a source of data, 3

Housing authorities in New Jersey, to build middle-income housing, 185-86

Housing Authority, see Newark Housing Authority

Housing Code, 77-78; see also Code enforcement

Housing in Newark: houses lacking central heating, 13; NHA's view of, 15; NHA has best data on, 53, 107, 117, 119; deterioration of, 62, 66; expanding the supply of, 78, 84; for Negroes, 149-51, 154-55; see also Middle-income housing

Housing officials, 107; view of urban renewal success, 2-3; goals of, 15; view of grass roots, 135

Independent boards and authorities: appointment of board members in Newark, 44-46, 58; business bloc's views on, 95; and administrative empires generally, 179-80; and "political" considerations in Newark, 182-83

Industrial park proposal (East Ward), 110-11

Industrial redevelopment, see Jeliffe Avenue Renewal Project; Slum clearance and redevelopment

Innovation, the political basis of, 5, 169-71

Integration, racial, see Racial issues

Integration, social: and low visibility of urban renewal system, 163-64; of urban power structures, 165-66; methodological implications of, 165-66, 171-72; of urban renewal system in Newark, 166-71; of various types of systems, 166, 168-69; and output of systems, 169-70; and pluralist politics, 169-71; and structure of systems, 174-83

Interaction, patterns of, in the urban renewal system, 6, 166-67, 172-73

Interest groups: in urban renewal programs, 4, 6; NHA seeks acquiescence not participation, 60, 167-69, 173-75; underorganized in Newark, 65-67, 135-36, 164, 177, 182; and the citizen committees, 73-74, 174-75; and the civic leaders, 104, 112; and citizen participation, 135-36, 163-64; Negro groups and Central Ward renewal, 136-37, 154-56, 164; the urban renewal constituency, 149-51, 153, 164; won't jeopardize projects, 167-69, 180-81; and model of pluralism, 170, 177; in Newark city politics, 182-83

Interest rates, see Mortgages for redevelopers

Irish, 40, 189

Ironbound neighborhood, 149

Italians: as public housing tenants, 40; and the North Ward project, 117, 137-41, 151-53; voting behavior, 144-47

Italian Tribune, 138, 140, 153

Jeliffe Avenue Renewal Project, 8, 14; origins, 20-21, 98-100; and NCNCR, 80; later stages, 100, 109, 185-90

Jews, 40, 48

Kaphan, Samuel, 122

Kaufman, Herbert, 168, 176

Keenan, James, 6, 43

Kelly, Augustine, 37-38

Kennelly, Edward, 6, 32

Labor: as redevelopers, 27, 51; representation on NHA Board, 48, 51; in city

Labor (*Continued*)
politics, 65, 182; representation on NCNCR, 74

Land-use planning: the urban redevelopment or renewal plan, 34, 115; disputes over public housing on commercial sites, 94; residential versus nonresidential uses in urban renewal, 94-111, 187, 190; public versus private uses, 109; density of public housing projects, 124; and the North Ward Redevelopment Plan, 141-43

Lawyers, 61, 73

Lee, Richard, 170

Lehman, Jack, 6, 9, 25

"Liberalization" of federal aid, 101-2

Liberals in urban renewal, 65, 67

Library, Newark Public, 22

Local government, *see* City government

Mannheim, Karl, 172

Martin, Roscoe, 170

Mass participation, *see* Public opinion and participation

Master Plan: origins, 114-15; and NHA, 116, 119; updating of, 119-20, 130, 132-33; and Demonstration Grant Project, 132-33

Matturi, Alexander, 6, 137-38

Mayor, office of: role in urban renewal projects, 30, 104, 123; powers defined in *1954* Charter, 44-46, 49, 51, 181; future position at City Hall, 58-59, 183; role in urban renewal system summarized, 166, 172-73, 181, 183; *see also* Carlin, Leo; Addonizio, Hugh

Mayors: and urban renewal programs, 5; strong mayor, 165

Mayor's Commission on Group Relations, 148-49, 156

Melillo, Joseph, 6, 138, 144, 146-48

Mellon, Andrew, 101

Memphis, 186

Mercer Street public housing project, *see* Central Ward Renewal Project

Methodological implications, 165-66, 169-72

Metropolitan Corporation of America, 23-24

Meyner, Robert, 22

Middle class, *see* Class

Middle-income housing: as the major goal of NHA's program, 15, 95-99, 103,

105; rentals in renewal projects considered too high, 17, 25, 27, 96, 129, 132, 185-86, 190-91; rejected in Clinton Hill project, 83-84; NHA's flexibility on housing goals, 96-99, 101, 109-11; North Ward housing tenanted, 184; Addonizio urges more housing in Jeliffe Avenue project, 190

Minneapolis, 3, 186

Moran, Stephen, 6, 43, 115

Mortgages for redevelopers: insurance provided by FHA, 2, 4, 107, 186, 190-91; legislation on low-interest capital, 78; local firms refuse to provide, 96, 101-3, 107; interest rates and rentals in new housing, 186, 190-91

Moses, Robert, 25, 179

Munger, Frank, 170

Murphy, Vincent, 115

Museum, Newark, 22

Mutual Benefit Life Insurance Company, 71-72, 96-97

National Association for the Advancement of Colored People, Newark Branch, 153

National Association of Real Estate Boards, 70

Negotiations: role in urban renewal success, 4-5; as part of project planning, 14, 34, 140, 143; and political settlements, 87, 91-92, 126-27, 168; civic leaders poor at, 87-88, 91, 177; and diffusion of the urban renewal system, 92; as a device in central planning, 127-29, 131, 133-34; as a norm of the urban renewal systm, 167-68; low visibility of, 173-74, 183

Negroes: feasibility of redevelopment in the ghetto, 18-20, 185; as public housing tenants, 40-41, 151-58, 164; representation on NHA Board, 48, 51; as NHA's constituency, 52, 149-51, 164; immigration to Newark, 62, 148-50, 163, 182-83; poorly organized, 65, 164, 182-83; and the white civic leaders, 74, 154; and the Central Ward project, 88-89, 137, 142, 154-58, 162, 187; Negro leaders, 137, 150-57, 187; dispersion within the city, 149-52, 154-62; white response on racial issues, 151-53, 156-61, 187; voting behavior, 159-60

Neighborhood groups: as urban renewal

participants, 5; opposed to clearance, 29, 50, 135-43, 156-59, 162, 164, 173-75; and the civic leaders, 61, 66-67, 162

Neighborhood rehabilitation and conservation: defined in federal law, 18; as part of the Central Ward project, 18-19, 79-87, 90-91, 125-26, 185; as a goal of the civic leaders, 63, 70; as an alternative to clearance, 75-78, 83-84, 88-89; defining rehabilitation areas, 75-78, 88-89, 132-33; state enabling legislation on, 78-82, 123, 173; local ordinance on, 81-87, 125-26, 173; assisted and unassisted programs, 88, 112; as NCNCR's goal, 88, 188; and CPB, 123; and the Demonstration Grant Project, 132-33, 188; and citizen participation, 164, 174-75, 182; illustrating a limit to NHA's power, 169; and the Jeliffe Avenue project, 190; *see also* Newark Commission on Neighborhood Conservation and Rehabilitation

Neighborhoods, predominately white: opposed to clearance, 136-37, 142; racial invasion of, 148-53, 157-60, 186-87; and public housing, 151-53; and the *1958* election, 158-61

Nevin, Joseph, 6; appointment, 12; and the administrative agencies, 32, 117, 121; role in urban renewal success, 37-38; and the NHA commissioners, 51; and NCNCR, 83, 90; and CPB, 117, 121; and the City Planning Officer, 128-29; retirement, 189

Newark: renewal success, 2-6, 17, 28, 184-86; power structure, 65, 181-83; population trends, 147-50, 182-83; *see also* City government; Electoral politics; Housing

Newark Airport, 99

Newark College of Engineering, 22

Newark Commission on Neighborhood Conservation and Rehabilitation, 9; origins, 70-72; and the politicos, 71-72, 78-79, 111; internal organization and problems, 72-75, 78-82, 125, 182; and NHA, 73, 75-92, 96, 172-73, 175; and code enforcement, 74-78; the distribution of local rehabilitation powers, 78-87; and Central Ward renewal, 79-87, 90-91, 125-26; dealings with federal agencies, 80; attitude toward "politics," 87, 90-91, 112; status of its re-

habilitation program, 87-88, 187-88; and grass roots opposition, 88, 187-88; and CPB, 123; and the professional planners, 125-26, 130, 132, 162; role in the urban renewal system summarized, 166, 168, 172-73, 175, 182

Newark Economic Development Committee: and the Jeliffe Avenue project, 20-21, 98-100; origins, 70-75; goals, 93-95, 103-5, 108-9; and the politicos, 93-94, 100, 103-6, 111; and NHA, 93-111, 172, 175; Subcommittee on Highways, 95; Subcommittee on Financing Enterprises, 98; Subcommittee on Industrial Sites, 98-100; and Penn Plaza, 100-3, 106-8; Subcommittee on Penn Station, 101-2; as lobbyists, 101-3; role of professional staff, 103-5, 109, 125, 182; public relations activities, 103-5, 168; and the planning office, 125, 127, 130, 162; role in urban renewal system summarized, 166-68, 172-73, 175, 182; dissolved, 188

Newark Housing Authority, 6, 7, 9; as focus of the study, 4-6; the staff as conscious strategists, 10, 36-38, 167, 173-74; substance of policies, 10-28; NHA commissioners and the staff, 11, 46-51, 188-89; decision-making process summarized, 12-15, 60, 168, 175; and the business bloc, 20-21, 59, 93-111; staging of projects, 28-36; and the administrative agencies, 30-32, 121-22; and the local press, 32-33; importance of the professional staff, 36-38, 46-51, 105, 125, 174-76, 188-89; and "political" considerations, 39-43, 47-48; and the city commissioners, 39-45, 48, 181; staff appointments, 42, 45, 47, 189-90; accommodations in the substance of policy, 43, 60, 96-103, 109-11, 126-29; political resources of, 43, 75, 89, 112, 116, 119-20, 172, 175-76, 178-82; and Mayor Carlin, 44-46, 49-50, 52, 55-59, 111, 172-73, 176, 178, 181-83; and electoral politics, 53-56, 181-82; and the neighborhood rehabilitation bloc, 59, 75-92; and the planning bloc, 59, 115-33, 182; and the politicos summarized, 59, 181-83; maintaining the insulation of its policy making, 60, 111-12, 115-16, 173-76, 180; and the civic leaders, 66-70, 111-13, 175-78; and neighbor-

Newark Housing Authority (*Continued*) hood opposition, 135-43, 147; accommodations in policy refused, 141, 143, 152, 155-56, 176-78; and the Negroes, 147-64; and the public housing opposition, 151-53, 156-64; relocation policies, 156-58, 162; and the race issue summarized, 161-63; and citizen participation, 163-64; role in urban renewal system summarized, 166-69, 172-83; recent policies, 184-88; and Mayor Addonizio, 189-91; *see also* Project planning; Public housing; Slum clearance and redevelopment; Urban renewal program

Newark Housing Authority commissioners, 11, 69; role in renewal politics, 40, 46-51, 55, 180, 188-89; appointment of, 44-46, 55, 188

Newark Industrial Development Commission, 188

Newark Industrial Park (Jeliffe Avenue project), 185

Newark *News*, 33, 66

Newark Plaza Redevelopment Project (Penn Plaza project), 184

Newark *Star Ledger*, 33

New Haven: urban renewal achievement, 3, 186; Dahl's study of, 164, 169-70

New Jersey Association of Housing and Redevelopment Officials, 22, 78-79, 185

New Jersey Association of Real Estate Boards, 69, 78-79

New Jersey Bell Telephone Company, 102

New Jersey Legislature: enabling legislation on federal redevelopment program, 11; state universities' expansion, 22; bill requiring local referenda on public housing, 69; enabling legislation on neighborhood rehabilitation program, 78-82; bill on locally financed redevelopment, 102-3; proposed amendments to Municipal Planning Act, 124; Fox-Lance-Crane Act, 185-86

New Jersey Limited Dividends Housing Act (Fox-Lance-Crane Act), 185-86

New Jersey Local Housing Authorities Act, 11

New Jersey Local Redevelopment Agencies Act: amendments on neighborhood rehabilitation, 82; requirements on local approval of projects, 115, 117-18, 120, 173-74

New Jersey Municipal Planning Act, and local planning agencies' role in urban renewal, 5, 114-15, 117-18, 120, 124, 173

New Jersey Optional Municipal Charter Act (Faulkner Act), 44-46, 58

"New Newark," 103-5, 178

Newspapers, *see* Press

New York City: urban renewal in, 1, 3, 186; Sayre and Kaufman's study of, 168

New York metropolitan area, and public housing, 163

New York Metropolitan Regional Council, 163

New York Port Authority, 179

New York Triborough Bridge and Tunnel Authority, 179

Nonpartisan politics, *see* Electoral politics

Norfolk, 3, 186

Norms, in the urban renewal system, 105, 166-69, 171, 177

North Broad Street proposal (light industrial), 110-11

North Broad Street Renewal Project, *see* Colleges Expansion Project

North Newark neighborhood, 149, 152

North Ward: as site of project, 16-17; site-resident opposition, 136-42; small business opposition, 142-43; voting behavior, 144-48, 159-60; racial composition, 149

North Ward Redevelopment Project, 8, 14; Columbus Homes (public housing project), 8, 141, 151-53; origins, 15-18; crisis over redevelopers, 23-24, 143; staging, 32; local approval, 44, 115-20; grass roots opposition, 69, 117, 136-48, 151-53, 187; role of the business bloc, 96-98; project planning as an issue, 119-20, 123; and racial issues, 137, 151-53; and electoral politics, 143-48; middle-income housing opened, 184

Oberlander, George, 6, 174; named Planning Officer, 126; and NHA, 126-33; and CPB, 127; and the citizen committees, 127, 129-30, 132; and the capital budget, 130-31; and the Demonstration Grant Project, 132-33

"Obstructionism:" charged to local agencies reviewing NHA's plans, 80, 123, 178; charged to grass roots, opposition, 174-75, 178

Onondaga County Republican Party (Syracuse), 170

Opposition to clearance, 4-5; at the grass roots, 135-36; success of, 135-36, 139-48, 161-64; incidence of, 136-39, 141-43, 147-48, 163-64, 187

Organizations, see Systems, social and political

Palmer, H. Bruce, 6, 103

Parker, Jack, 7, 9, 24-26, 105-6

Parking Authority, 94

Parking problems, 63, 74, 94-95, 143

Parks, 124

Participants in urban renewal politics, 4-6; roles, 166-69, 171-78; motivations and commitment to the renewal system, 171, 176-78; mostly professional staff people, 174-75; and the slackness of the system, 177-78

Participation in urban renewal, see Public opinion and participation

Passaic Valley Sewerage Commission, 54

Penn Plaza Redevelopment Project, 9, 14; origins, 26, 74, 100-3, 106-8; and the City Council rebellion, 56-58, 169; renamed Newark Plaza, 184; recent progress, 184, 186

Pennsylvania Station, 100

Pettigrew, Theodore, 6, 51

Philadelphia, 1, 3, 186

Pittsburgh, 3, 100-1, 186

Planners, professional: and NHA, 60, 85-90, 124-34; origins and number of, 85, 88, 114-15, 120, 123-24, 132-33, 182; the City Planning Officer, 85-89, 124-33; and NCNCR, 85-90, 188; and the Central Ward project, 85-89, 125-30; and the Demonstration Grant Project, 89-90, 132-33, 163, 187-88; and CPB, 124-27; and the administrative agencies, 129; and the capital budget, 130-31; fail to become central renewal coordinators, 130-33; role in the urban renewal system summarized, 131-33, 166-67, 172-73, 175-76, 182, 187-88

Planning, central: civic leaders advocate, 65, 123; citizen committees avoid, 74-75, 93; absence of in Newark renewal, 91-92; underdeveloped in Newark government, 114-15; NHA's view of, 115-16; and the politicos, 115-16; and CPB, 119; attempts to revive, 120, 123-24; and the capital budget, 120, 130-31; through bargaining, 127-30; institutionalization of planning controls, 128-33; versus "project building," 129; a ten-year urban renewal plan, 131-33; current attitude of renewal participants on, 133; required as part of a workable program, 163-64; as an issue in urban renewal politics, 175; see also Central Planning Board; Project planning

Planning agencies, local: powers in urban renewal and public housing, 5, 115-17, 120; proposed changes in New Jersey legislation, 124

Pluralism, 170-71

Policy making: subsystems form around, 165-66, 169-70; and pluralist politics, 170-71; policy-making politics, 182-83

"Political" considerations: defined, 39; and NHA, 39-43, 47-48; and the NHA commissioners, 47-48; and the City Council rebellion, 52, 57, 159; the civic leaders criticize NHA on, 63; and CPB, 119; significance summarized, 181-83; recent developments, 189-90

Political parties, see Electoral politics

Politicos: role in project decisions, 30-34, 128; defined, 39; and public housing politics in the 1940s, 39-41, 63; NHA commissioners as, 47-51; urban renewal and city elections, 55, 143-48, 159-61; and NHA summarized, 59, 64-65, 70, 164, 180-83; and the civic leaders, 60-67, 72, 75, 82, 100, 103-6, 111, 120; and the planners, 114-16, 119-20, 122-24, 130-34; and the Negroes, 137, 142, 158-61; and neighborhood opposition, 137-38, 140-41, 143-48; Negro leaders as, 153-54; shift in attitude toward public housing, 158-59; role in urban renewal system summarized, 180-83

Population trends in Newark, 147-50, 182-83

Power structure, see Cities; Urban renewal system in Newark

Press, 90-91, 132-33, 138, 163; relations with NHA, 33, 55, 80, 120; and charter revision, 51; keeping controversy out

Press (*Continued*)
of the newspapers, 92, 109, 127, 167; ethnic newspapers, 138, 140, 153; generally supports public works agencies, 180

Pressure group tactics: civic leaders abandon, 63-64, 112; neighborhood groups employ, 138-41

Private enterprise: in neighborhood rehabilitation, 88-89; as a solution to the renewal problem, 93-95, 99-103, 108-9, 112; federal aid not seen as a threat to, 102; *see also* Business corporations

Project planning: process of, 12-36, 60, 167, 173-76; project feasibility, 16-17, 136, 185; staging, 28-36; NCNCR and the Central Ward project, 84-86, 89-91; and the planners, 115, 119-20, 123, 125, 128-31; staging and neighborhood opposition, 140-43, 152; and the grass roots, 142, 164; and the Negro leaders, 155-56; as an issue in urban renewal politics, 175; *see also* Land-use planning; Site selection

Property owners, opposed to clearance, 66, 135-38

Public housing: federal aid for, 1, 4; in the Central Ward, 19-20, 151, 154-55, 184; voting behavior of projects, 39-40, 55-56; tenant selection policies, 39-40, 141, 151-58; NHA's policies in the *1940s*, 39-41, 63; and "political" considerations, 39-43, 47-48; and the success of urban renewal, 43, 59-60, 180; Carlin critical of, 50, 159-63; and the civic leaders, 63-67, 69, 76-77, 94-96, 140, 162; CPB approves sites, 115-17, 120-25, 127; neighborhood opposition, 140-41, 151-53; income limits for tenants, 141; and racial issues, 151-64; and Negro leaders, 154-55; and relocation, 156-58, 162-63; creation of Tenant Relations Division, 158; future of NHA's program, 159, 161-63, 187-88; constituency support for, 164

Public Housing Administration, 4, 12; role in the Central Ward project, 121-23; role in the North Ward project, 141

Public opinion and participation: public for urban renewal kept small, 141-42, 164, 173-75; the urban renewal constituency, 148-51, 153-56, 164; acquiescence, not participation, sought, 164, 167, 173-76, 179-80; and the urban renewal system, 182-83

Public relations: NHA's use of, 32-33, 164, 178; the business bloc as publicists, 96, 103-5, 108, 168

Public works: to be coordinated with urban renewal, 5, 30-32, 130-31; and the Master Plan, 114-15; Negro areas neglected, 154-55; and administrative empires, 179-80

Public Works, Department of, 116

Puerto Ricans, 142, 149-50

Rachlin, Albert, 7, 98-100

Racial issues: and private housing, 89, 150-51, 156-58, 162; in public housing and urban renewal, 147-63; and the *1958* election, 158-61

Real Estate Board of Newark, 61; and NHA, 68-69, 89; and neighborhood opposition to clearance, 69, 138, 140; and NCNCR, 70, 76

Realtors: industrial realtors and the Jeliffe Avenue project, 20-21, 98-100; and "political" considerations, 42, 50-51; as civic leaders, 61-70; and NCNCR, 71-74; as opposition to urban renewal, 87, 89, 96; role in the urban renewal system summarized, 177-78, 182-83

Redevelopers: as crucial participants, 1, 4, 15-30, 36-37, 174, 180-81; and racial issues, 15-20, 152, 185; public institutions serving as, 21-25, 110; role in project planning, 24-30, 32, 129; absence of "political" considerations in selection of, 36, 41; the civic leaders and the selection of, 78, 97; local corporations refuse to serve as, 94, 96-98, 103; and the Jeliffe Avenue site, 99-100, 186-87; NHA relies on nonlocal firms, 105-6, 110-11; tax relief for, 185-86; interest rates on loans to, 185, 190-91

Redevelopment, *see* Slum clearance and redevelopment

Reform movement, 61; and conservatism, 65; and central planning, 120

Reichenstein, Harry, 7, 52-53

Reilly, Joseph, 37

Relations, established, 6; sought by NHA, 15; embody settlements, 111;

and central planning, 124, 131, 133-34; and grass roots opposition, 135-36, 139; and racial issues, 161-63; and the general public, 164; summary of, 166-69, 172-78, 181-83; Addonizio leaves intact, 189-91

Relocation: the relocation plan, 4-5, 34; and "political" considerations, 42-43, 48; and Central Ward renewal, 89, 91, 150-51, 156-58, 162; of small business, 141; and racial issues, 156-58, 162, 187; and public housing, 162, 187-88

Rent control, 66

Rents in new middle-income housing, 17, 25, 27, 96, 129, 185-86, 190-91

Residential redevelopment, see Middle-income housing; Slum clearance and redevelopment

Resources, political: of NHA, 65, 108-9, 111-12, 172, 175-76, 178, 180; of the civic leaders, 111-13; of CPB, 115-16, 119-20; of the professional planners, 125, 131, 133; of the grass roots opposition, 139; of public works agencies, 179-80

Rinaldi, Mariano, 7; as Executive Secretary of CPB, 116-19; as Business Administrator, 130-32

Rodino, Peter, 7, 138

Roles: as focus of the study, 6; in the urban renewal system, 59-60, 92, 111-13, 133-34, 166-69, 171-78; in city politics, 165, 182-83; and political analysis, 170-72

Rooming houses, 136

Rosenberg, Irving, 51

Roseville neighborhood, 149-50

Rutgers University, 21-24

St. Michael's Hospital, 185

Save Our Homes Council, 138-41, 153

Sayre, Wallace, 168, 176

Scudder Homes (Mercer Street public housing project), see Central Ward Renewal Project

Segregation, see Racial issues

Seton Hall Redevelopment Project, 9, 14, 21-23, 56, 184

Seton Hall University, 21-22, 24-25

Settlement, political: NHA and the politicos, 59-60; its role in the urban renewal system, 59-60, 167-68, 173-79; NHA and NCNCR, 87; NHA and the

civic leaders, 111-13, 124; NHA and the planners, 126-27

Sewers, Department of, 121

Site residents: as opposition to clearance, 5, 38, 135, 173-75; in the North Ward, 69, 117-19, 136-41, 144-48, 151-53; and NCNCR, 84, 89; in the Central Ward, 122, 136-37, 142; mostly nonwhite, 142, 149-51, 164, 187

Site selection: local approval of sites required, 5, 115-17; site feasibility, 15-18; process described, 15-27; defining clearance and rehabilitation areas, 19-20, 75-78, 83-84, 89-90, 129, 132-33, 188, 190; and economic development goals, 20-21, 94-95, 98-100, 186-87, 190; redevelopers' role in, 24-27; "political" considerations in, 39-41; NCNCR refuses role in, 78; for rehabilitation project, 83; disputes over public housing sites, 95, 120-25; site changes in the Jeliffe Avenue project, 186-87, 189-90

Slum clearance and redevelopment: for residential uses, 1, 17-18, 94-97, 99, 101-3, 105-10, 190; for nonresidential uses, 1, 20-23, 27, 96-103, 105-10, 112, 190; defining clearance and rehabilitation areas, 19-20, 75-78, 83-84, 89-90, 129, 132-33, 188, 190; civic leaders' initial views on, 63-70; NCNCR's views on, 77-78, 83-84, 89-90; NEDC's views on, 94, 97, 101-2, 109; and citizen participation, 163-64; see also City government; Federal aid for urban renewal; Financing of urban renewal projects; Land-use planning; Middle-income housing; Newark Housing Authority; Project planning; Site selection; Urban renewal program

Slums, see Housing in Newark

Small business, displaced by clearance, 89, 121, 135, 141-43, 175

South Broad neighborhood, 149

South Broad Street Renewal Project, 9, 14, 56, 89; origins, 25-26; recent progress, 184-86

South Ward: racial composition of, 149-50; voting behavior, 159-60; opposed to Jeliffe Avenue project, 186-87

Spatola, Gerald, 7, 47-48, 50, 188-89

Spot clearance, 83-84, 88, 188

Spruce Street merchants, 121

Spruce Street public housing project, *see* Central Ward Renewal Project

Stabile, Raymond, 6, 120, 122-23

Staff, professional: citizen committees lack, 73-75, 80-82, 90, 104-5, 112, 182; CPB lacks, 115, 119-21, 132-33, 182; as a political resource for NHA, 176, 180-82

Stonorov, Oscar, 7, 26, 107-8

Subdivisions, 115, 119

Suburbs, flight to, 61-62, 94-95, 153, 182-83

Superintendent of Schools, 31-32

Systems, social and political: output, 92, 167-68, 171, 180; normative self-image, 105; visibility to outsiders, 163-64; subsystems in city politics, 165-66; and methods of political analysis, 165-66, 171-72; recruitment and socialization, 166, 169; norms of, 166-69; integration of, 166-72, 174, 177-78; role differentiation, 168-69; and pluralism, 170-72; structure of, 172-78; slackness of, 177-78

Tax rates: urban renewal supposed to lessen, 57, 68, 96; the civic leaders' concern over, 63, 65, 68, 93, 95, 109, 114; effect of public housing on, 63, 94, 158-59; and tax deal for redevelopers, 96, 185-86; and redevelopment for public uses, 109

Tennessee Valley Authority, 179

Third Ward, 18; *see also* Central Ward

Tobin, Austin, 179

Torppey, Vincent, 162

Tung-Sol Electric Company, 97

Turner, Irvine, 6; as Negro leader, 52, 54, 136-37, 153-54, 159-60; views on urban renewal, 153-54

Turner Construction Company, 9, 25-26, 106

United Hospital Foundation of Newark, 27, 184

United States Congress, *see* Congress

United States Housing Act of *1949*, *see* Federal Housing Act of *1949*

Urban League of Essex County, 153

Urban Renewal Administration (formerly the Division of Slum Clearance and Urban Redevelopment), 8, 9, 55, 60, 97; and local urban renewal programs, 2, 4; as a source of data, 3, 186; and NHA's renewal policies, 11-12, 15, 18-20, 26-36; and NHA's staging of projects, 26, 116, 131; and NCNCR, 79, 88; and Central Ward rehabilitation, 79-80, 83, 85-87, 90, 126; and the Jeliffe Avenue project, 99, 186; and the Penn Plaza project, 101-2; and the City's one-third share of project costs, 130-31; and the Demonstration Grant Project, 132-33; and the workable program, 163-64; role in the urban renewal system summarized, 174, 180-81; and recent events, 185-88, 190; *see also* Federal aid for urban renewal

Urban renewal agencies in Newark: significance of vesting redevelopment powers in the housing authority, 11, 43, 64-65, 180; proposals for new redevelopment agencies, 57-58, 63-64, 93-94, 102; coordination of, 91-92, 124-34; jurisdictions of, 91-92, 168, 188; proposed reorganization of, 92, 132-33

Urban renewal program: defined in federal law, 1, 15; successful programs, 1-3, 27-28, 121, 184-86; political aspects defined, 4-5; NHA policies summarized, 10-28; the urban renewal area, 18, 79; and electoral politics, 55, 143-48, 159-61, 189; setting priorities in, 75-78, 91-92, 132-33, 188; and central planning, 91-92, 133-34; impact of racial issues summarized, 161-63; and citizen participation, 163-64; proposed expansion of, 185-86; Addonizio's views on, 189-90; *see also* City government; Federal aid for urban renewal; Financing of urban renewal projects; Land-use planning; Middle-income housing; Newark Housing Authority; Opposition to clearance; Project planning; Site selection; Slum clearance and redevelopment

Urban renewal system in Newark: to be focus of the study, 5-6; output and diffusion of, 91-92, 175-76; self-image, 103-5, 178; the civic leaders' role, 111-13; the planners' role, 133-34; repels threats posed by outsiders, 135-36, 163-64; and threat of racial issues, 161-63; low visibility of, 163-64; to be described as a social system, 165-66; integration of, 166-79; integration and output, 170-71; structure of, 172-78; slackness of, 177-78; preconditions for its emergence, 178-83; the future of, 183; recent threats, 189-91

Vailsburg neighborhood, 149-50
Vieser, Milford, 7, 97-98
Villani, Ralph, 7; relations with NHA, 30, 40, 43-44, 118-19; and other city commissioners, 43-44; and CPB, 115; and the North Ward opposition, 118-19, 138, 140-41, 144-46, 152-53, 159-60; and local elections, 144-46, 159-60

Waldor, Jack, 52
Walker, Albert, 189
Warrence, Samuel, 7; importance in the renewal program, 37-38; and the NHA commissioners, 50; and the Clinton Hill Neighborhood Council, 157-58

Washington Park, 109
Watts, Charles, 68
Webb and Knapp, Inc., 110
Weequahic neighborhood, 149-50
Welfare, public, and Negro immigration, 159
West Hudson–Essex CIO Council, 51; see also Labor
West Ward: racial composition, 149-50, 157, 162; voting behavior, 159-60
Wollmuth, Edmund, 7, 63-64, 67-69
Workable program, 163-64
Wright Homes (Spruce Street public housing project), see Central Ward Renewal Project

Zeckendorf, William, 7, 25, 27, 106, 109-10
Zeller, Joseph, 6, 120, 123
Zoning, 117, 119, 124

ABOUT THE AUTHOR

Harold Kaplan, who received his Ph.D. degree from Columbia University, is Assistant Professor of Political Science at York University, Toronto. In the summer of 1959, during part of his research for this study, he was employed as a Redevelopment Analyst by the Newark Housing Authority. He is currently engaged in a study of metropolitan planning in Toronto and other Canadian cities.